FUNNILY ENOUGH

by

Sophie Neville

*for Alycia
with love
Sophie*

FUNNILY ENOUGH © Sophie Neville 1991

Illustrations © Sophie Neville

All rights reserved

The moral right of the author/artist has been asserted.

http://sophieneville.net

Also by Sophie Neville

RIDE THE WINGS OF MORNING

MAKORONGO'S WAR

ASHTON HOUSE PUBLISHING

Walhampton, Lymington, SO41 5RB, Hants, UK

Funnily Enough

by Sophie Neville

The 2013 International Rubery Book Award-winning true story

"It is extremely well written, eminently readable and will sell very well indeed." Charles Foster, Author

'...very readable, thought provoking and funny. Things you've always asked yourself and never really answered are addressed with humour and incisiveness.' Margrit Duncan

'I am having no difficulty being swept along by the narrative, becoming wholly absorbed by your world and the way you describe it. It is entertaining and amusing yet in the background there's an unspoken tension gathering momentum as to how things will all end up... it has me hooked!' Lucy Thellusson

"I laughed a lot. The characters are well drawn and it reads very easily." Alastair Fothergill, Producer of Wildlife Films

"I must tell you I laughed out loud in the tube three times yesterday reading your script ~ I doubled up!!" Lucy Thellusson, again

"...your book gets better and better. I ended it wanting more." Mark Chichester-Clark, Composer

"I can dip in and out of it ~ it's a hoot!" Diana Vernon

"Just right for me. I think it would serialise well in a newspaper." Jane Whitbread

"I was glued to your book and kept reading bits out loud to my husband" Henrietta Mayhew

'Absolutely superb.' Rev. Canon Andrew Bowden. 'My wife keeps reading bits out aloud to me.'

"I don't know why but it gave me tremendous hope – it's also extremely funny. I want to give copies away to a number of people." Sue Bowden

'*Funnily Enough* was an absolute joy to read and it is so nice to see a refreshing take on the hectic workplace environment.' Heather Holden-Brown, Literary Agent

"…all plaudits to you for trying to describe and find humour in your darkest hour." Clare Francis, Author

~ FUNNILY ENOUGH ~

AUTHOR'S NOTE

This book is based on a diary kept in 1991

It is dedicated to my long suffering parents and all those who supported me through that year

~ SOPHIE NEVILLE ~

~ CONTENTS ~

South Africa, 1991

April ~ He maketh me lie down

May ~ Be still and know that I am God

June ~ I got to wondering

July ~ Unhealing healing for ultimate healing

August ~ Anything is possible

September ~ He will direct your paths

October ~ More of your grace

November ~ Where does the wind come from?

December ~ He comes with healing in his wings

January ~ One step at a time

February ~ Out of the mire and clay

After all that

~ SOPHIE NEVILLE ~

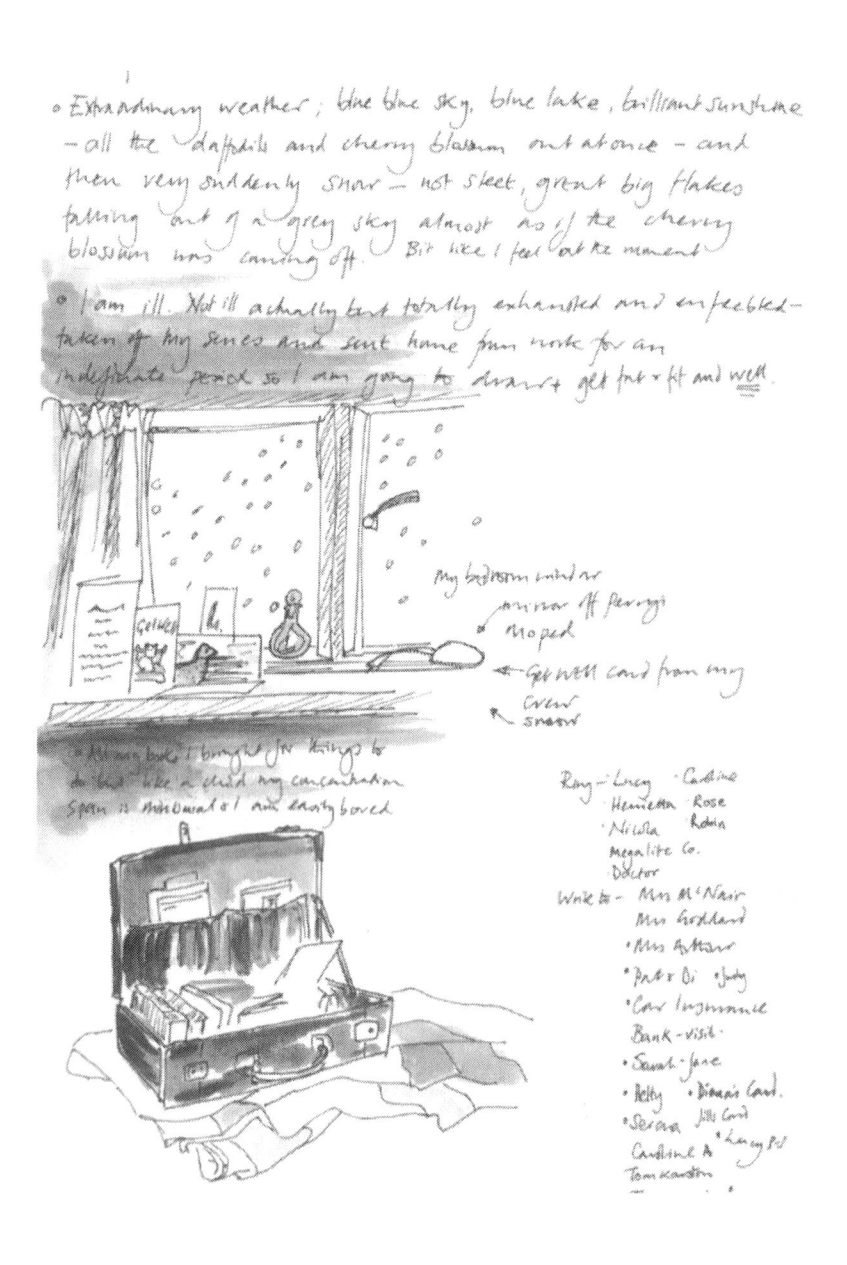

- Extraordinary weather; blue blue sky, blue lake, brilliant sunshine - all the daffodils and cherry blossom out at once - and then very suddenly snow - not sleet, great big flakes falling out of a grey sky almost as if the cherry blossom was coming off. Bit like I feel at the moment.

- I am ill. Not ill actually but totally exhausted and enfeebled - taken off my series and sent home from work for an indefinite period so I am going to darn't get fat + fit and well.

South Africa 1991

21st March ~

'I wish you could stay longer.'

'So do I,' I said, as we walked round to heave my luggage into a waiting car.

'Sophie, I wanted to ask: would you like to consider becoming my partner in the horse safaris?'

'Really?'

'Really.'

'I'd love to, Sarah-Jane but I can't. I've too many commitments.'

'Uncommit.'

'It's not that easy, I'm half way through my contract with the *BBC*.'

'London will be horrid,' she insisted.

'Yes, but,' I said, leaning against the car, trying to explain, 'I've agreed to direct a long-running drama series.'

'I know.'

'It's such a good opportunity. I can't turn it down.'

'I would have loved your help here.'

'Rebecca might come. She's a fantastic cook.' Sarah-Jane and I pulled ourselves up onto the boulders so that we could see her little camp below with the horses milling around in the kraal. I tried hard not to cry.

'It's good that you came.'

'Yes, it has been wonderful, much more than a holiday.' I stood looking out across the vast, wild country through which we'd ridden. It was still early in the morning and quite cold. The mountains were standing dark against the rays of the rising sun. A huge grief welled up inside me; I didn't want to go at all. Tears started streaming down my face.

'Sarah-Jane.' A voice came out of the darkness. 'You left your revolver under the front seat of my Land Cruiser.' The Game Warden had come to look for her. Time for me to go.

'Goodbye, Sarah-Jane. And thank you for such an amazing time. I'm sure things will work out.'

'Come back as soon as you can.'

'I will. Goodbye.' I drove off towards Johannesburg and an aeroplane that would take me back to what I thought I had to do.

APRIL ~ He maketh me lie down

England, 1991

9th April ~

Extraordinary weather; blue sky, blue lake, brilliant sunshine – all the daffodils and cherry blossom out at once, and then very suddenly, snow. Not sleet, but great big flakes falling out of a grey sky almost as if the cherry blossom was coming off. It's a bit like what's happened to me.

I'm ill. Or not ill, I don't know, but I'm totally exhausted. Enfeebled; like a sea creature stranded on a beach, with the tide receding. Everything was going well until I conked-out at work. I've been taken off my series and sent home to my parents' farm. By the *BBC* doctor. For an indefinite period.

I suppose that when you just can't move there must be something wrong. My father had to drive up to London and bring me home to Gloucestershire. I sat slumped in the car, shaking and unable to speak, but I'm going to stay here now, in my old bedroom, and get fat and fit and well.

I'd better be careful; I think it's quite easy for stranded sea creatures to start feeling sorry for themselves. I knew an actor who once had a small part playing a sand monster in *Doctor*

Who. His scenes were filmed on Brighton beach in January. 'We monsters had to lie under a thin layer of sand, staying still until the director shouted "Action!" Then we would emerge and bear down, scarily, on the Doctor and his assistant' (a buxom girl wearing a leotard.) They ended up having to do it again and again, take after take.

'I got quite used to being buried and waiting around for the crew to set up the shot again.' After the seventh take the monster found himself lying under the sand for what seemed like hours. 'I thought I would just take a peek to see what was happening.' The entire beach was deserted. It had started to drizzle. The crew must have moved on to the next location. 'I felt so stupid. I didn't have any money on me and had to walk back through Brighton to the unit hotel, all cold and stiff in the soggy sand monster costume, trying not to frighten old ladies or children in pushchairs.'

10th April ~ There are stars above my bed here, here in my room high up at the top of the house. The windows are set in the eaves and look out into the treetops and across the lake. Our house is in a deep wooded valley so you can't see far but are wrapped in sound. That is what's so wonderful ~ the birdsong and the rushing water as the lake spills over, water falling twelve feet into the river flowing past the mill and away down to the sea.

'I wish you wouldn't interfere, Martin.' I've heard this war cry from childhood. It's my mother in normal state of chaos bustling about and shouting at Dad, who presumably, was trying to help. I'm going back to sleep.

11th April ~ I have the concentration of a five-year-old and can't do a thing. This is my symptom. It's no good; I'm meant to be working. My throat is on fire.

Perhaps I should have done a bunk and stayed in South Africa after all. It wouldn't be cold there, it would be sunny and I wouldn't be ill. I'd be riding across the plains with the wind in my hair and wild animals all around me.

Apparently I have a syndrome: post-viral fatigue. Yuppie 'flu, of all things. The doctor at work took a long time examining me.

'How long did you have to prepare for this drama series of yours?'

'Three weeks, but I caught 'flu so it ended up being less.'

'And how long do you normally need?'

'Oh, three months. But I only finished editing the last series in February and couldn't start any earlier.'

'Why didn't you take some leave, Sophie?' he asked.

'I did, I took two and a half weeks' holiday and went to South Africa.'

'I'm surprised you came back.'

'I had to.'

'So you got off the plane at 6.00am and walked straight into a meeting.'

'How did you know?'

'Yes, well you have to be pretty fit to do your job.' He became very strict. 'You can't attempt to do it when you're in this shape. I don't want you to return to work unless you can look me in the eye and say you've been playing tennis every day for ten days. End of story. Keep a diary of how you feel, even if you only write five words a day, and take a list of symptoms to your G.P.'

It's a bit of a shock. And a real nuisance. I went down with something vile for two endless weeks in January, then I'd been ill with a similar virus for ten days over Easter. It could have been a bug I caught on the aeroplane flying back from Johannesburg. My family doctor gave me antibiotics, which had made me feel so much better that I'd returned to work as soon as I could. I couldn't not. We had rehearsals, I had scripts to prepare, and we had meetings, lots of them, and there were numerous locations to find.

In effect, I didn't say 'Cut' early enough. I'm always forgetting to say 'Cut' and then stand around wondering why the actors continue to walk down the street. This time I should have stopped myself sooner. I collapsed after the first day of filming. Very embarrassing.

12th April ~ Census day, of all things. We are about to become statistics and the media seems obsessed with it. England can be so parochial. I dreamt about warthogs last night, and zebra running in the dust; there were great herds of eland and giraffe standing against the mountains. And I was riding past on an Arab horse. I wonder if heaven will be like that? Do you think we'll get there and find it covered in wildebeest?

I seem to sleep all the time. But my friend James is always nodding off and he seems ridiculously healthy. I hadn't seen him for ages but he drove up from Bristol especially to see me, bringing my old boyfriend Alastair. They both happen to be working at the *BBC Natural History Unit* and smelt all officey. It was lovely to see them but a bit jarring:

'How are you!' James shouted, in his cheery Etonian voice.

'Not feeling very well.'

'Never mind,' Alastair shouted back. 'A couple of days in bed will sort you out.' And giving me a slap on the back he took James off to look for a hobby. Hobby as in bird of prey. They only returned to eat. Why Mum is so enchanted by these two I don't know.

'Oh, but darling,' she said, as soon as they were out of the house, 'Alastair is tall, dark and good-looking and I suppose you could describe James as cuddly. Don't you want to marry them?'

'Not just at the moment.'

After supper Alastair gave James a plate of ice cream, not realising that he'd started snoozing on the sofa. James woke so suddenly he flung the bowl against the wall. The ice cream went splat! and dribbled, melting, down the radiator.

13th April ~ must focus on getting better.

It's quite busy here. I've been living in London for so long that I didn't realise what my family was up to. Atalanta Blue has come to stay. She's my niece, aged one, and has arrived with an extensive wardrobe of baby-grows. My incredibly efficient sister Perry has left instructions: pinned to the mantelpiece is a schedule of what Atalanta has to do and when.

- 7.00am ~ Wakes
- 8.00am ~ Eats
- 10.30am ~ Sleeps
- 12.30pm ~ Eats
- 2.30pm ~ Sleeps
- 5.00pm ~ Eats
- 5.30pm ~ Bath
- 6.00pm ~ Plays
- 7.00pm ~ Sleeps

What a life.

Perry has gone to make an advert for British Gas, her blonde hair bobbed, her pink suit pressed. She left in a furious temper because she slept the night in Mary-Dieu's old bedroom. The smoke alarm kept going off every half-hour like an alarm clock. It was indicating that the batteries were running down. Poor Perry. She didn't know this, couldn't find what it was and ended up sleeping in Dad's study, as there's a bed there. Only she was unable to sleep due to my coughing. To make extra space Dad's put the bed on top of a chest of drawers, which means that anyone sleeping on it is rather close to the ceiling and my bed's on the floor above. Does this sound mad?

14th April ~ Mum's been trying to lose weight again. It puts her in such a bad mood. Her classic way of dealing with anything is to scream. It usually works; we all leap into action and scurry about doing things for her. The screaming is exacerbated when she's irritated about something or hasn't had enough to eat. Surely after all these years she must realise that dieting doesn't work for her. I think the problem is that she insists on wearing baggy sweatshirts and tracksuit bottoms, which are most unflattering. They would make me look podgy and I'm a size 10.

'I don't care what I look like, for you lot,' she shouted, turning on the whizzer to make more spinach soup. 'I want to look slim for a part I'm going up for at the King's Head in Islington.' I bet the play doesn't even get off the ground. She's always going to futile auditions, despite the expense. Mum couldn't resist auditioning for *Peter Pan* once. My sisters and I somehow couldn't imagine her in flight.

'Not to play Peter. I thought I might make a good Mrs. Darling.' Once at the theatre she had to stand on the stage, looking out into silent darkness in the old fashioned way, and sing a song. 'I sang *By yon Bonny Banks*, as it's about all I can sing, and had just got to the bit about my true love, when a voice from the back shouted, "Stop. Stop! You don't look a bit like a sexy green crocodile."' And that was it. 'They were looking for a Mrs. Darling who could double as the crocodile in a sparkly bikini thing. I'm sure I could play a reptile if it was required.'

Dad has had an argument with his rotavator. He calls it a tiller. It's a big red and white machine with handles like a plough and four rotary blades that churn up the vegetable garden.

He'd lent it to a friend who had managed to wear out the drive-belt. Instead of replacing it with an expensive Honda belt, his friend thought he'd buy a cheap one. This idea has nearly killed my father. When he put the tiller into reverse the drive-belt slid off and the whole thing leapt back at him, with the heavy blades turning madly right between his legs. And I mean right between his legs. They could easily have gouged out his stomach. As it was they caught his trousers, tearing and whipping the material round until his bottom was exposed and his right thigh was held in a tourniquet. The lower blades just missed his knees, slicing right through the rubber of his gumboots. Fortunately the engine then cut out. He couldn't move though; he was pinned to the thing and awfully embarrassed about crying out for help, as he was quite naked around the middle. He said that luckily he found a hanky, which he put over his private parts.

As the vegetable garden is down the lane, 400 yards from our house, Dad knew we'd never hear him and became rather worried about whether he'd ever be found. In his desperation he hacked away at the material twisted round his leg with a piece of stone and finally managed to get free. He's a bit shaken. Mum is trying to be sympathetic but thought the whole episode very funny.

15th April ~ A huge *Get Well* card has arrived, signed by my entire cast and crew. It's a picture of a crocodile in bed with a thermometer in its mouth. Not a very sexy looking one. My P.A. had written 'Rest: don't feel guilty about spending time in bed, you work too atrociously hard.'

I'm reading a book about the French Revolution but I can't take it in; my brain seems to have shrunk to the size of an apricot.

Mum went around in a Police car today with a video camera, in an attempt to catch speeders speeding. The life of a J.P. (Justice of the Peace.) She absolutely adores being a magistrate. Having always complained about public lavatories, it gives her a title suitable for bullying people to do something about them. And, she always had an aptitude for prosecution. I can remember waiting at the traffic lights when we were little when Mum sharply informed a boy on his bike, 'It's getting dark, you should have your lights on.'

'So should you lady,' he answered back. He was right; she hadn't turned her own headlights on.

Alastair came to see me, leaving a trail of destruction. It comes naturally to him. In the last few years he has broken the dishwasher, sloshed coffee all over the Persian carpet and split open our pink bath. He stood in it. For some reason he got in without any water, which was just as well as Dad found a live electric wire running underneath. Rats had gnawed off the plastic insulation.

It's sweet of Al to come over, but it's rather enervating having him around. Like many high achievers, he switches from being frantically outgoing to being totally self absorbed. I just wish he could understand that we love him for who he is and not for what he can achieve.

I don't know; he's crazy about what he does; Alastair is even more engrossed in his work than I am. His great passion in life is birds and he loves, loves, loves making films about them. I once asked him what was the most important thing in his life, thinking he might talk about his faith or his family, his health or even perhaps me. He said, 'Peregrine falcons.'

'Oh. What's the second most important thing in your life?'

'White fronted bee-eaters.'

James says he finds it somewhat annoying; not the bird fetish so much as the desire to get up so early in the morning. Al says he's sure everyone thinks he's bonkers but doesn't care. The great thing is that one is whisked along with his enthusiasm and where it takes you; out to see gannets on the Farne Islands in sparkling sunlight and high seas or off to remote parts of Morocco to find the flamingos and egrets he last filmed in the Camargue. Surprisingly good fun. A group of us girls went out to Kenya one Christmas to see him when he was making a film on the white fronted bee-eaters with Simon King. Al was so focused on the project that when we returned from a long and adventurous journey to Lake Turkana he didn't even say Hello. Mind you, he was battling to complete a sequence with a mongoose. (They predate on bee-eaters.) It wouldn't do what Alastair wanted at all and that can be extremely frustrating. I had the idea that Marmite might smell like a female on heat. They got a shot of the mongoose sniffing a bit but somehow the Marmite got everywhere. Under Alastair's arms, on Simon King's pigtail, all over the mongoose, and I was covered in it. Mongooses don't smell very nice either. The idea of making wildlife films suddenly lost its charm.

16th April ~ My littlest sister Mary-Dieu, aged nineteen, has a baby girl aged one. She's called Daisy, has no schedule at all and arrives with a huge pile of laundry. It's pretty difficult looking after her as she normally sleeps in bed with my sister and objects to being plonked in a cot. But she's come to stay because Mary-Dieu wants to go 'Clubbing'. Night clubbing. The thought alone exhausts me.

Daisy is a delight. Her big eyes and curls make her look like a little imp with a question mark on top of her head. I really didn't know what to do with her, but found Atalanta's baby-walker behind the sofa. Daisy thought this was great and spent all afternoon whizzing about my room. I rather need a baby-walker myself.

Nicola, one of my best friends from school, came over. She looked at Daisy with horror and then said in a small voice, 'I'm pregnant,' sounding like a frightened sixteen-year old. She isn't sixteen; she's twenty-nine and has been married for two years. I think it's exciting that she's going to have a baby. I showed her the schedule, which is still hanging on the sitting room mantelpiece.

'Oh, Sophie, I thought that was for you.'

'Yes. I suppose it could be.'

'Do you manage to keep to it?'

'No, we're always behind.'

Daisy is sleeping with Mum in her bed and my father has migrated to his study. I lie alone in my high four-poster, looking at the card of the crocodile. Mary-Dieu (Dieu as in mildew) was nearly four when we adopted her. I was fifteen. She was the sweetest little thing, easygoing, bright and extremely articulate. Our only problem, and it was quite a hazard, was that she was, and still is, radically outspoken. She could state the obvious at embarrassing and inopportune times. We all had to go to court for her formal adoption. Mum knew that the old judge only had one hand. The other had been replaced by a hook. We were all terrified that Mary-Dieu would declare, 'You've got no hand,' or something and had been drilling her frantically. Instead, she walked into the court, paused in the doorway, and when sure of everyone's attention, looked at the judge, looked up at Mum and said, in her clear piping voice, 'I no say anything about the hook. I just tell him to be careful of the crocodile.'

17th April ~ Mum came plodding upstairs to ask if I wanted Rufus Knight-Webb to come and see me. I looked at her a little oddly. I know that Jesus wanted the sick to be visited but I'm not sure I should have so many people in my bedroom. Rufus is the son of our old G.P. and I haven't seen him since he was adolescent. He's an artist and lives in London; I'm sure he won't want to come.

'You've absolutely got to see his wife. She's beautiful.' I'd no idea they were downstairs.

Mum was getting impatient with me. 'It's all right, they live in a squat.' She was referring to the chaos in my room.

Rufus' new Yugoslavian wife is beautiful. Startlingly so. In the way she is, as much as how she looks. She speaks not one word of English. Rufus, in contrast, hadn't brushed his hair for a long time and spoke without drawing breath.

'I'm painting with ultra-violet in the dark,' he told me. I could just imagine it. Rufus in Peckham, painting in the dark. I showed him the luminous stars stuck to the ceiling above my bed. His works of wonderment need to be illuminated by a black light or something. Weird. (How can you get black light anyway?) They're going to James' dance in May, when we all have to dress up as soap opera stars. I tried to persuade him to go as a carrot and represent *The Archers*.

My photos of South Africa have arrived from the developers. Oh, how I wish I'd never come back. The horses look so beautiful. I'm sitting on a big black Friesian with a flowing mane and tail. There are shots of us riding with the game. Shots of us walking through the mountains. Well, me walking, Sarah-Jane striding. I must've known her for twenty years. She has a wild and free life. And I mean a life in the wild, where she has freedom. Strong minded and independent, she's torn away from convention and does what *she* wants. And why not? About five years ago we drove down through Africa and, although she had no money at all, she decided to stay and start her own business in tourism. Rebecca was on that trip. I'm going to send her some of these photographs and persuade her to get out there. It's very much her thing.

18th April ~ Syndrome worse today. Achy back. I can hardly do anything at all. It's so frustrating; being unproductive goes against the grain of my essential make up. I'm not even much fun to talk to. But surely I'll be better in time for James' party?

I went to see my family's General Practitioner. She peered down my throat. 'Yes, well this is infected for sure, but tell me, do you always push yourself to the limit?'

'In what way?'

'Were you getting stressed-out at work?'

'I was under a great deal of pressure, but I'm used to coping with that. It can be all quite exhilarating.'

'How long have you been doing this job?'

'I've worked for the *BBC* for about eight years, and have been in this particular job, directing stuff, for three.'

'But is it a stressful job?'

'Yes, it's up to me to come up with the goods; the filming is pressurised,' I admitted. 'I work with children who are only allowed on set for a limited time, so I have to operate at a fair pace, directing with two cameras, but it's not as if I was getting particularly anxious or worried. I enjoy it.' I do, I love my work. I didn't go into the details but it was the stupid recce that nearly killed me. These times of planning and reconnaissance are normally fun, but we had no time at all. I was going to have to film difficult sequences from a canal barge and wanted everything to be well organised. It was all rather difficult to envisage. Instead of delegating, insisting my production manager chose the locations, I'd spent a Saturday cycling miles up a gravely towpath and I think I pushed myself too hard physically. The only stress was on my muscles, which I'd thought would be good for me. But I was still on antibiotics and must have felt better than I really was.

'Well, you have had two bad bouts of 'flu this year. I'd say you definitely have post-viral fatigue.'

'How long can I expect to be ill for?' I asked.

'It's hard to say.'

What I somehow never managed to explain was that while I was with Sarah-Jane I recognised the fact that I was badly in need of a long break; a proper sabbatical.

I staggered back from the surgery, sank into bed and spent all afternoon in a deep, hot sleep. Mum came back from Gloucester looking pretty exhausted herself. She told me that Mary-Dieu was still in bed when she'd returned Daisy at half past five. In the evening. Honestly, even I get up before then, and I'm meant to be in bed.

'Her basement was filthy,' Mum reported, 'so I set to, scrubbing away. Mary-Dieu just sat on the sofa smoking, and watching me.' Mum hates cigarette smoke. 'I don't suppose the night clubbing was much fun.' Mary-Dieu's lived in Gloucester for two years but hasn't many friends. She seems to lead a nocturnal sort of life that I suppose cuts you off from the world after a while.

Mum, worried about christening her granddaughter, once asked Mary-Dieu if she had a church. 'Yeah, I belong to The Church of Can't be Bothered.' It's her choice but she must be so bored. Poor Daisy has to put up with all the muddle and smoke and the darkness of this ~ I don't know what you call it ~ alternative lifestyle. Mum was quite funny though, going on about the mess; her own room is just as bad. The things she has on her windowsill alone: piles of letters, Agatha Christie books, wire coat hangers, one shoetree, empty boxes, her old specs (I bet she's been looking for them for ages) and we are not allowed to interfere. Mary-Dieu knows this of course.

19th April ~ Woke up with a stiff neck, feeling turgid and somehow compressed. It seems I'm unable to do anything productive. I ended up sitting slumped by my bookshelves reading about a boy who was dying, called William. I was completely caught up by the story. His mother, Rosemary Attlee, tells the first part. Now I'm reading the journal William wrote in the last four months of his life. He was nineteen. It's a spiritual journal and so touching. All true and much better reading than the French Revolution.

This diary of mine ought to be a spiritual diary but I'm shy about what people might think. I mean, it's very personal. I used to think faith was a private thing, but we're not going to learn anything by internalising what we experience. Anyway, it's exciting hearing about what God's doing in people's lives. I don't know if what's happening in mine will be. Where do I start? I'm in the middle of so much. Start where I am now. Not a good place because I feel that nothing spiritual is happening in my life at all. I feel clogged up intellectually (and can hardly spell. I've just spelt hour: OUR and her: HAIR).

Should people pray when they're ill? Well, yes, I've so much time on my hands. I ought to try to get closer to God. He really is here the whole time. That I have noticed. It's a staggeringly beautiful spring for a start. These last few days I've been sitting quite motionless for ages, just soaking in all that is around me. I look out of my bedroom window at the cherry blossom. It's spectacular. In the past I've been so busy filming that I've missed this extraordinary sight for years. Now it seems as if it's out just for me, undaunted by wind or snow. Do people just get so busy they fail to appreciate God's presence in their lives?

20th April ~ Tried to pray. Can't; too groggy. Must, must keep my intellect at least ticking over by writing more creatively. It's essential to persevere. And take risks.

P o e m
If it wasn't for all the mud and rain
Reality wouldn't be the same.

Better try harder.

Try brain exercise. Must read newspaper. Reach for *The Times*. Ghastly news:

It says that an estimated 100,000 people have just died in Bangladesh, killed by a cyclone. That's an awful lot. But then you read (well, I read in Bill Bryson's book) that 1,360,000 people in the USA are airborne (flying over it) at anyone time; that must be about 5,000 aeroplanes; more. Dad says unless a load of planes are in the air, there's not enough runway space for them to park up. Can't bear to think about it. Give up. I don't think I'm very well. Perhaps I could write about being ill for the advance of medical science.

I was just beginning to feel dejected when Mum appeared bearing ten pairs of the most enormous knickers I've ever seen. Five pairs white, five pairs 'flesh tone'. Tamzin, who claims to be my most down to earth sister but is really quite glamorous, had just sent them to her for her birthday. Being a housewife she doesn't earn any money, so my brother-in-law Johnty had had to pay for them. What an hysterical present. Mum had asked for knickers and told her to get the biggest possible, but these are VAST.

Dad, seriously concerned now about safety aspects of handling garden machinery, is writing an article about his experience with the rotary cultivator for *The Kitchen Garden Magazine*. They'll just think he's nutty.

21st April ~ Nicola has kindly given me some emu oil for my skin. Real emu oil, all the way from Australia. The Aborigines say it has wonderful healing properties. The only problem is that it makes me smell like a roast chicken.

I'd love to be married like Nicola, but it's just as well I'm not. I can't bear anyone touching me at the moment. You don't when you have 'flu and I feel like one does the day after the fever has gone, only this day seems to be going on and on and on. I must thank God for all the good things. He is in control. Control over a sick girl smelling like an emu.

Dad came back from buying plants looking relieved as he learnt that he's not the only one to have an absurd relationship with a motorised plough. The man who runs the nursery, who after all is a professional gardener, said he started his rotavator in the garage and for some unknown reason it leapt into reverse too. The thing pinned him to the wall, blades spinning frantically within inches of his person. Like Dad, he was all alone and there was no way of escape. He had to wait until it ran out of petrol, which took about forty minutes.

22nd April ~ Why, after specifically trying not to be, have I ended up being foul to people? All day. I don't mean it; I just don't seem to have the mental agility to say what I feel without hurting people. I've made Mum feel guilty about eating too much. And I don't think people should feel guilty about food.

It's ridiculous to say a cream cake is evil or that chocolate is naughty. No wonder people get confused about sin.

Why do we sin at all? It's insane. It only hurts other people and makes us miserable. Separates us from one another… and God. I know. Sophie the sin expert, with no mother in sight so I can't apologise. She's put a spotty hanky round her head and gone for a long walk with her otters. They go off down the lakeside to an old wooden caravan where the otters can dry off. She can just about catch Jims there and then walks back with both of them sitting on her shoulders so they can't escape and get run over. This works until you get stuck in the mud and lose your gumboot.

I don't know why otters like clinging to your shoulders but ours always have done. They like being able to look around and balance quite easily with their flat tails hanging down your back. We have tame Asian short-clawed otters; Bee (she's called Bee because otters smell of honey) and Mr. Bee or Jims. He's very naughty and will dive down the front of your jumper given half the chance. It makes you all wet. My mother came back soaked.

'Mum, can animals sin?'

'Well, the dog's just stolen half a pound of butter and most of it's all over the sitting room carpet.'

Pippa rang to say that she's taking my plants into care, otherwise all is well with my little flat. She rents my spare room there but is on location so much she's never around. After forwarding my mail she'll be off again, working on a period drama.

23rd April ~ Feeling crotchety today. I once saw someone wearing a badge saying:

> PLEASE BE PATIENT;
> GOD HASN'T FINISHED
> WITH ME YET.

I need to wear one now. I must be driving everyone dotty. I've been pestering James when I know he must be busy editing his film on invertebrates. He doesn't think animals can sin in the same way as humans. 'You can't convict them of theft when it's an instinctive reaction. When you teach them obedience you get a learned, rather than a moral response.' (He's a zoologist, but I can't help thinking he is making excuses for the naughty spaniel he's attempting to train.) He reckons that if an animal's actions could be labelled as evil, you would probably find that they had been initially mistreated or damaged by man.

I'm always amazed at how considerate and gentle animals are. Mum describes the otters as being quite polite and they are. They warn you before they bite.

I suppose some sins are pretty insidious but I know when I'm guilty; I have a spiritual faculty especially there for the purpose: my conscience. It gets blunt if I ignore it but I've just realised that I've eaten a whole big bar of chocolate in one go and it wasn't naughty; it was sheer greediness: gluttony incarnate. And I'll get spots.

Rebecca rang to thank me for the photographs. 'I'm flying to South Africa,' she declared. 'Off to live in the bush.'

'Are you? When?'

'Tomorrow.'

'Goodness. How wonderful.'

'I'd already made plans when your photos arrived, but it was your letter that persuaded me to go.'

'Did I write?'

'Yes. At Easter.'

'Do take some chaps.'

'Chaps? I'm hoping there will be lots of men for me there.'

'I mean things you ride in,' I said, bossily.

'I hardly see myself as a cowboy; I'll be too busy cooking or slaving away for Sarah-Jane to ride.'

'You'll love it. There are animals everywhere and she has a sweet bull-terrier.'

'I want to go off travelling around Madagascar,' she added.

'Oh, can I come? My cousin's working there.'

'Are you still stuck in bed?' she asked.

'Yes.'

'When are you going to get better?'

'That's the problem, I really don't know.'

24th April ~ When I was breaking down in the office, I kept muttering, 'Oh Jesus. Help; give me strength.' A prayer of desperation. I was trying hard not to cry but had fallen down under my desk and was grasping the edge of the filing cabinet, determinedly saying to myself, 'I can cope, this is just a dizzy spell.' Only a huge pile of scripts slid on top of me. Then the Manager's Assistant came in, discovered me groaning under this mound of pink paper, heaved me up and off to see the doctor. 'Well, Lord, I'm still ill. If you're in control, please tell me what's happening.'

I lie looking at the ceiling. Nothing's happening. I'm not getting any better. One thing's for sure: this illness just proves how terribly weak and vulnerable I am. It's made me realise the astonishingly obvious fact that I only have one body and it's not disposable. It is certainly not meant to be demolished by slogging away on some wretched series. As my Department Manager, said, 'In the end, it's just another television programme. If you were run over by a white van I would have to replace you.'

Had I let working in telly become my idol, my *raison d'être*? Alastair says if we let our jobs totally define us, it is of course gutting if they dissolve overnight. I have a horrid feeling that I'd let pride slip in too. I didn't mean to boast, it's so ugly, but when people at a drinks party ask you what you do, they never fail to be impressed when you say that you work in TV or the media. Pathetic isn't it? The self-justification I think I held in place, was that it took so much hard work and determination to become a television director I felt I deserved to be able to say something for myself. None-the-less, like grotty old T-shirts, these vanities have to be flung out. I want God to be able to accept me, *use* me. Otherwise what's this life all about?

24* April

Now I've been taken from having *my own* way, from *my* work, *my* social life and *my* travelling; from self-fulfilment. I suddenly have the status of a child and have no alternative but to fold up my ambition and let God take over.

I'm going to fight this sickness all the same.

25th April ~ I've just been reading through my diary of last year. I'd written, 'You can only fight effectively when you have surrendered to God.' How extraordinary. That's what I was working through yesterday. Perhaps it didn't go in deep enough the first time. I must have slid backwards.

Meanwhile, here and now, in Gloucestershire, our village church has had a Rogation Service, held outside, to bless all the animals and crops. My mother thought this great, and decided to take, not the otters who can travel around fairly easily in a Port-a-pet cage, but Leonard, her spotty donkey. I don't know why. She had to walk him at least five miles over the hill. He wasn't keen but our dog, Jake, went along and helped herd him there. They arrived on time but awfully hot and thirsty. Mum said that Jake, who is a big Airedale-cross, was panting so loudly when the service started, everyone was straining to hear.

'The rector had a bucket of holy water that he'd been blessing the wheat fields with,' Mum said. 'He went to get it so that he could sprinkle the guinea pigs a bit and found Jake had just finished lapping it up. He'd drunk the lot.'

26th April ~ I can't believe this. The day before I fell ill I wrote in my diary, 'There is a purpose to *closed* doors.' I suddenly felt a bit desperate this morning and rang not our rector but Gordon, the pastor at the church in London I've been going to. He's a young South African who always looks as if he's just walked off a beach but has great wisdom. I asked (shyly) if they could pray for me now. He said they had already been, (to my amazement) and would persevere. He said God does have plans for us, that he keeps saying so and he wouldn't say it if he didn't mean it. I looked up the verse he gave me: 'For I know the plans I have for you,' says the Lord. 'They are plans for good and not for disaster, to give you a future and a hope.' (Ooo)

27th April ~ One thing is that when I lean back into trusting God, I feel a wonderful warm glow that I can only respond to by literally going, 'Phew, it's going to be all right.' I actually woke with a headache feeling groggy and dozed until 11.00am and then slept for another three hours after lunch, on a bed Dad made up for me outside in the garden. He has heard from the rector that Leonard was the only male donkey at the Rogation service and had made rather a lot of noise braying at all the girl donkeys. Mum hadn't said anything about that.

Still feeling fuggy and tired, with itchy ears and a tight chest; frustrated by my own inactivity. I can't seem to organise myself at all. I collect together a basket of things from my bedroom, stagger downstairs, and then discover that I've left something important in my room, like the cordless phone. I don't have the energy to go back to the top floor and fetch it, or answer the telephone when it rings in the sitting room. It happens every day. My friend Griz said her second pregnancy was like this.

Griz, who reckons that we ignore the spiritual side of our lives at our peril, was in the first ever Bible study group I went to, at university. I can remember her saying that loyalty, love, honour and understanding are the rocks that we must cling to no matter what. She says she still 'sees through a glass darkly' but wrestles on.

Griz is a great witness, not by what she says so much as how she lives. You can see from her eyes that she has the love of God inside her, and it pours out in all directions. She's incredibly generous and kind, always able to see things from another person's point of view.

I suppose if people confuse faith with religion, Christianity will freak them out. They think of the words 'born again' as some ghastly sixties phrase. Mum thought it was.

'No, Mum, Jesus said it 2,000 years ago.'

'Did he?'

'Yes,' only I couldn't remember exactly what or why, so I've had to look it up too. 'OK, it's at the beginning of *John*. Jesus said: "The truth is, no one can enter the Kingdom of God without being born of water and the Spirit. Humans can reproduce only human life, but the Holy Spirit gives new life from heaven. So don't be surprised at my statement that you must be born again."'

'Oh, OK,' Mum said, and went on washing up.

28th April ~ 'It doesn't say 'born again' in the King James Version.'

'Well, it does, it just says, "Verily, verily I say unto thee," instead of "The truth is".'

It's not the analogy of re-birth that gets to Mum at all, it's the cynicism in our society that has built up behind the phrase that makes one feel all twitchy about using it. If you say 'I'm born again,' people think you're a weirdo. And Mum doesn't want the people in our church to start clapping.

It's just my poor body that needs new life now. I seem to be stuck with a morning-after-the-night-before 'flu just-after-the-fever-has-dissipated feeling but I'm not going to think about it. I'm going to think about what I can see. Sheep. We have sheep here. They live on the bank, eating cowslips and are terribly noisy today. Dad says that with the weather warming up they're getting itchy, but they can't be shorn yet. The nights are still too cold.

I can see Dad from my new green bedroom here in a corner of the garden. He's building a boat and has just finished the mizzen-mast. It certainly has a great deal of character. Never have there been more brass fittings on a dinghy. He's going to call it *Tulip*. He made the hull at a boat-building course in Tower Hamlets when he had to work in London for a year. My friends said they'd see him walking through the City in his gardening clothes. Dad is always making amazing things; he's a great doer and giver. As for me, I want to be a doer but don't know what I can do (physically do) about anything. I've no option but to hold on tight and hope God will see me through. Having to learn to trust.

29th April ~ I've been meditating about sheep. They have to trust the shepherd. No option. A shepherd will shoot a rogue ewe if she's more trouble than she's worth. All the trusting sheep have to do is eat grass, put on weight and look after their lambs. The fleece, the most productive part, just grows. In fact it's often of much better quality when it grows in adverse conditions.

I'm a bit like an itchy sheep waiting to be shorn. I think this is called impatience. It's easy enough to say, 'Trust in God', but actually living that through is hard when nothing tangible seems to happen. I've become so independent, so used to making things happen. I want things to work out now, instantly, my way. I'm like a headstrong horse champing at the bit rather than a good sheep.

A combination of impatience and making a lot of noise does get things done. And not done. I wish people were more patient and trusting at work ~ we could accomplish a great deal more. Determined criticism, backbiting and gossip always divides a team, undermines leadership and slows things down. It must be the same when you're working for God.

Mum has let the otters play in the house again. She says it's the only way she can catch Jims after their walk but I wish she wouldn't. They swim around in the loo and then insist on coming to dry off in my bed. I'm not being at all patient about this, I can tell you.

30th April ~ Since the weather's improved I've been sitting outside just looking. I'm beginning to notice all sorts of things. It's quite exciting. Everything's coming out here, celandines, wood anemones, even fragile, wild geraniums seem to be thriving despite the storms. The woods are full of bluebells and wild garlic. Sunlight is bouncing off the Cotswold stone walls of our old house. On the bank the buttercups are coming out. And I've missed all this for years.

In his journal, William Atlee, the nineteen-year old boy who was dying, looked at trusting God. Like me he was wondering when to take the initiative himself. He says:

'The driving force should be (the) love of spreading God's love to others.' Later he concludes, 'the Holy Spirit and the love of God should start you inspirationally into works of love. So one has to look to oneself before others. Clean out your own back yard before you try and tend other people's.'[ii]

I had to read this a few times. What I think he's saying is that if I'm a headstrong horse it's love that should be holding the reins, keeping me in check or spurring me on. He's right about having to sort ourselves out. The only way we can possibly flush out the gunk and bad habits is through repentance. It isn't just a saying sorry either. It has to be an intentional and complete turn round.

But what do people do about forgiving terrorists motivated by retribution three hundred years old, who aren't making a mistake but think that murdering your child is a righteous thing? Very, very, hard. I've found it difficult enough having to forgive people I like. God does say we have to leave the judgment to him, which I suppose is a bit of a relief.

MAY ~ Be still and know that I am God

1st May ~

'Did you go and wash your face in the morning dew?' Mum asked. I did not. She thinks that if you wash your face in May Day dew you'll be beautiful forever and had us all doing it when we were little. I'm not superstitious and feel ghastly.

Must keep brain going. Go brain go. Read paper. In the news today it says four terrorists have been blown up by their own bomb. 'Vengeance is mine,'[iii] sayeth the Lord.

We can't condemn others willy-nilly, or even criticise really. There's usually some point that we know nothing of which makes the action comprehensible. OK, Mum has to condemn in court but it's her job; she has no personal agenda. It's as fair as it can be; the magistrates have to listen (endlessly) to all witnesses and accounts before dealing with those who break the law, and I suppose God does the same. The comforting thing for us sinners is that he's more merciful than my mother.

The gardening magazine has accepted Dad's article, well; an edited version aimed at amusing the readers. They're calling it *A Tiller Fights Back*. Now I'm trying to work out if the machine was taking vengeance on Dad. He's not in any way like the terrorists.

I rang up Tamzin, hoping she would make me laugh.

'Terror,' she said 'is big business. Did you know that people who design roller coasters are called Terror Technicians?' What a job title. Imagine putting it on your passport.

'It's May Day,' she went on. 'Did you wash your face in the morning dew?'

2nd May ~ I woke for the first time feeling sleepy rather than debilitated and ill. What a luxury. I was able to drive myself to the doctor's. Yesterday I couldn't possibly have done it. I was so muddled on Monday that I'd thought I had an appointment, getting Dad to drive me all the way there, only to discover I was supposed to go today.

Once at the surgery my brain started to fog up. I sat in the waiting room trying not to vibrate with fatigue, thinking of what my doctor had said about stress. It's a bit of a difficult thing to quantify because different things stress out different people. Tamzin's husband Johnty finds it relaxing to drive round the M25. I suppose unforgiveness is bound to stress you out since it entails lugging someone else's sin around.

Dad told me that stress was originally an engineering term. I've heard it defined as 'a result of losing control of a situation'. Was I feeling out of control just because it was such a rush at work? I suppose that drives some people over the edge but stress can also be purely physical; athletes repeatedly put their bodies under stress on purpose. It can be exhilarating; isn't whizzing around in a roller coaster something we do for fun?

'Ah but it's only short term. You rest afterwards and your body gets a chance to recover. It's relentless stress that seems to weaken the system.' Apparently the adrenal glands enlarge and you have to rest, physically and mentally in order for them and your battered immune system to recover or you'll catch every virus on the bus.[1]

I went over a list of my ills with my physician who has a good, analytical brain and a resolve to crack problems.

Physical symptoms:
- I look a bit better but *still* feel 'flu-ey.
- Am sleeping a lot, but wake dehydrated in the night and lie in an ill fug for hours.
- Very weak. Breathless on exertion eg: walking up stairs.
- Feel achy, especially in my legs and still don't want to be touched.
- Continuous sore throat.
- I cannot cope with physical stress. I went into shock when the parrot nipped me yesterday, becoming cold, shaky and needing to go to the loo. (I would normally just stick my finger in disinfectant and get on with life).

Neurological or cephalic symptoms:
- Exhaustion. That's the only way I can describe it. It's not tiredness, I'm absolutely shattered the whole time. I feel like a ninety-year old woman.

- Incredible lassitude. (Uncharacteristic).
- Often can't concentrate for more than twelve minutes.
- Can't take in everything visually or audibly; loathe watching television.
- Have abominable short-term memory; keep forgetting things.
- Continual nightmares.
- I don't seem to be able to cope with any form of mental or emotional stress. It's as if my brain has been overloaded and is shutting down.

I wanted to know how long I can expect to be ill for. My doctor gave me a long and sympathetic look, said that I must, 'Give it a wee while yet,' and has taken more blood for another glandular fever test. The first test proved negative, but they can check again. I'm not anæmic. She says the problem that medics have with diagnosing post-viral fatigue or chronic fatigue syndrome (it's also known as C.F.I.D.S. ~ chronic fatigue immune dysfunction syndrome ~ in America) is that there is, as yet, no test for it. There's also no treatment. What they must do for me now is to run negative checks to see if I haven't contracted anything else. 'A sore throat can be a warning signal, the first symptom of a variety of conditions. A congenital disorder might be coming to the surface.' She's going to test me for thyroid problems and blood disorders next. Deary me.

The doctor emphasised that I should eat lots of good, fresh food. Oh I do. (She doesn't know my mother). I was surprised that she didn't seem enthusiastic about vitamin tablets. I had a real binge on them on Sunday, eating all the ones I could find in the house. Well, one of each kind. Having swallowed them with gusto I then read the labels that said they needed to be chewed with meals. Well I swallowed the lot first thing in the morning. Goodness knows what's happening to my stomach. Now I've just learnt that the vitamin B complex Mum gave me came from the vet and is something to stop the dog going bald. She says it's my own stupid fault for not reading the label properly. Dad said I ought to go on a proper course of Bob Martin conditioning tablets.

3rd May ~ The editor of the gardening magazine wants me to draw a cartoon of this Dad of mine being attacked by the rotavator. He says he can't explain it to his illustrator. A professional commission. I sat outside on a flowerpot and tried to get Dad to pose. Sort of. It was freezing cold and he got uncharacteristically irritable. We couldn't replicate the position. Mum came out at a critical moment and burst out laughing. Dad got really upset. I think the grievance against the machine is coming back to him.

Have decided it's impossible to work with my parents' emotions running high, let alone try to draw something complicated like a tiller on its side. And when it's so cold. Why am I doing this when I'm ill? I'm never going to get paid for it. I'm glad it isn't the way I have to earn a living. Thank God for National Insurance and sick pay. Mind you, I've paid enough into that particular scheme over the years. About twenty thousand pounds, would you believe?

Now Mum is shrieking and screaming. She's never going to get ill because she always externalises her stress. I wish it wouldn't have to come our way. My throat is burning. Nothing's ever her fault. Blaming others is not a good answer. It doesn't solve a thing.

I'm sitting up in bed trying to work out who or what to forgive and have got stuck. If I blame the magazine editor then I can forgive him, which is easy, as his motives were completely professional and benevolent. It's actually the fault of Dad's friend who started all this, only Dad doesn't bear a grudge because he said he would have fitted a cheap drive-belt too.

At last I've worked out what that the blame-games we families play should be called: unforgiveness. That's what they amount to. Someone told me that the way to cope is to separate the person from the grievance. We have to go on loving the person, but we can hate what they do when it's wrong or hate what they say that isn't right. We can forgive the person without condoning the crime. I mean, you can love the man, but hate the alcoholism. He probably hates it too. I'm not an alcoholic but I'm still busy being selfish. Looking after yourself is one thing, but becoming a self-centred old cow is another. I'm meant to be able to give my best to other people and 'die to self', no matter how I'm feeling.

I've just been downstairs for lunch. We have two visitors from Los Angeles who are friends of some mad Californian that Mum met on a film set. They're soft spoken and hesitant, the sort of people who you find yourself saying sorry to when they've knocked a glass of water over. I always end up saying the wrong thing. It goes like this:

Her: 'Awe, *Sophie* – now that is the most beautiful name.'

Me: 'Do you think so? I've always thought it sounds like a French tart's.'

Her: 'My grandmother was called Sophie.'

They didn't eat much, probably because they saw our kitchen, but told me it was 'because we are actors.' (Only pronounced ack-tours). I looked up at Mum.

'Oh well, I'm an actor,' said Mum, licking her spoon with a look of resignation on her face.

'Yes, but, well…. What you have is not fat; it's becoming!'

'Becoming fat,' Dad said.

I think they think the mad friend is mad too.

'But he's a *dear* man,' she kept stressing. 'He's the *on-ly* man I know who is still friends with all the masses of women he's slept with, as well as his ex-wife; it's *extraordin-ary*.'

'How incredible,' said Mum, who I don't think has ever actually had an affair or knows the grief involved. She was entirely taken in by them, and then what happens is that she begins to laugh in the wrong places, and all the parrots start laughing too. We have three parrots. Coming from the States, they said things like, 'we were school sweethearts, married at school, had a child at school.' And Mum, who doesn't know that school can mean university, was laughing because she couldn't work it out, and the parrots were laughing, only then they said the child had died. It was all becoming surreal. Awful. And terribly tiring. The good thing about being ill was that I was able to apologise at that point and slink off to bed. This wasn't a good way of dying to self, but still.

4th May ~ Daddy, who always thinks of others before himself, sweetly, went all the way to my flat in West London on his way to a lunch in the City because Pippa is still away and I'm longing to get my mail. Once there he rang up to ask what I needed. I said I wanted to hear my answer-phone messages. It was pitifully disappointing. He played them down the line. The only one was from me to him. But then Dad must have wandered off because it kept on playing old, old messages I certainly didn't want to hear. I kept yelling, 'HELLO? HELLO DAD,' in this empty house here trying to get him to stop it. Now I'm sure the mail will be of no interest at all. (I was secretly hoping that I'd won a huge prize in a competition).

I'm busy wrapping up little parcels for God. There are a number of pretty deep concerns that I have ~ mostly for other people, but some for myself and the direction in which I'm meant to go. They're all things I can do little about, which I've already prayed for pretty comprehensively, now metaphorically wrapped up and posted heavenwards. One package is my work; the other is where I live, another my possible marriage. (This one is a bit bulgey). I mean, ultimately we've got to be doing what God wants, where and with whom. We're going to lose out otherwise, aren't we? Or waste a lot of time. He knows what I enjoy doing and what would be best for me. It's a bit scary though; means being ready to drop everything and go anywhere, whatever the cost. I know that. God wants us to grow but that could mean having to face tough challenges. I suppose I'd better hold on to what I have lightly and be ready to change or I'll never get anywhere.

One of my parcels is for Mary-Dieu. At the moment she's going through a bad patch and none of us know what to do. She's certainly depressed, she has postnatal depression, but it's going on and on and on. And it's rather an odd version because she's had it since before she fell pregnant. Mum took her clean laundry back last night and found her still in bed at 6.00pm. She's not sick, she just watches television all night and doesn't go to sleep until 6.00am. Daisy was running about in a saggy nappy and kept sitting in her pushchair to ask Mum if she'd take her for a walk. But Mum felt she had to do all the chores ~ again. This action in terms of practical help doesn't seem to be what Mary-Dieu wants at all. Or do much good. She just seems to sink deeper. It doesn't change her for the better; we can't change her. She's smoking forty cigarettes a day, and did so when she was pregnant, but you try stopping her. The social workers can't, she just screams at them. (Tamzin says she enjoys screaming at them.) Dr. Knight-Webb is her Psychiatrist, but he says he can't get through to her. The only person who can is little Daisy. I just pray they'll be kept safe.

Some parcels get added to, but I'm naughty. I worry ~ I unwrap them and fuss when I know I should just be grateful that God has everything in hand ~ a sure sign that I still need to learn about trust.

I can't believe this; while I was writing this down, Mary-Dieu rang to say she'd been going to fetch Daisy from Clamber Club with her friend Sharon, and had just crossed the road when Sharon was knocked over by a van. She was badly hurt and Mary-Dieu had to take her to Casualty. Golly. And I've just been praying specifically for her protection. Why Sharon and not Mary-Dieu? You see Mary-Dieu is disabled. She had polio when she was eighteen-months-old and can't walk very well. She can get about but certainly can't run away from white vans in the street. And my Manager had been hypothesising about white vans; I wonder just how often they do knock pedestrians over?

5th May ~ Am feeling like a fragile little package waiting before God, just like Abraham and Mary...Not that I'm expecting a baby.

Griz came to see me today with her babies, her little children Paddy and Eliza, which was a joy. She confirmed quite emphatically that she felt as I do when she was pregnant and although she's not a doctor she thinks the cephalic symptoms might have something to do with a shortage of chemicals reaching the brain. Goodness. Better take more vitamins and enzymes to activate the system.

'Cut down on sugar,' Griz advised. 'It's meant to inhibit your immune system.'

'Golly, and I thought it gave you energy.'

'Only superficially. Refined sugar can also cause havoc in your gut by promoting candida. Onions and garlic are terribly good for you. They're meant to cleanse the blood.'

'OK, lots of cleansing onions and garlic.'

I took the children up to see the otters. Paddy who is three was fascinated and Eliza called out in delight as the otters stood upright and put out their little webbed hands to say hello. They live in an enclosure in the wood with a stream running through it. There's also a bathtub there in which they love showing off to visitors. Jims dived and rolled in the clear water. Bee joined him and they dived again. Oh that I had their vigour. Griz had to admit that they don't eat either onions or garlic and yet are incredibly healthy. I suppose their bodies produce natural sugars.

6th May ~ Mum and Dad came back from acting in a drama series called *Trainer*, shot on Bath racecourse. I'm not sure who or what Mum was playing but Dad had a small part as a gypsy, which he'd been looking forward to for days. Since he only started acting in his retirement his two lines were a great excitement. He brought me up supper on a tray and said the oddest thing happened. At the end of the day an old badger appeared from nowhere and scuttled down the racetrack to the finishing line, where he paused as if to receive applause. And applause he got, from the entire crew and crowd of extras who cheered him more wildly than any horse that had run all week.

Mum plonked herself on my bed with a cup of tea that she then proceeded to drink herself. She was so excited, dying to tell me about Susannah York whom she'd met on the set. They'd once been at R.A.D.A. together (Royal Academy of Dramatic Art, no less). Apparently Susannah York used to rush upstairs two steps at a time but all I could do was lie still and make groany noises.

'Pippa was there.'

'Uuh.'

'She sends you her love.'

'Uh, um.'

'I wore Tamzin's new underwear.'

'Uh?' (Tamzin is tiny; a size 8.)

'You know, the new underwear she gave me. It was nice and respectable when I was changing.'

'Umm.'

'They put me in a wig with a huge hat and a lovely, pink, silky costume. Pippa said...'

'Umm.'

'...it made me look like a mobile marsh-mallow.'

7th May ~ It's a beautiful, blue skied, windy day. I've been lying in the garden gazing at all the different colours of green. It's so wonderful and enriching to be able to see in colour and yet I normally take it completely for granted. I still have so little strength. For some stupid reason I decided to tidy up the sewing drawer. I couldn't manage it and had to leave everything half sorted out all over the floor. Mind you, no one's been able to sort out that drawer for ages.

I can't think why I started. I can't even manage to do the things I need to, like polish my shoes or take a bath. Slept all afternoon. The dog joined me. 'Jakey-wakey-woozey', Mum calls him. He can't achieve much but it doesn't seem to matter. He's very happy. Jake did get a job once. He acted in a film playing 'Dog'. The exciting thing was that Spike Milligan was his voice. The otters were in it too. Mum is very proud of this and makes all our visitors sit through the whole video, but it's funny to watch. Jake says: 'Umpy, dumpy, dumpy. Wot hove we got here? Ooo dear.' Idiotic stuff like that.

Even if he did have Spike's communication skills, there would be only so much a dog could get up to. I've been made differently, having been given two hands, intellect and intuition. It's embedded in the nature of my soul to make things, to build, to produce ideas and interpret others. Created to create.

I wish the mere practicalities of life didn't take up so much time though. Because we have bodies we have to go to such a great deal of effort just to keep them fed and clean, clothed and healthy. If we were just spirit we wouldn't need to do anything practical at all. We won't have bodies when we're dead. It must be much easier to be good and true if you aren't preoccupied with survival. Would addictions to cigarettes or alcohol evaporate or become an absolute torment since they could never be satisfied?

It says in the Bible that we'll have some sort of resurrected body in heaven, but that there won't be sickness or pain. Good. I suppose most people will need new body parts by then.[iv] Apparently we will be able to recognise each other and communicate, so James will have a lovely time chattering away. There must be lots of fascinating dead people there, so he wouldn't be bored. Martin Luther said, 'If you're not allowed to laugh in heaven I don't want to be there.'

My granny's been to heaven. She was terribly hurt in a horrific car accident in Nairobi when she was only twenty and died, clinically, but retained her spiritual faculties. She said it felt as if she was floating down a river in the dark. It got lighter and lighter until she could recognise faces. Her memory and emotions were fully intact. She said it was lovely being there. Then, Wham! She was back in hospital. A doctor had injected adrenalin straight into her heart and revived her. They could do that sort of thing in Nairobi back in the 'thirties.

I suppose if all you knew was anger and hate, then when you died fear and its allied horrors would just roll you along into endless hell. It would separate you from God and you'd certainly be bored, burning and endlessly frustrated whether you were pestered by addictions or not. It's interesting working out what's going to happen when we kick the bucket. We need to know where we're going. And to get a grip on ourselves here and now.

Maybug

8th May ~ Dad and I have just been eating Ryvita for lunch. Just as I'd finished Dad said, 'Ooo look,' and about twenty

weevils dropped out of his Ryvita. 'Aren't they sweet?' Well, I didn't think so. I must have eaten a whole load. I thought the Ryvita tasted funny. I reckon we have to watch out for demons in the same way.

I can sin sitting by myself in bed all day. I'm brilliant at it. An addict. I'm like a kid hooked on computer games. My favourite game is called 'if only'. Do you know that one? I easily fall into the trap of worrying about past decisions. Instead of just forgiving myself for being myself, I start thinking, 'if only...' and can end up seething with hatred and jealousy, murderous thoughts spinning in my head. My consciousness is invaded by inadequacy, hopelessness and despair, and yet I can't resist playing the mind game. There are others: one's called 'worry about money'.

Dogs aren't immune. Jake can't resist biting horses' heels, which is jolly dangerous. If he gives in to temptation and starts chasing sheep the farmer will have to shoot him.

9th May ~ I'm beginning to see that I'm also addicted to reading Dick Francis thrillers. It's not the horses, it's the excitement, the pressure put on the hero. Stress. The greater the stress factor the more hooked I become. When it comes to escapism and entertainment we love observing how others cope with anxiety and pressure, don't we? The great draw to watching television is the tension ingredient. It's what makes the snooker so gripping. Perhaps I've just been a stress junkie. Better try to pray for everyone I know who's under stress.

Later: I keep getting side-tracked. It's intriguing. Today I discovered:

- People are happiest and work most efficiently at 19°C. (Too chilly for me.)
- Playwright is spelt playwright and not playwrite. (I never knew.)
- 8 out of 10 people on earth live in cities. (Dreadful.)
- 1.6 million pay upper bracket tax in the UK. (Well I'm not one of them.)

But the gardening magazine has given me £85 for the cartoons and they're going to be published in *The Kitchen Garden*. Yes! I'm going to sit here and sing praises to God.

Later still: Mum and Dad have gone out to watch a film they once had little parts in: *The Saint*. Mum in an action movie. She was a big fat babushka. Dad was a butler. The house sounds empty. It's been a quiet day. Now radiant evening light is streaming into my room. The land gets increasingly beautiful.

Rosemary Attlee writes, '…against our very nature we (learn) that there is nothing more practical than trusting in Christ. He's especially close to the suffering and broken hearted.' Back to trust again. I've been thinking how trusting dogs are. They trust actively. It's pretty amazing. I now realise that the reason we need to wait patiently is because God needs time to work and heal. Most of our wounds are emotional. I suppose that before you can build a new relationship you often need to have another healed. It's trust that provides the environment for love. It gives us security but we are still vulnerable, constantly put under stress with weevils, enticements and pressures from all sides.

C.S. Lewis says that love itself will involve hurt. To love makes us vulnerable. Romantic love is the most risky. It hurts to be separated from loved ones, we ache when they're wounded and it's devastating when our commitment is trampled on. It's worse when we find that we've done the trampling and destroyed something precious. Our lives are so precarious I'm just left feeling I absolutely *have* to ask God to steer mine, to let Jesus take up the reins. The reality is I'm trusting him to protect me from myself.

10th May ~ Dad couldn't believe I didn't know how to spell playwright. He explained that plays aren't written but forged, tempered and wrought, like a blacksmith working iron. Television programmes are certainly wrought. Wrought and fraught. If a playwright is a playwright and I write my own documentaries, does that make me a wroughter? A wroughter daughter. With a tempered life. It all sounds quite Icelandic.

The one book review that Mum did in all her years as a presenter for HTV was called *God Bless Love*. I found it in the playroom. It's a compilation of children's writing by Nanette Newman.

> 'You must take care of Love – if you don't it goes bad.'
> James, aged 5
> 'Love is hard to do to people you don't perticuly like.' (sic)
> Deborah, aged 10

> 'I know what love is, it's the stuff they sell on the telly.'
> Clara, aged 4

Dad said he did take the dog to work on another film but it was not a success. It was a comedy series with a huge crew being made in the centre of Birmingham. Jake never goes to town and felt terribly insecure. He wouldn't do anything Dad said, got all nervous and just kept trying to hide... until teatime when he overtook Rowan Atkinson in the race for the tea table and pulled the whole thing over. Urns of boiling water, iced buns and sandwiches went everywhere. No one thought it at all amusing; in fact they were all furious.

Are we like that? Do we try to hide from God and then, overcome by our own physical desire, pull everything over on top of ourselves in our panic and greed? Perhaps it's the other way round.

With our dog, or when you're training a horse, respect isn't just granted; it needs to be earned. It's an active commitment with trust being built through time and experience. If you're me, you make mistakes and the horse goes bucking off into the distance, trailing its reins. This always makes me feel desperate at the time but it doesn't matter too much, as it's not going to break down my relationship with the animal. What is crucial is being consistent, that I don't fail him, as that will break trust hard to regain. It's the same with people. As always it's living it out that's difficult. Tamzin said, as we listened back to recorded messages once, that I don't come across well on the telephone. She's right. In Pippa's words I sound like the Wicked Witch of the West. I must make an effort to show people I value them and be more affirming.

We must build each other up, recognise each other's worth and everything God has poured into us. We can't like everyone we meet, but we must try to be positive. It's absolutely central to everything. Loving is something I have to strive to achieve. The dog doesn't seem to find it complicated.

'Let your gentleness be evident to all. The Lord is near.
Do not be anxious about anything, but in everything,
By prayer and petition, with thanksgiving, present your
requests to God.'

from *Paul's letter to the Philippians,* read by John Peters at the Gulf War Service.

Granny has just rung from Bedford. A 'black youth' came into her bedroom in the middle of the night. She sat up in bed and said, 'I don't think you're supposed to be here,' in her old fashioned voice, and flung a huge pot of Ponds cold cream at him.

'Granny! What happened next?'

'He ran away.' Blimey.

11th May ~ Mum says she did a whole load of other book reviews, 'Well, I interviewed the chap who wrote about Paddington Bear and then chatted away to Clement Freud about his *Grimble* books. I made him sign them all for you children.' She has just dragged Dad off to some wildlife park where they're lecturing on otter conservation to a group from the Women's Institute. Dad says he's petrified.

Tamzin and Johnty came to lunch looking very smart but then I always think of Johnty wearing a tie because he works so hard. They helped me no end ~ making my bed, lighting the fire, and picking vegetables. Tamzin even sorted out the sewing drawer and put everything away. She is so practical. I was very touched. Johnty stood looking in amazement at all the books I'm reading at the same time. He only ever reads *Autosport*.

Maud, Tamzin's black Staffordshire bull-terrier, watched their every move. They're off to Jamaica for two weeks. Maud must know they're going away. She's not stupid. Bull-terriers, I am assured, are very sensitive.

Johnty ate bread and cheese for lunch as he doesn't trust our kitchen. He wandered around with a cloth muttering, 'Survival of the fittest.' He's always horrified by the 'fridge which is crowded with suspicious looking tubs of yoghurt, most of which are horrifically out of date. Tamzin says that I can't possibly make Mum feel guilty about food.

'It's her love, her passion. People don't feel guilty about something they relish.' They left to take Maud, Atalanta's booties, a bunch of broccoli and a letter marked *Confidential* to Perry's house.

'Come here, Sweetness,' Tamzin said, calling her dog. 'You know Sophie, Johnty must have loved me very, very much. To think, he married me despite the state of the kitchen.' She closed the gate and disappeared.

I went to bed, exhausted, only to be invaded by James and his puppy-dog. We sat by the lake watching her play, drinking a fortifying port he brought along. (Port is meant to be good for your throat.) His spaniel tried to eat Daisy's green Ninja turtle puppet and we tried to eat Mum's beef burgers. Then James promptly lay down on the sofa and slept. I watched telly ~ more alert than him. But I am grateful. James, who seems immune to the mess we live in, shows his love as a friend by coming over here and bringing the most wonderful presents. He's incredibly generous and seems to know just what I need. I appreciate the gift of time more than anything. James loves talking and all us girls just thrive on chat. He's ended up with so many female friends that when he gets married we'll have to give him a hen party. I reckon a lot of men don't spend enough time developing their communication skills. They can make a noise but are incapable of listening. It must be hard on their wives. And ultimately hard on the husbands when they don't feel appreciated in return.

Mary-Dieu is astounding, she's closed down and depressed at the moment but she hasn't always been this way. She used to concentrate on having fun and making people laugh. She can be enormously loving, telling you outright that she loves you and giving you a big hug. It's wonderful. You suddenly feel valued. Such bold expression always blows me away but I never know what to say next. I can't take a compliment; must be too English and repressed. I don't know if I find expressing love verbally all that easy. I'm like Mum and Dad; I show love by helping people. Perhaps Mary-Dieu just needs to be told that we love her every day. She certainly doesn't respond in any way to offers of help. Never has done. I suppose she just can't accept love expressed in that form.

Perhaps Mary-Dieu doesn't have English reserve because she isn't English. It must be harder for her than we can imagine. She comes from Vietnam and, though her father was from California, she ended up here. When Saigon was under siege at the end of war, she was three years old, staying in the American/Vietnamese orphanage and dying of amoebic dysentery. An Englishman called Pat Ashe was out in Vietnam desperately trying to help the children of the war. Reports from witnesses elsewhere in Vietnam were so horrendous he thought the Communists would literally slaughter any child with American blood.

The *Daily Mail* sponsored an aeroplane and they brought ninety-nine children back to England. I don't know what the British Home Office thought of this, but Mum was there to meet the plane. She found nothing had been organised. There were a few volunteer nurses rushing around but no one could see that the children were desperate to go to the loo. Mum got stuck in and said she was so busy she didn't sleep for three and a half days. Then she was asked to take two children to Guildford Isolation Hospital. She fell completely in love with Mary-Dieu who was adorable and, being fair with huge eyes and a snub nose, looked just like her own child. She felt she couldn't leave her anyway; there were no night nurses and with six different tropical diseases Mary-Dieu needed a lot of attention. Mum kept thinking she would die but Mary-Dieu pulled through. She's a survivor. After six weeks Mum rang up Dad and said she wanted to adopt this little girl. Dad went off to a jeweller's shop and had a little silver bracelet engraved with Mary-Dieu's name. Mum's telephone number was on the other side so that whatever happened she could always call on us for help. What happened was that Pat Ashe decided it was right for Mary-Dieu to come to us and she did. Forever.

12th May ~ Had a dreadful nightmare about burglars and massive pots of Pond's cold cream. Now very, very tired this morning; spent. It hurts to swallow. I started to ask, 'Why this illness, Lord and how much longer and when are things going to start happening?' But I'm answered by the feeling that I do need this time and, 'How do I know that things aren't changing?' If that's the case, I ought to be *thankful* for being in this situation. I could be dying of dysentery in Saigon.

It's another beautiful day, which makes it easy to be grateful. The whole garden is showing me that although things seem to happen slowly to us, God is actually working with incredible power and force. All the leaves on a tree come out in a matter of four weeks or so. Pretty quick really. You can't hurry everything. You can't go around opening all the flowers. You'd hurt them and why bother when they're going to open naturally, all in good time.

Five weeks seems a long time to be in bed but it isn't a long time at work. Not when you're frantically busy making something. God must be continuously creating. Or re-creating. Through conviction and cleansing he can rework the corrupt world into a new thing if we just begin to let him in. He's the only one who can change mis-spent lives. I only ask that he'll change me. We all need our hearts changing the whole time otherwise the years will flit by and we'll find that 'nothing was gained under the sun.' To quote King Solomon more fully, this was me:

I denied myself nothing my eyes desired; I refused my heart no pleasure.

My heart took delight in all my work, and this was the reward for my labour.
Yet when I surveyed all that my hands had done and what I had toiled to achieve,
Everything was meaningless, a chasing after the wind; nothing was gained under the sun.

Granny says the most important work of all is prayer and I have a lot of opportunity for that. God be in my mind and in my thinking.

13th May ~ Today I entered four competitions hoping to win a holiday in Paris, a car, £50,000 and a set of saucepans. Very materialistic and no good to me at all should I die tomorrow, but still.

Daisy is with us without any shoes. Granny rings the whole time about the rooms she's renting out at the top of her house. 'A trainee solicitor is coming to look round ~ she's Nigerian.' As it turned out the girl didn't like the rooms and turned Granny down. I now keep getting bulletins that no one else has rung. The apartment is OK, as it's nice and high up, but the bath is in the kitchen. No one will want it. (Unless they like frying onions while they're having a scrub.)

Granny has spent her entire adult life enduring illness. The car crash in Nairobi injured her internal organs. Her liver, pancreas and duodenum were ruptured. She initially made a good recovery but, exacerbated by a bad wartime diet, her system kept producing too much insulin and she could not regulate her body temperature naturally. She cannot stand the cold. Until recently she was housebound, forever thinking she was going to die. Mum says she can't have been shopping for forty years; she has everything delivered. She isn't reclusive, but illness has cut her off from the world. Held in time, she still has the accent and vocabulary, the outlook and manners, certainly the clothes and the hair-do of someone living in the early 1950s. A bit like the Queen.

Granny now has new drugs, which regulate the insulin and enable her to venture out and even get up to Scotland, but she still regards herself as an invalid. In many ways her secret has been to be content with what she has, and what she can do. But it has to be said she's become used to doing very little. She has never, ever had a job.

I feel I'm beginning to get better and am able to move. But I must finish my letters. I'm writing all the letters I'd never had time to write. It's my shy way of being able to express what I feel and show my appreciation to people. God be in my pen and in my writing.

The kitchen has just filled with smoke and generally got me in a shaky state. I put the oven onto BROIL instead of OFF, then the phone rang upstairs. Now what was going to be for supper is a black, sticky mess. I still can't manage to do anything right. God be in my actions before I burn the house down.

14th May ~ Still haven't polished my shoes. I'm trying to think up a limerick about riding bicycles in order to win a Raleigh Pioneer. Not very good at this. Don't feel I would ever be able to ride one anyway.

I saw my first wasp today, which is early. Also saw a tiny caterpillar. I've been thinking about waiting on God and his timing. I hate wasting time and it's the thing I usually find hardest to give people. It's such a precious commodity. But, if we give God our lives then our time on earth is his to use, his to give away and his to protect. It's fascinating. If you look at the world there are seasons for everything, even in the tropics. Times when everything seems to lie fallow, followed by times of incredible spurts of growth with insects buzzing around pollinating everything. There's a reason for it all. The frost in winter kills the bugs that would otherwise get out of control. Jesus says clearly that if we ask for something in his name we'll be given it. He isn't slow to fulfil his promises.... as he sees slowness.

Mum and Dad have arrived back from Bedford where they went to present Daisy to Granny, who has never met her. She's the only granny I know who doesn't like babies. 'Nasty, wriggly things' was her description. You can't argue with her. My parents were tactfully planning to do something about the rooms; the ones at the top of the house that were rejected by the Nigerian trainee solicitor. It transpired that Granny hadn't even been up there. Poor Dad ended up clearing the horrendous mess left by the last occupants. He said there's no loo. The tenants have to use the one half way up the stairs.

15th May ~ I've decided that I must get dressed every morning, even if I end up lying about in my clothes, so I'm sitting up in bed wearing a Viyella shirt and two huge baggy cardigans over corduroy trousers. I can't bear the idea of wearing anything tight.

A postcard arrived from Rebecca saying that she has adopted five heron chicks. Sarah-Jane added that they've given all her guests fleas and that everyone is riding along scratching, and am I sure I haven't got tick bite fever? Tick bite fever? I did come back with a bite on my foot that went rather black, but I never developed headaches, and I know it gives you blinding ones. Perhaps I have some other weird tropical lurgi.

Mum has taken to calling Daisy 'Impy Cudworth'. This was actually a Birmingham accountancy firm in the early 1960s. The strangest things lodge in my mother's memory. Anyway, I spent all morning making Impy Cudworth a pair of pixie boots (very smart green corduroy ones with red silk trim) when Mum arrived back from town with a pair of horrid pink toddler booties. Huh.

Mum had been in court trying a pathetic man who keeps nicking things just so that he can stay in prison. 'He had dreadlocks, was wearing a T-shirt saying, *Legalise it*, and apparently had a problem with maggots in his crotch.'

'Oh, Mum really.'

'Of course none of the other magistrates noticed what he was wearing,' she went on, 'but *I* did.' You wouldn't think Cirencester could produce such characters but it does. And because it does, my mother gets to be a J.P. and I have to look after Impy while I'm ill. She's very good, but chews my books.

Dad is off canoeing and Granny rang to tell me that a builder, an electrician and a decorator are coming to look at the rooms. I don't suppose it's with a view to living there.

Mum is after a cure for my illness. Something that has more impact than emu oil.

Mum: 'I think what you need is a blood transfusion, darling.'

Me: 'I don't want someone else's filthy blood, thanks.'

Mum: 'You can have mine!'

Then she reckoned I needed my gall bladder out, or acupuncture: the search for the cure to the syndrome continued. Eventually she got talking to my old nanny Muriel, whose sister Maggie had M.E. for a year (a year!). Maggie got straight back to me. She said there's no difference between chronic fatigue syndrome (C.F.S) and M.E. (*myalgic encephalomyelitis*)[2], just that M.E. comes in different severities, probably depending on when you start to rest. For rest, and total rest, even when you're having a feeling-better splodge, is what you have to do. 'Be positive, don't let yourself get depressed, eat plenty of fresh fruit and vegetables and lots of vitamins, particularly vitamin C, B complex and zinc.' I haven't been very good about the zinc and so went and took a whole load tonight.

When she was ill herself, Maggie didn't know what M.E. was and tried to fight it, working whenever she could, because she was running her own business. I'm horrified to hear that she was ill for a whole year. Perhaps I should rest even more. The only good news is that, after the initial virus has abated, there's no evidence for M.E. being contagious. Muriel gave me an address for Action for M.E. and Chronic Fatigue and a paperback called *M.E. and You*. All I know is that the whole time she was talking, all I wanted to do was go back to bed.

Apparently 120,000 people in Bangladesh have died since the cyclone ten days ago but in those ten days, as many babies have been born in that country. It does put my life back into perspective.

16th May ~ Daisy is doing the gardening, flinging clumps of buttercups around. Dad showed me a grass root that was hard and sharp. He tells me it probably has greater tensile strength than iron. Henry, our ancient macaw, is in his tree again. I wish someone would nail a box up there so that he could live in it all the time. Much nicer for him and much, much nicer for us. They're driving me mad, the parrots. Mum has put all three in the dining room, so there's no room left for us to eat there anymore. They've been dominating the scene since Christmas and are making our lives a misery, yelling and shrieking whenever you pass by to get to the kitchen. 'Hello Henry,' the macaw screams, aggravating the others. When Mum lets out Josephine, her blue-fronted green Amazon, the noise level diminishes but only because she's busy pecking the veneer off the furniture. She ('dear little soul') has completely ruined a corner cabinet and took a chunk out of one of the ladder-back chairs. Dad found her tearing apart a Georgian picture frame surrounding an ancestor who would have been horrified. We keep being given these birds when they outlive their owners. Desperate relatives come round when their auntie has been put into a home. Mum adores the parrots but what will I do when they outlive her? Josephine can be quite violent.

I'm lying on my garden bed, having a medicinal glass of sherry, and trying not to think about it. It says in the paper:

- 25 million people died of 'flu in 1918. 'Virus' means poison in Latin. As viruses (viri? vires?) are not bacterial but chemical they can only replicate in cells. They operate by entering a cell, growing in it and killing it. (Could viruses be akin to grudges?) 'We are protected by the immune system. Itinerant viruses are ones that only affect a few people. They can grow and spread by a change in human activity and behaviour. For information on Ebola, Rift Valley, Lasser Fever... write to: Emerging Virus, PO Box 7, London W3.' (Odd address. Very odd having to write to a disease. Never mind, I'm going to ask it/them if M.E. is triggered by an itinerant virus or just a vengeful one.) ~ *There was no reply.*

- A meteorite landed in the garden of an old aged pensioner last Sunday. There was a picture of him in *The Telegraph* looking awfully pleased with his stone. In 1989 a rock weighing 400 million tons missed the earth by only a few hundred thousand miles. Someone calculated that if it had hit earth it would have killed 100 million people. (Oh yes, what if it had landed in the Pacific Ocean?) I'd love a meteorite to land in my garden. Just a small one.

- The Aquatic Reeds Research Centre at Sonning near Reading has discovered that when barley straw rots it can help combat algae problems. (What? Oh, in rivers. I thought this was medical research for a moment. I must be getting paranoid.) The straw creates an ideal habitat for invertebrates, which encourage more fish. (Of course.) They're putting wire cages full of it in the Pang. (I'll tell James.)

- The planet Neptune has a moon called Triton and Pluto has a moon called Charon. (Good for them.)
- Here we are: Chronic fatigue syndrome. Although anyone, of any age can contract this mysterious syndrome it's three times more common in women than in men. (I wonder why?) It's more prevalent in women than diseases such as multiple sclerosis or lung cancer. (Really.) The Japanese call it 'low natural killer syndrome'. (Do they now.) 'M.E. or *myalgic encephalomyelitis* means involvement of the muscles (*myalgic*) along with inflammation of the brain and spinal cord (*encephalomyelitis*), but this may not be an accurate description as there has been very little sound scientific evidence to show inflammation. The World Health Organisation has it listed as a disease of the nervous system.' (That means I need to see a neurologist, surely.) Abnormalities in brain function have now been demonstrated hence the decision by some doctors to change *encephalomyelitis* to *encephalopathy* (= a less specific disorder of brain function). One thing's clear; no one has been able to discover much about M.E. I would come down with a mystery disease.

I don't know why I'm drinking this sherry; it makes me feel peculiar. Alcohol does these days.

17th May ~ The Soap Opera party was good fun. James' family had been busy for weeks making preparations. Unlike me; I'd been in bed all day and by 6.00pm was still tired but

Mum and Dad persuaded me to go and I'm glad they did. I felt like a vegetable but, thinking of the advice I gave Rufus, went in gumboots and dungarees, wrapped up warmly in a Barbour as Ruth Archer. Rufus himself was actually looking quite hunky in an orange hard hat, climbing boots, and puffa jacket as *Twin Peaks*. His new wife, who after all doesn't speak English, must think we are all barking. I mean, his parents wore outrageous sailing gear as *Howard's Way* and started cackling with Mum and Dad, who were dressed in hideous outfits as Texans from *Dallas*. Is she left with the impression that all English people go to parties in horrible old clothes? Not my friend Diana; she was looking fabulous in a gold medieval gown with a high cone-shaped head-dress, as a character from *Blackadder*.

I couldn't think whether the series had been a soap opera or a comedy, but since Diana is flamboyant and about six foot tall she certainly brought a touch of drama to the scene. Alastair went as a Rasta for some reason. He makes a most scary one. He was wearing a crocheted hat with dreadlocks dangling from it but smelt normal and didn't seem to be scratching excessively. 'I'm Nigel from *The Archers.*' I can't begin to think that Nigel would have been a Rastafarian. He was an upper-class twit.

Everyone had brought their dogs. Rebecca would have loved it but they were a bit bouncy for me. I tried not to move and so sat as still as possible to conserve energy, only making six moves all evening. Move III : went through to supper. James had *promised* that I would sit next to two sexy men, but all I got was someone's deaf old father, dressed as a monk, on one side, and a hole on the other. But Claire Berry was on the other side of the hole and we had fun. She'd just recovered from typhoid. Her eighteen-month old baby had it too. Terrible. They contracted this from eating raw baby sweetcorn, from Marks and Spencers. I said she should complain. She laughed and explained that, actually, she was the Vegetable Buyer for Marks and Spencers. They were horrified to discover that the vegetables coming from the Third World weren't washed; they just look clean. She's certainly going to see that they're scrubbed now. The supermarket shelves are going to have little signs pinned to them saying, *'We recommend that these vegetables are boiled.*' I spent the rest of the evening wondering if I ate a raw and exotic vegetable back in April but can't remember.

18th May ~ Diana stayed with us after the party, only I might say she got to bed a great deal later than I did. We spent the whole day lying on the lawn, me on my outside bed, Diana on the newspapers, talking about our little worlds and the people in them. She's meant to be writing a ditty on surgical rubber gloves for the London Rubber Company for whom she toils, but you can't do that sort of thing on a Sunday. Instead we made our way through four papers and decided I'm going to win a Caribbean holiday.

Diana says she has no desire to go to church. 'Boring,' she pronounced, shaking her mass of curly hair. 'Most of my friends are happy clappers but I just can't get it,' she went on, trying to teach herself to tango from a diagram in the *Sunday Times*.

Late in the afternoon we went to pick rhubarb and broccoli, which we wrapped in the newspaper. I'm sending it back with Diana to pep up her urban diet. I have to say the London Rubber Co. supply their marketing executives with alarmingly sleek black vehicles. Alastair calls it 'the condom car'.

19th May ~ 'Please tell Diana to bring me a stock of Marigold rubber gloves next time she comes,' Mum said. 'I want to try out any snazzy new colours.' They're her favourite item of clothing. One of the few things that Perry and Mum have in common is that they both adore their rubber gloves. And they get quite upset if anyone borrows them.

The doctor calmly wrote me out a chit keeping me off work for another month and told me that the average duration for the syndrome is three months – three. I'm stunned. She says that tick-bite fever would have cleared up in a week, especially since I was on Tetracycline. An under-active thyroid can cause both mental and physical lethargy, but the test shows that isn't my problem. I do have low blood pressure. She's pretty sure that I have chronic fatigue and that, while it's important to 'take a little gentle exercise,' I must rest, avoid getting stressed and wait it out.

I've noticed the flowers on the ash tree are out. We have little grebe on the lake and migratory waders. I wheeled my garden bed so far from the house that Mum and Dad lost me at lunchtime. I'm still here again at the end of the garden with some awful old knitting of Perry's to keep me occupied. It's pink with batwing sleeves, started so long ago that the colours and pattern are long out of fashion. I realise that I'm slipping with my prayers for others. I'd like to become a great prayer warrior but lack self-discipline and get continual interference. It's no good. God doesn't want me to be half-hearted. He says that he'll spit us out if we are lukewarm.[v] I once was given the guide P.R.A.Y: **P**raise. **R**epent. **A**sk (for others, then for)

Yourself. I'm going to lie here, knitting, and change the world through prayer.

20th May ~ Solomon arrived today. He's twenty-three and has absolutely massive feet. Mum fell in love with him at first sight. He does have a dear face and suits her perfectly. I think he must be a cold-blooded Dutch carthorse. He has a moustache. I've never seen one on a horse before but he certainly has one, take it from me. He belongs to a straight talking man with a completely shaven head and tattoos all the way up his arms, who doesn't own a field. I don't know what Solomon will think of the sheep but Dad says they make good friends for horses. He also has spotty Leonard, Leonard the Donkey, to keep him company. Jake tried to snap at Solomon's heels, which I thought was idiotic considering the size of his iron-clad hooves.

The cow parsley is out and I've noticed the leaves in the beech tree, translucent and green, have just emerged. All the woods are white with flowering wild garlic. It has been a lovely sunny, sunny day. I thought I saw a chimpanzee in the cherry tree but it was a black crow; a big, sleek, black crow. They're marauding. There's one at the end of the lake, which eats the coot's eggs from her nest as she lays them. I know it's natural but I can't help finding it upsetting. I wish Dad would go and shoot crows.

Alastair rang to tell me that a secretary where he works at the Natural History Unit in Bristol, was so depleted by M.E. that she had to stay in a wheelchair and could only just manage to feed herself. Now he's read in the newspaper that an eleven-year old boy became 'paralysed' by M.E. and was thought to be psychiatrically ill. 'Five years later he's much better but still can't speak.' A cheering phone call. I'd better not go to any more tiring soap opera parties.

A creepy photographer came to photograph Mum and her otters for a women's magazine. Did he make a meal of it: great white screen, reflector umbrella, lights, masses of gear and self-important looking silver boxes all set up in the garden. I could tell he was flirting with me; 'You've got the wrong girl mate, I'm not impressed with your equipment or Leary glances.' Of course I was too shy to say anything. He had a scrawny male assistant with a ponytail and awful, shiny shell-suit bottoms with which he did such unattractive manoeuvrings that I had to leave the scene.

I'm being critical and judgmental, aren't I? Prayer warriors are not meant to wear this ugly attitude. 'Lord, help me to see the good in all people as you look for it in me.'

21st May ~ Mum very, very upset. She reacts by lashing out in tears and fury. She won't say what is wrong, just that she wants to give everything up and go and work as a nanny in Australia. Well, I'm upset because I'm missing a party at Syon House tomorrow; Crispin Odey is getting married again. How does he manage it? I haven't managed to get married once.
Action for M.E. has sent me a newsletter and pamphlet. Goodness. I wish I'd been able to read all this before. It seems that I'm not the only one going dotty: Clare Francis, the Chairman, says that 150,000 people in the United Kingdom have M.E.[3] Although anyone can suffer it 'most commonly affects fit, hard working people aged 20-40 in occupations with increased exposure to infections, especially enteroviruses.' She was a round-the-world yachtswoman. Like a teacher, it seems I was at a higher risk working with children. They say,

♦ 'There is, at present, no definitive treatment for M.E., but patients diagnosed early and able to rest in the first year of illness and avoid relapses have a better chance of recovery. This is in contrast to the benefits from hard exercise often experienced by those unfit or mildly fatigued following depression. *Exercising beyond safe limits for people with M.E.*

can exacerbate M.E. symptoms and lead to a prolonged relapse.'[4]

'Oh Jake, listen to this. It says here,

♦ 'Around 60% of people with M.E. improve significantly, although they may not regain full health. Up to 20% may become severely and chronically disabled. However 20% of people are likely to make a full recovery in two to four years. Early diagnosis and advice on managing the illness can help recovery.'[5] (Yikes.)

I didn't know what I was up against, that M.E. can be so seriously disabling. And yet I still don't know for sure if this is the illness that I have. 'What should I do Lord?'

The phone rang. It was 10.30pm and I was in the bath but heaved myself out.

'Is that Mrs. Neville?'

'No, it's Sophie. Can I help you?'

'Sophie?'

'Yes.' It was Sarah-Jane, sounding very small, six thousand miles away.

'There has been a bad accident. Rebecca is in intensive care. She has serious head injuries and is in a coma. I can't reach her parents. Can you handle things in England for me?'

'I need your contact numbers,' I muttered. 'Tell me what happened.' I was grabbing pencils, wrapped in my towel, dripping from the bath.

Rebecca had been driving a big Toyota 4WD along a main road when the front tyre blew out. The loaded vehicle rolled down a bank. She couldn't have been wearing a safety belt because she'd been flung out of the window at such speed that she skidded along the tarmac on her head and shoulders. The girl sitting beside her had been kept in by her seat belt and was fine. She stopped a passing car and managed to get Rebecca taken to casualty.

'She's alive but could have permanent brain damage.'

'Is she in Johannesburg?'

'No, a run-down Afrikaans hospital in the Lowveld. I think they're moving her to Pretoria tomorrow. I know a brain surgeon who says he'll do his best to help.' Goodness. Sarah-Jane's good in a crisis. I spun into an awful dither. There I was, in the middle of the night, trying to track down Rebecca's family and not finding it easy. I made call after call. Her parents, it turned out, were on a driving holiday in France. Her sister was too busy to fly out. I managed to find her old boyfriend who said, 'Will she be a vegetable?'

22nd May ~ Sophie the liaison officer. I was in such a state I got tight with the stress, but it was good to have something useful to do. I rang James and all Rebecca's other friends, explaining the situation and encouraging them to send letters to the hospital. I made them promise to ring the friends whom I don't know. Then I set to and prayed earnestly for Rebecca's treatment and recovery. For her complete healing. It was I who encouraged Rebecca to go back to South Africa in the first place.

The news brought things back into perspective for Mum who told me why she'd been so upset. The Chairman of the Magistrates told her off for speaking as she did to the man with the maggoty problem and the dreadlocks. I know what the problem is. No-one else wants to sit on the bench with her. Too embarrassing. She told one man who came before the court to take his hand out of his pocket. He couldn't. He only had one hand. She's going on a J.P. training weekend tomorrow so we left it that she would talk to the chap in charge. I think Cirencester is a bit tame for her and that she'd have more fun in a tough area like Gloucester where she goes anyway to see Mary-Dieu and Daisy.

Nicola came to see me in the afternoon with her neurotic sheepdog, Polly. I made her look at all my photos of the horse safaris. She wouldn't believe me about Solomon's moustache so we went to inspect it. This turned into a drama because it entailed trying to keep Polly away from the sheep, which started rushing about in all directions, just like me in a crisis. My energy level was near zero and I could only totter along. I kept talking about Rebecca whom Nicola doesn't know. Then I showed her more photographs to try and explain. There was one I took in January of Rebecca with some piglets. I burst into tears, muttering, 'We might lose her, and it's all my fault,' which was ridiculous. And faithless. And just made Nicola feel awkward. It's a good thing she's known me for a long time.

A stone sculptor came round to sketch the otters. He said he'd been erecting a statue in the middle of a pond at the Barbican Theatre yesterday when the caretaker rushed up, screaming at him to get out. Apparently there are terrapins in that pond capable of biting off body parts... He'd better not try swimming with our otter Jims.

The lilac is out and the flies have arrived; life goes on.

23rd May ~ Dad has had another awful gardening accident. I don't know how he does it. He was mowing along the edge of the lake on his sit-upon mower. He wanted to do the edge neatly but got too close and the whole machine toppled into the water. Dad was caught underneath with his foot trapped in the clay lakebed. Underwater. Somehow he managed to hold his breath and dig himself out. He was just able to struggle free and come up to the surface in time.

Dad amazes me; he changed his clothes, pulled out the mower with his car and now he's only concerned about the impact of the water on the diesel engine and hydraulics. All Mum said was that he's lucky we don't have terrapins.

Perry, Robert (her husband) and Atalanta arrived ~ with Perry's new vacuum cleaner. No one else I know would bring one with her. She'd just bought it for £490 and attacked the sitting room directly upon arrival. She was out to prove how filthy we are; as if we don't realise anyway. This new thing vibrates and sucks down to seven inches. Well, Perry had a wonderful time getting out what is reputedly our skin scale (the instruction manual calls this 'body ash') and emptying the bag of dust with glee. She did all the beds (especially where our feet go), the chairs and floors and even has attachments to do the ceiling. Robert says he has to stop her talking about it at dinner parties. Atalanta also showed signs of interest, which is ominous.

Perry kindly made a stir-fry for lunch (light but healthy). I persuaded Robert to try to shoot a crow, but of course all the crows disappeared and he just trudged around a bit with the air rifle cocked. He's a major in the British Army; why isn't he better at shooting things? I don't know what the neighbours think. They currently have a builder pouring cement into their cellar.

I still feel like a wrung out dish-rag. I spent four hours in bed after Perry's visit. When I eventually staggered downstairs James had arrived with a bottle of wine. We drank it with Mum and watercress soup. I then wasted a substantial amount of energy trying to persuade him not to put his dog in pup, on account of the fact that she's still a teenager and there are too many dogs in the world.

James has moved into a cottage owned by someone called Shanda Lear. What a brilliant name. All her friends came to inspect him and I got the impression that he'd been overwhelmed by horsy girls. We lay across my bed later trying to think of what we could send Rebecca. He said he'd been praying for her, which is good news. He doesn't normally talk about things like prayer. I don't know why it should be shy making but it is, isn't it? I later had great fun describing his visit here to her in a letter. Not sure if she'll be up to getting the true meaning of that girl's name.

The *Action for M.E.* association is going to send me all the scientific articles on chronic fatigue from *The Lancet*. Goody gumdrops. Charlotte, a friend from work who besides being a television researcher is a qualified aromatherapist, rang to recommend: Dr. Mary Loveday, Harley Street Specialist and neurologist. (I rang. Her receptionist said she has a six-month waiting list. Great.)

24th May ~ Mum returned in a good mood from her J.P. training weekend, where she seemed to have drunk a lot of booze whilst learning about licensing laws, but is still bent double from unblocking Mary-Dieu's waste pipe on Friday.

Alastair arrived later and generally strode about exhausting me with his display of vigour. It's absolutely impossible to discuss abstract ideas with him. He likes facts. Quite funny; this is how he chats up girls:

Al: 'What's the longest animal in the world?'

Girl: 'I've no idea.'

Al: 'It's a ribbon worm.' (Apparently, a dead one was washed up on some beach measuring 180 foot.)

Al: 'What's the fastest bird in the world?'

Me: 'Peregrine falcon.'

Al: 'No; wrong. Not in powered flight. It's an eider duck.' (I can't imagine this without thinking of an airborne eiderdown.)

Al: 'What's the most common bird in the world?'

Girl: 'A sparrow.'

Al: 'No, storm petrel.' (Have you *ever* seen one?)

He rowed me up the lake in Dad's new boat and we came back for a lovely supper Mum had made which we ate at the big green table outside. I think Al was a bit apprehensive about the food until he was faced with a wonderful pudding made from meringue, cream and mango. He isn't remotely worried about Rebecca, says she's as tough as nails and will pull through in no time.

Alastair is making a series on Antarctica, or hopes to, and so Dad brought out all his books on Shackleton. A relation of ours called Eric Marshall was on the first expedition. He was the doctor.

I had to lie down, which meant Alastair coming upstairs and generally devastating my room; into all my invitations, magazines, books and textiles, like a large toddler. 'Will you make me some silk boxer-shorts? Or a bowtie?' Then, with everything everywhere he looked round and declared, 'Sophie, you know your room really is a mess.' He can't talk. His own bedroom is known as 'the rhino pen'.

25th May ~ First dragonfly.

Still feeling ghastly despite lovely weather. Better ring Dr. Loveday again; see if I can scrounge an appointment. Seem to have a problem with my nose. As a child I had terrible hayfever and pretty bad allergies. No one knew it but I was seriously allergic to feathers. This problem is exacerbated if you have a Granny determined to wrap you up under leaky old eiderdowns. I nearly died of asthma one year. It wasn't something common or well understood then. Dr. Knight-Webb was convinced I had bronchitis. He prescribed bottle after bottle of penicillin, which would lie half-finished in the 'fridge... I don't think that can have been exactly beneficial to my developing immune system. Maybe it's reduced the power antibiotics could have right now. I hardly get asthma these days but have a continually blocked nose. Why, I don't know. I'm allergic to cats but we don't have any. Perhaps it's some other heinous thing.

I sat up in bed answering some letters that arrived from the office. When I just couldn't bear to be inside any longer, I went out to lie in the garden bed. Despite her bad back Mum went to Gloucester and brought back Impy Cudworth. (Miss Daisy.) It took Mary-Dieu fifteen minutes to open the door. Inside her basement it was baking hot ~ heating full on and the curtains drawn with the windows closed. Sealed up in her solitude while I lie in the garden in shorts, ill but happy as anything. 'Oh dear God, I think she must be much iller than me, just in a different way. Help me to try and understand her better. Please protect her. Hold her in your arms.'

Impy arrived looking yellowish and cross but she's content now even though confined to an old playpen. Mum found it in Gloucester. She saw it abandoned in someone's garden and just asked the man for it. She doesn't want Daisy to fall in the lake. I can't believe it but the sun is so hot I have burnt legs. Funnily enough, when I was well I found it exhausting looking after small children, and vaguely irritating, as I didn't have the patience. Now I'm more on the level of an eighteen-month old baby myself I find it much less of a strain. Impy loves the numbers book I made her out of buttons and I chat away to her about the colours. I can't wait for her to start talking.

Mum had a hugely tall visitor ~ a chap of 6'8". He did look odd standing next to her and Impy who isn't even 2'8". We started talking about anti-biotics. Mum gave this complete stranger the graphic details of how Tamzin, having drunk a whole bottle of banana-flavoured penicillin by mistake, had to be forced to drink salt water and was held upside-down by the ankles, until she was sick on the dining room floor. What Mum didn't explain was that Tamzin was two-and-a-half years old at the time.

At last I have news of Rebecca. She's in intensive care, drifting in an out of consciousness. The surgeon didn't operate, just stitched up her head. She doesn't have any health insurance.

26th May ~ Dreadful morning. Stayed in bed. Nicola came after lunch by which time I'd perked up and begun to enjoy myself. We lay in the sun chatting. Impy emerged from sleep and we went for a walk down the valley and back up the towpath alongside the old canal, looking at the incredible variety of wild flowers; pink campion, periwinkles, borage and trees greener than green. Somehow the walking and talking did me good and we returned to let Daisy run barefoot on the lawn. I actually remembered to give Nicola her wedding present, a mirror, and, as she said, we ought to have them outside, as the reflections are too beautiful.

'I love the white doves you have here,' she said as we walked to the car and the birds rose up around us.

'Oh, do you? I loathe them.'

'Why?'

'They seemed like rather a romantic idea at first, but they don't keep to the dovecot and have mucky roosts all over the place. They can spread about twelve different diseases. Come and catch a pair if you like.' She thought not.

So many enticements in the newspaper:
- 'Shape your own future!' (How I would love to). 'Today's difficult residential lending market conditions have created an exciting high profile opportunity for a talented and ambitious…. Debt Recovery Professional…' then it goes on to tell you that, 'You will have an outstanding track record in the collection of unsecured personal debt. Interestingly you indicate the remuneration sought.' (I don't believe this; they need debt collectors so badly you can ask for whatever salary you want.)

I was thinking about my own opportunities and options. Have I, and am I, making the most of my life? I'm determined to work in the office less and spend more time seeing the world. At least being ill has allowed me to live here in the country, spending time with my parents and Daisy. Like being on holiday it has enabled me to relax and be myself. Perhaps I ought to change my job to accommodate the way I want to live. Perhaps I'm in for a change away from television anyway. James thinks I ought to start drawing more seriously.

27th May ~ I went riding. Mum suggested it and got Solomon ready for me, so I went up through the woods. Solomon did not particularly agree with where I wanted to go but we only plodded about. Still, I was exhausted by it. Not a good idea. The fatigue struck me down in the afternoon and I spent about three hours lying in a stupor unable to move or read. I felt sad and moany. Untrusting. How do I know how things would be if this hadn't happened? Maybe by conking out now I've avoided contracting some terrible degenerative disease and will end up living a lot longer. I've hardly been in a car in the last seven weeks. You never know, I could have avoided being in some horrific pile-up on the motorway. I could have been travelling in Africa with Rebecca. I wish I could fly out to help, but Sarah-Jane said today that it looks as if she's out of danger and is going to be fine. What a relief.

I can't understand why I should be knocked sideways by riding; I've always ridden, I was born on a horse. No, that's a lie. I was born in this four-poster bed. I arrived early and was delivered by my great-grandmother. She was Scottish. Mum said she tied one of her legs to the bedpost with a towel and pulled on the other. 'Brace yourself,' she shrieked. 'You're going to split from side to side.' The horror. I'm sure Granny wanted to be there as well, but she was too ill. She sent Mum one of those rubber dog's bones to bite on so that she could bear the pain. It was a blue bone. I found it years later in a cupboard. Dad was banned from all proceedings, of course, except that he'd had to dig a hole to bury the placenta in the herbaceous border.

28th May ~ I'm all alone in the house. I feel better today, much better than I have been and very peaceful. I've been lying in the garden listening to wood pigeon. I'm meant to be at a party in Wiltshire. Perry and Robert are going.

My awful gritty throat does seem to be calming down, so perhaps my immune system is jerking back into life. I now realise how much my body has needed this time of recuperation. Total rest. Too bad if I'm non-productive. I must just try to appreciate not having to do anything.

Daddy pointed out that aged sixty-two this is the first spring that he has ever been free from the worry and commitments of running a business. We rush away our lives.

All the same I wish I could have gone to the party; the only dramatic thing that happened today was that a dove landed on my head in the washing machine room.

Our neighbour came round in the evening asking if she could borrow a baby-walker. She explained that two of her six Dachshunds have slipped discs and she wants to try and get them walking again. We tried with an agile one but it's difficult to get a grip on a sausage dog. After a long session we decided that it would be hopeless.

Granny has gone to stay with my Aunt Hermione who lives by Loch Lomond. To make a bit of extra dosh Hermione has made her dining room into a craft shop. Mum thought it a good idea to install Granny as a shop girl. Mistake. My cousin says she terrifies all the customers. And worse. She's not even into decimal coinage yet. When asked the price she'll say, 'Oh fifteen bob' and take 75p for something that is worth about ten times the price.

29th May ~ I was lying in the garden utterly absorbed in my book when I looked up to see another little dog; Tessa. I turned over to find James trudging towards me. He'd brought me three sketchpads and an incredibly expensive box of pencils.

James explained that he wanted me to start painting. He showed me a rather naive watercolour of running zebra that a friend of his had painted in Kenya saying that when she exhibited in Cirencester everything sold. I thought, 'Goodness, I could do better than that.' James saw this and looked pleased. He must know about the catalyst of a challenge and is a great encourager; that's a valuable gift.

It must have been at least 3.30pm and I'd already eaten but James had brought cold white wine, smoked salmon and French bread. I found a lemon, made a herb salad and brought out the Ryvita. I tapped the packet a bit to make sure there were no weevils while James took everything out to the table under the willow tree. It was a delicious lunch. I hid from him the terrible secret that it was exactly what I'd eaten, alone, two hours earlier.

We rowed down to the field beyond the lake. I wanted to see if I could find a meteorite, but didn't have the strength. I lay watching as James searched but he got distracted exploring all the little things there. A kingfisher darted past and I saw a dipper with two fledglings, which I thought quite special. James said they have to learn to dive into the rushing water as they live off caddis fly larvae. They're the funny long things you find in streams covered in little bits of stone and shell. James rowed us back and we lay on the lawn talking about painting. And gossiping. It's a terrible habit, but I can't resist and James always has all the inside info. He says that Alastair's accumulated so many parking tickets he has received a summons and now his car is sitting on the forecourt of the *BBC* with not one, but two punctures. He once got H.M. Customs and Excise into a tizz by trying to bring a small population of termites back from Uganda in a jam jar. He was most upset when they were confiscated.

Mum and Dad returned from their separate ventures and soon we all had supper together. I made James tell us about the girls he lives with and what they do all day long. They're attractive girls by all accounts, but he seemed intent on changing the subject. He told Mum that the *BBC* are planning to make a series on carnivores called *The Velvet Claw* and that a chap called Paul wanted to ask her if the otters would mind being in it. They wouldn't mind a bit. Like girls they thrive on attention.

30th May ~ I woke not feeling so bad and was down happily for breakfast outside at the green table quite early. I sat eating paw-paw and lemon with coffee, glad not to have to exist off a diet of caddis fly larvae.

I'd gathered all my art materials into a basket ready to produce a great masterpiece but decided to write to Rebecca first and found it was all I could manage. Then my parents decided to have a raging row about a colander of all things. They'd lost it. (Scream ~ 'It all your fault.'- Scream). How can they get so stressed about the location of a sieve? I suddenly felt devastated and went to bed until at least 3 o'clock. I can't fight when there's no fight in me.

The phone rang. Granny has done an awful thing. I can't believe it's true, but it is. My cousin Olivia reported that a large Asian family arrived to see round the craft shop. Now Granny is quite tall and forbidding. Born in Malaya in 1913 she is what you might call a daughter of the British Empire. An Imperialist through and through. She let the family into the hall, and while staring straight at them shouted back to the kitchen, 'Hermione. Hermione, you must come at once. There are natives in the hall.'

On with the battle: Perry told me to ring a girl called Caroline who had M.E. badly for ten years, suffering severe fatigue, pain, collapse, partial paralysis. She eventually paid a great deal of money to go to a dietary clinic in Knightly for three weeks and found she was chronically allergic to certain foods ~ soya (which most domestic livestock are given to eat), wheat and milk. She said that, after going on a fast, she took her pulse rate before eating certain foods. It was 62. She ate a plate of beef and her pulse rate rose to 102 so quickly she fell unconscious. She said life was dismal before the diagnosis. She's obviously had loads of tests... I've only ever been allergic to inhalants, but I'm going to try giving up wheat for a while to see if it could be a problem. I've always just gobbled up anything and everything regardless. Perhaps I ought to consider what I consume more carefully.

31st May ~

'Oh no James, I can't paint feeling like this. And how could I ever make a living out of it? I'd have to live in a commune like Rufus, and would never have enough money to buy shampoo. All I can do is lie and read. I'm drained for two days by your visit alone.' He's not here. I lie in the garden watching clouds, gazing at the lake. It's quite beautiful. The trees are turning a darker green and the flowers are more rigorous. Dad spends his days planting and mowing. There is a pochard on the lake, beetles, a spider that looks like a mustard seed on legs. There's so much to do and draw and study in all its minutiae. And now I have time to look and time to smell and time to listen and feel this peace. Time to enjoy stillness.

No, I can't. It's incredibly noisy here with the thundering waterfall and the pigeons; no wonder we all shout at each other.

And it's a Bank Holiday so there is the neighbour's chain-saw, tooting cars and passing children screaming at the parrots, sending them into a shrieking frenzy. This gets the otters going, 'Squeak, squeak, squeak.' But it's always been like this. Mum thinks I must be getting more sensitive to sound. Can I be? I certainly can't bear bright light and am beginning to have to wear my dark glasses in bed. In the bedroom bed.

If I weren't ill I would be directing a television studio today, or trying to. It seems incredible. I know something; I would have missed this spring, missed out on smelling the wild garlic.

Bang! It was a baked potato exploding in my hand, hitting my face with searingly hot pieces that shot out from its middle. I stood by the stove, rocking on my feet unable to take the shock but realising it was a miracle I could still see. I must have forgotten to prick the potato before I put it in the oven. It was only a little one but there are white bits all over the kitchen. Mum told me to go back to bed.

My cousin has been bravely tackling Granny about calling people natives.

'But Olivia, I was born in the Far East and brought up in Tanzania, I have a deep love for indigenous people.' What can one say? She's not racist it's just that, with her language stuck somewhere in the 1930s, these words come whizzing out of her mouth. To her the term 'natives' is the same as saying there are Spaniards, or Scots for that matter, in the hall. And Granny is a native Scot.

All attempts at staff training have rather backfired too. Granny breaks every Trade Description rule Hermione tries to comply with. This, apparently is her latest sales spiel:

'Jam!' she declares, 'made by my daughter.' (Kitchen as yet unknown to Health Inspector.)

'Soap!' she says shoving people's faces into a pile of highly scented soap stacked up on a shelf above the hall radiator. 'It's all made by my daughter. With natural chemicals.' (This is untrue.)

'Shells, from Loch Lomond.' (They're seashells from the Pacific.)

Hermione once said that the trick to selling an Aran sweater was to get the customers to try one on. Olivia said that she heard muffled shrieks coming from the dining room yesterday only to find some poor tourist being jammed into a tight, itchy, traditional Aran jersey, Granny heaving at the hem. In her zeal to sell she'd forgotten about the customer's arms. His little hands were sticking out at the bottom quivering. I know how he feels, Granny dressed me for years and it's a terrifying experience.

I found the colander. It was outside by the compost heap.

JUNE ~ I got to wondering

1ˢᵗ June ~

This day was spent in bed. Mum has had to put a sheepskin under my bottom sheet to stop me getting bedsores... I ask you.

I've done little more than read ~ Rosamund Lehmann ~ and pluck away at an awful little tapestry Granny herself once gave me to finish. I see it as a kind of therapy. Corrie ten Boom, who went through hell in a German concentration camp during the war, reckons that God's plan for our lives looks like a tapestry that we can only see from the back. It often looks messy. But it has to be like that; it's the way something intricate and complicated with lots of colour is made, and that's that. We can't work out the design until it's finished and we can see it from the other side; from God's perspective. When I look at my tapestry the plain background, which is necessary for the whole picture, it's quite neat at the back. But then there are times of order in our lives as well as what seems like utter confusion. I expect it's the same for everyone. We wouldn't want our lives to be a single plain sheet of stitching even if both sides were neat. It would be dull and God would get bored making it.

The problem with this tapestry is that I'm running out of red wool. Because Granny must have started it in the 1950s, I'll never be able to match the colour. I've been thinking that all the red ought to go. It might have been fashionable then, but it doesn't work with interior colours today. I could plough ahead but it'll be much better if I unpick the red. I don't want to spend all this time on something that looks hideous and will end up not being used. Is God's work in our lives like this sometimes? Does he have to un-pick bits when we've made mistakes, wrong decisions or can't bear to change? Do we have to suffer being taken away from a partnership or position, in order to be joined to someone or something that's going to be so much better, more useful and infinitely more beautiful in the end.

Perhaps it's not as simple as that. We've been given free choice after all. John Irvine, our vicar in London, says God has a perfect will and a permissive will. He has great plans for us but if we choose to spend our inheritance badly, like the prodigal son, he allows us to.

John reckons that just as he would let his little girl choose what to do with her day, so our Father gives us the choice. 'If she asks me I'll help her and I'll give her what she needs, although not always what she wants. I'll also watch over her and see she's safe. But if I don't let her make mistakes she won't learn, which could be disastrous later on. What's wonderful is when she finds an interest she's keen on; we can follow it and help her to reach her full potential in that area. The sad thing is that she keeps on asking me for a pony. I'd love her to have one, but it just isn't possible yet.' Oh yes Lord,

I want a pony and to be well enough to be able to ride one. Won't you make me better?

I have to do what I can. I've been off wheat for a week, much to Mum's annoyance. I took my pulse at lunchtime, which was 84-87, and then ate some bread to see if I have an allergic reaction. I was expecting to collapse, writhing in agony, but there wasn't any change at all. I'm going to eliminate dairy products from my diet next; milk, cheese, butter, cream and yoghurt.

'I would have thought,' Mum said in disbelief, 'that you could do with the calcium.'

'But I'm taking all these vitamins.' She thinks this is cranky.

I now feel infuriatingly weak and it's so cold I'm in bed again rather than lying outside. I've just been horrible to Granny. 'Please don't keep saying, "Oh poor you" like that, I'm trying to be positive about this illness.' She was so upset that she rang Perry twice. Perry was upset because she'd left one of her favourite shoes in a field at the party on Saturday, but pleased because she'd got a part acting a pregnant doctor in the *BBC* drama *Casualty*.

Dad had been to see Tamzin and was thrilled because she gave him a bottle of whisky he'd won in a raffle that her friend Raddy had organised. Mum grabbed it out of his hand as he walked through the door. 'Just what I need for the dinner party tonight.' I went down and joined them for a short time. They had invited the Pharmacist, his wife and a man who used to have a bakery shop in Tetbury. The food was good and Mum was larger than life. The poor Mrs. Pharmacist went to my parents' bathroom by mistake. This isn't a very comfortable place. There's no door and she couldn't find the light, so had to do everything in the dark. What she wouldn't have known about was that loo seat came off in 1979 and has never been replaced. Mum thinks sitting on the cold porcelain is good for you.

All through dinner I kept finding bits of potato, from the explosion yesterday, stuck in my hair.

2nd June ~ Mum and Dad made my bed properly and what with the sheepskin under me I had a marvellous lie-in. Only it wasn't a lie-in, it was a having-to-be-in. I was awake and could hear and see but couldn't move with fatigue.

I gulped a cup of tea and lay motionless even though I was sure the house was alive with burglars. What I thought was the alarm turned out to be the new telephone. It was James ringing to say that Rebecca is flying home next Wednesday. She's out of hospital and speaking fluently, but is badly grazed and very sore. We can be two crocks together.

I've received two journals which tell me all about which competitions to enter. I'm making a professional attempt to win a car, seeing this as an economically good use of my time. In fact I ended up sending off loads of postcards, entering draws promoting a variety of commercial products, which had nothing to do with cars at all. It's really a pathetic form of gambling and contemptible beyond belief but, as Diana says, 'Who cares?'

The Competitor's Companion journals themselves are hysterical. You can win '5 x lunch with Barbara Cartland at her home in Hertfordshire' and 'an unspecified number of shell-suits.' I'm going to make Tamzin go in for the *Chunky Dog Food* competition for which you have to send in a photo of your dog. She can enter one of her fat, black bull-terrier. For another competition you have to 'Take a photo that you think best captures the dynamic image of *Drakkar Noir*,' which is apparently a male 'fragrance'. I'll send that to Tamzin too. She can post off the same picture twice.

People write in to say what they've won. One man wrote to say he'd received: Two mugs, a soft toy elephant, electric scales, a running vest, £5.70 voucher and a tea towel. In a *News of the World* competition he won a piece of scud missile.

I entered lots more competitions and then had to ring a lady called Evelyn who'd left a message on the answerphone. She told me I've won a two-week cruise in the Caribbean. How exciting. It wasn't from a competition at all. They just drew my name from the electoral register.

3rd June ~ My friends Johnny and Mary are getting married in Northumberland today and I can't go. And Griz asked me to stay and I can't go either. Instead I'm going to see the Pharmacist's son Jeremy for acupuncture, 'aqua-puncture' as

James calls it... we'll see. I'm not too sure about alternative medicine. But Mum's set this course up for me and I don't want to be narrow-minded. My friend Mikie, who is a racehorse trainer, says it works on animals. He uses it on his horses, explaining that the needles alert nerves that stimulate body organs to repair themselves in the same way that drugs send chemical signals to the brain. An aspirin, for example can tell the brain 'no pain, thanks,' and so can a needle stuck in a nerve. Good Lord protect me.

The sun is shining for the first time in days and I'm outside, lying on the garden bed, feeling much better. I'm so excited about winning the Caribbean holiday but, despite having just won a bottle of whisky, Dad thinks these competitions could be dodgy and is sure the holiday I've won is some sort of con. Why should it be a con? I'm thrilled.

Later: I drove, shakily, to Jeremy's house stopping outside the newsagent's on the way. As I opened my car door I nearly knocked a man off his bicycle. Feeling stupid I staggered on, clutching the directions in one hand, until I found myself at a cottage in the middle of nowhere. There didn't seem to be anyone about. I was just wondering what to do when Jeremy came whizzing around a corner and steered me into his consulting room. It smelt of joss sticks and was hung with Indian cloth. Bits of what can only be described as 'pieces from the Far East' made up the furnishings. I sat in an upright chair opposite a little scribe's desk. After much 'Damning' Jeremy found ink for his fountain pen. He asked me about my health and whether I felt hot or cold. He took notes on the pattern of viruses, my lifestyle, how I'd slept recently, notes about the nightmares, about my menstrual cycle (Tamzin always calls this getting on your menstrual bicycle, but never mind) and he asked whether I had all the symptoms of M.E. It seems I don't. I'm not running a fever or battling with migraines. I do have some muscle ache but not 'severe joint pain'. Patients tend to get candida apparently. I don't seem to have tummy aches, nausea or problems with my digestion; all common symptoms. What a mercy.

So. That was it, the diagnosis prior to treatment. We must have talked for an hour or so. No needles. £50, but he did know about chronic fatigue and I'm assured that he's highly regarded. It was good to talk to someone who thinks he can do something about my condition. I tottered back home to bed.

Evelyn has just rung back. 'When would you be able to come to our promotion?' Promotion? Ha. I haven't won a holiday, they were just tempting me to come to a timeshare sales bash. What a swizz. Mum and Dad returned from a not very thrilling day filming in Scunthorpe, full of fish and chips and devoid of sympathy.

4th June ~ A better day.

Dad has taken *Tulip*, the boat he built, off to be displayed at the *Classic Wooden Boat Exhibition* in Greenwich. Mum took me to the village fête in Rodmarton. We wandered up the drive of the Manor past a tiny pony giving cart rides and suddenly seemed to be in the middle of a *Dog who looks most like owner* competition, which was bizarre and most alarming. A pug dog was being led around by a portly, middle-aged woman in a tight beige suit with black patent leather shoes and a brand new perm.

'Do look, it's absolutely priceless.'

'Shut up, Mum.'

I staggered on unable to take everything in but it was all happening sure enough: *Win a ride in a Noddy Car* and *Guess the weight of the pig*. There were raffles, draws and tombolas galore; gambling left, right and centre, and all in aid of the church.

The church itself was cool and still. It was filled with displays of christening robes and terribly bad flower arrangements that were all dying. They had proud little placards beside them declaring that Mrs. So-and-so had entered the dismal thing. Rather embarrassing I thought. Mum knelt down to pray in a prominent place, amazing the next lot of people who came in before they realised that they were in a church, built for this purpose.

I have to say that in the village hall was a most impressive art exhibition with a huge variety of styles. The artists round here are brilliant. I was intrigued at the range; they had everything from fluid charcoal sketches to intricate oil paintings.

    Why do some people's lives go more smoothly than others? It often has nothing to do with our choice. Look at those poor people in Bangladesh who lost everything in a cyclone. Perhaps our lives are like all these different paintings. Some flow freely like wonderful, glowing watercolours. Other pictures, like other lives, seem wrought with pain. The artist might find every intricate stroke takes intense consideration. At other times he has to plough on boldly and with great courage, making changes to days of work that risk mucking up the whole thing. Sometimes it just all goes wrong, but when I'm painting I try to work on through the mistakes. I'm often surprised by the outcome. My best drawings are actually rectified disasters.

5th June ~ Jeremy stuck the needles in me this time. He said, to my alarm, that he'd rung my doctor and they agreed that I should be off work for at least another three months. That is until the beginning of *September*. I can't bear it. He says that I'm 'Not too far gone for all that,' but I must rest. He agreed that Charlotte-the-aromatherapist could come and massage me but 'No other exertions, now.' He did not care for the idea of a magnesium supplement, suggested in *The Lancet*, and just told me to keep off cured meats, as they are, in Chinese terms, 'too hot for me.' Oh dear, I love salami. He said I'm suffering from heat and damp together. Yuck. He took a funny Chinese pulse and examined my mouth with a little torch. My mouth ulcers are, apparently, an indication of 'heat'. (Don't they just indicate that I'm run down?) I'm not sure about all this, but found myself writing out another cheque for fifty quid.

Why I drove to Jeremy's house I do not know. It's only ten minutes away but I nearly hit a dustcart on the way home. I'm stupefied, stunned. How could I fail to see such a huge object? I seem to have lost the co-ordination needed to steer effectively and fear I really will have to immobilise myself.

I found Dad looking after Atalanta. He'd plonked her in a boat that was lying on the lawn and she was happily fiddling with the fittings. Poor Dad, he had us four and is now looking after the second generation of little girls. Perry is with Mum in Cheltenham. They're both working on a television drama called *Dead Romantic*. What a title. Wish I'd thought it up. Tamzin rang, laughing, having just returned from a wedding in Hamburg. She thanked me for sending her *The Competitor's Companion* and says she's longing to win a lunch with Barbara Cartland, but would she have to go five times?

Olivia rang from Scotland to tell me about Granny and the python in the hall. I'd forgotten about that. It's huge; a terrible old stuffed one and must have been made into a standard lamp by some deranged taxidermist in Arusha. It used to hold a light bulb in its mouth and the electric fitting is still there, standing upright between two sets of barbed teeth. Granny, however, is inordinately proud that her father shot the snake on their coffee farm in Tanzania and has been horrifying customers with stories on their way out of the craft shop as well as on the way in.

I have to cancel going to my friend Rose's thirtieth birthday party in London tomorrow. What a shame, all my mates will be there. I do hate missing things. It says in the M.E. book that it's important to learn to say NO. Not an exciting word.

I find it difficult to accept that I can't be the painter of my own life. 'Lord, can I ask you to control this runny paint. Stop me from going too far in the wrong direction. Or in the wrong direction at all. I trust that you'll mix the colours because, from where I am on the canvas, I just can't see the whole picture.'

6th June ~ *The Velvet Claw* film crew arrived to record their sequence with the otters but it was pouring with rain.

Torrential. They could do nothing but sit around waiting for it to stop. It never did. I felt sorry for the producer but jolly glad I wasn't in his shoes. I stayed tucked up in bed and had another indulgent little spurt at entering competitions. It's amazing how many there are in the papers. I'm determined to win, rather than buy, a car.

Rebecca rang. She's back at her parents' house in West Sussex and sounded amazingly herself. She asked me over. Mum is driving within twenty minutes of their village tomorrow so, regardless of whether I'd have the strength, I said, 'Yes, please' and packed a bag.

7th June ~ Mum was taking the otters to give a series of lectures at a school in Petworth. It was good to get out of the house but, Gosh, what a bewildering journey. I hadn't driven with Mummy for ages. She was so frightened of getting lost she kept changing lanes without warning. I just kept saying, 'Don't worry, Mum, you'll get there,' and amazingly she did. Amazing considering that she came off the M4 at Junction 10 when she thought she was coming off the M25 at Junction 10.

The otters squeaked with delight when they saw Rebecca, who came veering towards us as the car pulled up. She was wearing a neck brace but looking cheerful. Mum delivered me like a child and hurried onward, the otters in their travelling cage looking out through the back window.

Rebecca has twenty-five stitches across her head. Shaved for this purpose, she has the alarming appearance of a punk rocker. The scar is extraordinary. Shocking. I can hardly believe she survived. Although she's suffering from a sprained ankle and terrible grazes over her back, she seems amazingly fit considering what she's been through. Her parents shuffled us into their conservatory and we talked of our symptoms like two old ladies.

I knew more about her accident than she did. She wasn't able to remember anything about it or her first week in hospital. All she knew of the second was that she hated it. No one had given her any information at all. 'They just looked at me as if I was mad,' she declared indignantly, 'and kept asking me questions in Afrikaans.' She'd actually been in and out of consciousness for nearly two weeks, and the other people in the hospital probably couldn't speak much English. But, poor Rebecca, she had to suffer indescribable indignities at the hands of clumsy and obstreperous nurses. She has lost all sense of taste and smell.

'That's brain damage.'

'Yes, Sophie, brain damage.'

We both slept after lunch and I stayed in bed while she was taken to have a haircut. All her lovely thick blonde hair was cropped short like a boy so that the shaved section was a little less conspicuous. Later we looked at her big stack of letters and Get Well cards. 'I had to bring them back, getting them meant so much to me.' I was pleased. 'One package arrived with such a huge Customs and Excise bill I refused to pay. There was an awful fuss. It must have been returned to England, because it arrived here yesterday.' She brought out the parcel, which contained a large, framed picture of James' dog.

8th June ~ Rebecca's father has banned the use of the word invalid as a bad label. Inval-ed invalids. He's right; if we're not careful we condemn ourselves. In my sub-conscious, buried deep throughout my childhood, I can hear Mum shouting 'I'm *sick and tired* of... (this, that or the other.)' And now this sick and tired thing has come upon me. It has come to pass. You are what you say you are to some degree. Or, by making such statements, do we let Satan have traction in our lives? I suppose once he finds something in us that belongs to him he can exploit it. If we live with a lie then he's always got something to blackmail us with, hasn't he? If we steal we go into partnership with him, don't we? So, if we spin into a fury and say something like, 'I'll never get well,' can he take that as a vow and hold us to it? He certainly doesn't play fair. It's hard because he seems to have such varied artillery at his disposal but I think the devil only knows us because we allow him to.

Rebecca's photographs have arrived back from the chemist. There was an amusing one of someone sitting on a horse looking at a magnificent giraffe. The horse had its head stuck out and was yawning. There were lots of the girl who was travelling with her at the time of the accident. 'Poor Miranda, her eardrum burst when the car rolled, but otherwise she's fine.' Rebecca was most pleased with the shots of the funny little heron chicks, one of whom was called Ron. 'I wish someone had taken a picture of the crash, or at least what the vehicle looked like after it rolled. I'm quite interested.' She said that complete strangers had been incredibly helpful. 'I didn't have to wait for an ambulance; there was no chance of getting one. A man just took me in his car. I don't remember the journey at all, but Miranda said he drove so fast that she thought we'd have another accident.'

'Was your treatment all very expensive?' I asked.

'The cost was a terrible worry, as I didn't have health insurance, but right at the end the South Africa government paid, saying that as I was a guest in their country they would look after me.' How amazing.

'I'm not sure if I would have dared stop to help with a car crash in the middle of the bush. You know Rebecca, I don't think I have the gift of compassion.'

'You're here with me, which is nice.'

'No, you're my friend which makes it different. I'm not naturally good at extending kindness to complete strangers or unlovely people. Mother Teresa can; I can't.'

'Work at it.'

I made Rebecca go into the village so I could buy a copy of the *Daily Mail* and enter a car competition, on the grounds that we needed the exercise. And I need a new car. Even Tamzin says that I can't drive a Chrysler Sunbeam forever. (I bought it because I liked the advert with Petula Clark singing, '*Put a Chrysler Sunbeam in your life.*') It has orange plastic seats and a trench-like dent across the roof from when the automatic barrier at the entrance to the *BBC* car park came down on top of me. Also, every time a passenger starts to unwind their side window you have to shout 'No!' before the glass plops out and falls down inside the door.

Rebecca and I walked/hobbled 400 yards past the church to the village shop. A portentous wedding was in session with an oversized bride in frilly white nylon and a groom in a pale grey suit, white shoes and an unfortunate skin condition. The flowers were yellow and everywhere. Just as we arrived 'one of the party', wearing a big floppy hat, squeezed into a Ford Capri, drove over the granite curb and gave herself a puncture. I had no compassion, just thought, 'She shouldn't have driven over the curb.' And I'm a snob. Rebecca, forgetting her unconventional appearance, was busy saying, 'It always happens when you're in your smart clothes, doesn't it.' Neither of us made good Samaritans though. Rebecca's mother arrived in her snazzy convertible and whisked us both off.

Rebecca couldn't remember anything of what we did later, which worried her. But I hadn't a clue either. Is brain damage catching? The truth is that we both have to remember that one function of pain is to ensure we look after ourselves –

physically, mentally, emotionally or whatever. We would be endlessly injuring ourselves otherwise.

I still want to find a meteorite but Rebecca wasn't keen to go searching in the fields. She looked at me and said, darkly, 'Watch out. One might fall on your head.'

9th June ~ I can't remember what has happened today. Rebecca said, 'My sister came, made a lot of noise and went away again. You fell asleep.'

'Did I?'

'Yes, dear.' We behave exactly like two old ladies in a nursing home. James rang to say he'd been chucked out of Shanda Lear's house, because of his dog. We are unconvinced. (No compassion.)

'James, did Miss Lear try to seduce you?'

'Well, she'd sit on the kitchen table in her towel and sort of flirt.'

'What did you do?'

'Do? I just wanted to eat my cornflakes.' He's coming for breakfast here tomorrow.

10th June ~ Rebecca made a cake. A one-egg cake as there was only one egg. Brain damage cake; the egg was meant to be for James' breakfast only we forgot, but then he didn't make it anyway. It turned out to be a useful cake as it fed an enormous number of people. They all turned up out of the blue: Rebecca's old business partner, an Army-ish man with wife and new baby, plus three Australians no one knew at all. It became quite a noisy conservatory.

Rebecca was shattered afterwards but is getting much better, and much more argumentative. I found her in the driveway feeling along the edge of a car window and looking incredulous. 'It can't be true. I just can't believe that I was flung out of so small a hole.' The fact that she's alive is difficult to digest. She's a walking miracle. Well, a hobbling one.

11th June ~ I had to lie down for most of the day. James arrived for supper, instead of breakfast, with Tessa the dog. He was wearing shorts with long socks and lace-up shoes. We decided he looked like a cross between a boy scout and a child molester. Suddenly, without warning, Rebecca stood up and started shouting, 'Rouse. Rouse!'

'What's happening?'

'Rrrrrouse!' called Rebecca, shaking her arms about.

'Is she going mad?'

'Rouse! Rouse!' She'd seen a mouse and was trying to get Tessa to catch it. The spaniel rushed about but missed the mouse, which zipped out of the conservatory unharmed.

'R.O.U.S.E.' said Rebecca, flopping down into a chair.

'Why rouse when it's a mouse?'

'**R**odents **O**f **U**nusual **S**ize **E**ndemic: rouse,' she said looking at us as if we were dim. 'It was the code name we used in South Africa for rats. We didn't want the safari clients to be too revolted. Sarah-Jane's dog is much better at catching them than Tessa.'

I've been reading more C.S. Lewis. He says that each man is like a stone sculpture. We have to endure the sharp taps of the chisel and the paring down and the polishing before we are fully created. Well, Rebecca is someone who really has received a tap on the head, and a shoulder polished by the Eastern Transvaal Highway.

I suppose what C.S. Lewis means is that we mustn't winge and whine if we are asked to suffer, because we won't know until much later how much we're actually gaining from it. 'But, why Lord, am I having to be ill?'

'So you will gain wisdom and understanding.' (And compassion?)

12th June ~ Rebecca is definitely recovering fast. I'm not. My parents came to collect me. We drove over the green hills of England to Shrivenham where the Department of Military Defence allowed us to visit Perry. Atalanta had lost the foot of the sewing machine but this is currently the only worry in Perry's life. Her house is alarmingly neat and well ordered. It always has been and always will be despite the presence of a toddler. She spends her free time making up soft furnishings in an attempt to turn the margarine coloured Army quarter into a place of designer living. Amazingly chic clothes fill her wardrobe with an array of different suits made by a tailor in Cyprus. I found her full of news of her thrift-shop bargains including a golden jacket, a silken number, she acquired for £7.50. All her immaculate garments hang on carefully padded hangers; there's not a wire one in sight. Unlike my cupboard.

I wondered where Tadpole, their dog, was but Robert had taken her to the office. Apparently this is quite fine if you're in the British Army. I think it might make up for being deskbound when he would have loved to have fought in the Gulf War. Perry, with babe in arms, said she's mighty relieved Robert didn't go off to face chemical exposure and risk of death.[6] He had to stay here at Staff College learning about biological warfare instead.

Perry knew exactly why James had been chucked out of Shanda Lear's house. 'He set fire to the kitchen curtains with the toaster.'

13th June ~ I've just spent a lot of money sitting up in bed: gas bill, telephone bill, poll tax for the flat in London I'm not using, which is aggravating, and a doctor's appointment I booked for £75. Mum is shocked at the price but I feel it's fine if it gets me better. Charlotte has arranged for me to see Dr. Mary Loveday, the specialist in M.E., at her home in Farnham, so it wouldn't be Harley Street itself, but it's the only way she can fit me in. Have just got to get to Farnham somehow.

The vet has taken away Henry, our green and scarlet macaw, not because he's sick but to star at an International Veterinary Convention in Cheltenham. He went off perched on the back of the vet's passenger seat screeching with glee. He's going to be an exhibit, illustrating a talk on psychological illnesses in birds.

Henry, it must be explained, has a terrible habit of plucking himself and the pale grey, exposed skin of his breast is hideous. Naked and bobbly. Alastair calls him, 'The oven-ready bird.'

Dad left with *Tulip* for a long weekend in France. He's going to the house where Monet painted, to re-create the barge scene. Mum won't go. She can't stand the idea of having to go to a French lavatory. Albert, our plumber, is going instead. Albert is both enormous and enormously strong. He has a rowing skiff, which he can lift out of the water with one arm. He doesn't say a great deal, but what he says is sane. And he's not frightened of loos.

I prayed that Rose would ring and she did. She said she was going to, had decided not to due to a sore throat, then changed her mind. I'm glad that she found it again. (Her voice). She has invited me to her husband Matthew's ordination in Wells Cathedral. I would love to go.

I sat up in bed later reading my diary for February when I was ill for two weeks. On the fourth day, when I'd been expecting to be feeling better, I wrote: 'Terribly cold with four inches of snow covering London. Lay, ill and weak, watching telly in bed; endless news of the Gulf War. Drained of strength I have limited concentration and a sensitive tummy. Terrified that this could be something serious.' Four days and I thought I was going to die. What a wimp.

14th June ~ It's sunny but incredibly windy. The cherry tree is bearing fruit and the wind's bringing the cherries down. They are rather small and don't taste very good. It's because the tree's never been pruned.

I managed to get outside with the *Wanda-phone*. It's just another cordless phone with a long aerial but saves me from having to move. Three of my friends have rung, which is wonderful as I was beginning to feel forgotten. A d v i c e: If you have a friend, who is ill for a long time, ring them up regularly for long chats. It can be more reviving and encouraging than a visit and is probably more convenient and less tiring for both.

One call was from my P.A. at work who filled me in on all the gossip and said, 'It's not the same here without you,' which is always comforting to hear. She told me that our department was moving to the new building that the *BBC* has built on the site of the White City greyhound stadium and that she would arrange for the contents of my office to be taken over in boxes.

In a serious effort to win a motor I have applied fifteen times to the *Daily Mail* Win-a-Car Competition. I still end up applying for things I do not want or need, like a weekend in Brighton or an awful tiring trip to California. I'm beginning to feel uneasy in my spirit about these competitions. They're not real contests involving judgement or skill. The ones I've been entering are just marketing ploys on the whole, and perhaps God, like Dad, wants to protect me from being conned. Am I being drawn into deception? It's a 'Game of chance' thing but not exactly problematical gambling. Definitely not a sin. Is it? I suppose you could say I'm wasting stamps, and my time. Perhaps my conscience is being pricked by the fact that I'm actually becoming addicted to it.

God tests our motives: what are mine? Greed? Avarice? Not really. It would be an effective and sensible use of my present time to win a car; I need one. But I can't deny that lust for more doesn't slip in. Perhaps it's because it doesn't glorify God. If he has promised to provide all I need, why ask Chance?

Have just read: '...a greedy person is really an idolater who worships the things of this world. Don't be fooled by those who try to excuse these sins, for the terrible anger of God comes upon those who disobey Him.'[vi] OK, I get the point. I can see that competitions are a way for companies to get hold of up-to-date names and addresses, but once down on a computer, the data could then be sold or used for something which you just might not want to become involved with.

I'm not quite sure what the acupuncture involves me in either, I feel uneasy about that too for some reason. 'Acupuncture is an ancient system of healing developed over thousands of years in China and other Eastern countries,' it says in an M.E. fact sheet that then goes on to describe the traditional theory behind it. They also say, *'This fact sheet is intended to summarise the pros and cons of an available therapy for people with M.E. It's not intended in any way to constitute or replace proper medical advice. Action for M.E. accepts no responsibility for the consequences of trying this therapy...* '(Ooo)

Life was changed by Daisy's arrival. She has come for the weekend with an enormous pile of washing. I let her run around the garden and try to eat grass and flowers and earth until she was rushing around so wildly I was worried she would plop into the lake like her grandfather. The boat isn't here so I had to put her in the playpen.

[sketch: Saturday 15th June. Another bad morning. I lie still peeping out from the sheets feeling sorry for myself. Bad. Untrusting. Rather odd shaped geranium on my window sill.]

15th June ~ Another bad morning. I lay peeping out from the sheets feeling sorry for myself. Bad. Untrusting. The newspapers are no help. I was reading in the *Mail* of all the layers of insecticide sprays that our fruit and vegetables are subjected to. Lettuces reared commercially can get sprayed seven times. Then someone like me eats them. I know these insecticides are meant to be harmless to humans but our bodies must have to deal with a lot of chemicals. That can't be good. You can wash them well, but do restaurants or work canteens always wash things like lemons and tomatoes when they look perfectly clean? Although the lettuces are crisp, they taste of nothing at all, so I don't suppose they have many minerals and thereby much goodness in them anyway.

Mum went off to a fête, which the good people of Michinhampton have asked the otters to open. Ridiculous, but they draw in a lot of people. I'm left here to look after Daisy. Having thought I ought to do something productive I completed the ironing; about four shirts and a lot of folding, as Daisy's gear doesn't warrant an iron. She wandered about playing happily with the clutter in Mum's bedroom. Later I liquidized some food for her, but she regurgitated it all over me, which meant changing her and washing my cardigan. And it finished me off. I suddenly felt awful; I'd overdone it. How pathetic. I realised I'd caught Daisy's cold and went to bed as soon as Mum returned, feeling hot and feverish, thanking God that I'm not a single parent trying to cope with active little children as well as this disease.

16th June ~ I felt pretty dreadful but walked Daisy down the lane a short way. We met our old family doctor, Chris Booth, who said what I needed was a Caribbean holiday. (Huh.)

Instead I spent the afternoon in bed with Dick Francis while Mum returned Daisy to Gloucester. Mary-Dieu had actually bought Dad a *Father's Day* card. I'd forgotten about this. She can beat me dead on the showing of love stakes when she tries.

Daisy's cold had gone to my head and the pressure was only relieved by soaking it (my head) in a hot bath. I was invaded by self-pity. Mikie says this is the arch-enemy but I allowed myself to wallow in it. And the bath.

I lay submerged listening to a tapping sound and what sounded like manic laughter. It turned out to be the vet, knocking at the door with our macaw laughing on his shoulder. I'd totally forgotten that he still had Henry and staggered downstairs in a bathrobe to meet them. Apparently the talk on bird psychology went well. At the end an old buffer stood up and started droning on about his own findings when the macaw interrupted him by saying, 'Hello Henry,' and all 129 vets collapsed in laughter.

17th June ~ I woke thinking I would never move again, but of course I did. I dressed and drove off to the surgery in Michinhampton. My doctor gave me a full and thorough examination – chest, stomach, heart, eyes, mouth, reflexes. I'm to have another blood test and a chest x-ray. I went over all my symptoms again, the fatigue, the muscle ache and lack of motivation. When I told her I was beginning to feel miserable about it, she started suggesting the whole thing might be psychological. How can an inflamed throat be psychological? It's totally physical, as is the fatigue. I refused anti-depressants point blank. I'm not a bald parrot.

Now I'm heartily annoyed, lying flat out in bed with the cold sitting on my head, feeling ugh. I can't be imagining all this, feeling sore is no fun but then I suppose psychological illnesses can give you genuine physical symptoms and I suppose all illnesses have a psychological dimension. Burton's *Anatomy of Melancholy* says, 'Hard students are commonly troubled with gouts, catarrhs, rheums, cachexia, Brady pepsia, bad eyes, stone, and collick, crudities, oppilations, vertigo, winds, consumptions, and all such diseases as come by over much sitting. They are most part, dry, ill-covered.' I certainly haven't got gout.

I was wondering what had happened to everyone when I heard a bedraggled noise and Mum came squelching upstairs. She'd been standing up to her waist in the river all morning helping the film crew get underwater shots of the otters for *The Velvet Claw*. She was frozen. This would have been me, filming my series on the canal; I know it.

Dad brought a shell-shocked Albert back from France. I don't think Mum would have enjoyed it. They ended up camping on the back of a flat-bed truck with a tent made from a tarpaulin slung over an oar. She was delighted to hear that Albert was absolutely horrified by the French *pissoirs*. She has found an ally.

18th June ~ It's a wet June ~ bushes of roses blowing in the wind under a dark, dark sky. Roses over the lake, pink roses hanging over the house, old fashioned smells everywhere.

I rang Mikie who kindly said he'd take me to Matthew's ordination, which is great. God's provisioning as he's a busy man with racing stables to build. I really want to go. And if all of this is psychological, then I can. Mikie never rests, always forces himself on, and he's paraplegic, in a wheelchair. He drives cars incredibly fast. I hope getting to Wells Cathedral won't be too terribly scary.

I had a bath to be clean for Charlotte but went to bed shaking afterwards. I'm flaked out just by taking a bath.

My friend Robin arrived for lunch looking very smart in a purple stripy shirt, purple socks and a purple rose, bearing purple chocolates. He's going to the ordination too, but taking the London train.

When I told Robin I'd been labelled an invalid invalid he said, indignantly, that some bank had just returned one of his cheques as invalid. He'd written the date in Roman numerals.

Charlotte arrived late but ravenous. She'd been at Highgrove to massage the Prince of Wales. She's not meant to say anything about this but was too hungry and excited not to. He'd asked her to come every day this week.

'But I have to go to Ascot tomorrow.' Charlotte told the Prince.

'No matter,' he said. 'After the racing go to a car with a crown on the door, parked in the Royal Enclosure. Get in and it will bring you here.'

But what does she do with her couch? This, not exactly small piece of travelling furniture, was now erected in my room. It has a special hole you put your face into which makes lying on your tummy comfy. I lay on two hot water bottles and Charlotte oiled and massaged. She worked hard and well and it was just lovely. She did my back, my face, my tummy, my legs, my feet. I had lavender oil for healing, rosemary for muscle tone, camomile and something else. It smelt wonderful. No wonder the Prince wants her to come every day. I went straight to bed afterwards and lay in an oily glow reading *A Year in Provence*. Feeling happy, I rang Rose to say I could come to their ordination picnic and then rung Diana who told me that she has, to her amazement, been promoted again (Ah, but the world of Corporate Finance isn't slow to recognise a bit of flair.) She said Charlie and Jane are having a baby in October and that Guy and Tanya are getting married in November. Everyone seems to be moving on except for me.

19th June ~ I found a cartoon in the *Daily Mail* of Prince Charles being massaged at Highgrove... either the secret is out or it was pure chance. I sent it to Charlotte.

Mrs. Booth took my blood. She said she thought, or rather Dr. Booth thought, that acupuncture releases endorphins that the body needs to keep you going. She's a nurse who has had post-viral fatigue herself and advised sunshine. She also said I must walk a bit. Yes; that is what my body's telling me. And I don't want to seize up. Or become like one of Burton's hard students and develop oppilations, whatever they are.

I walked to the vegetable garden. There was one white butterfly. We hardly ever see them anymore. Apparently a hundred years ago there were 100,000 butterflies to every individual that exists now. There are lots in South Africa.

I couldn't find our dog. He doesn't seem to be about much, which is odd. But I'm not going to worry about him. Granny rang to tell me that she's worried about me. I found myself telling her it's a sin to worry because Jesus told us not to. There's no point because God cares for us and will give us what we need. [vii] What we need but not always what we want. But, he also wants us to have our heart's desire. 'Really? A new car?'

'Seek ye first the kingdom of God, and his righteousness; and all these things shall be added unto you.'[viii]

20th June ~ A pot of boiling oil. Well, Charlotte told me to lie in a bath for twenty minutes with a cap-full of aromatherapy bath oil. I don't think it's a magic cure though. There wasn't enough hot water for a start and Mum had to keep coming in with kettles.

I feel rather bad about telling off my Granny but she insists on living a life of worry. She wraps it round her like an itchy blanket. Worry; the guilt of the future, as Olivia calls it. It's her addiction. That and the telephone. Not being able to get out she has resorted to living her life through others, ringing us all non-stop. It drives Mum dilly.

Mum is dilly. She's just been to the supermarket without her handbag. But the Lord provided richly. She seemed able to buy an incredible amount with money-off vouchers she found in her car and, like Joshua and Caleb, returned with great bunches of grapes. She's convinced that they give you strength.

'Not for you, they're for the parrots.' I did get to eat them but the first fruits were sacrificed to Henry.

Dad caught Solomon for me and I went riding after lunch. I just plodded through the fields. The dog didn't seem to be around, which was a good thing as I didn't want to get snapped at. I had a lovely time. I thought, 'Here am I, riding on wisdom.' What did King Solomon say about horses?

It's a complete wonder I enjoy riding at all. I learnt in a terrifying and unconventional way; Mum taught me. She bought a donkey, seated me on top and led us off to the Boxing Day meet. 'Armstrong,' I can here her saying. 'We called him Armstrong after Anthony Armstrong-Jones who had just married Princess Margaret.' Once there my donkey promptly fell in love with the riding schoolmistress' enormous grey mare and galloped after her. I managed to cling on somehow. Dad said that we went for miles, over the hills and far away. I was four years old. He had to run after me.

By the time I was seven, two long-maned ponies had arrived. They looked like creatures from the pages of a fairy tale; a *Grimm's Fairy Tale*. They were hard mouthed, malicious creatures no one else wanted, and caused us endless embarrassment. It's horrid being in the centre of a jumping arena when your horse refuses to jump. Perry had a stubborn, opinionated bay mare that once rolled in the ash from an old bonfire on the way to a Pony Club rally. It seemed so unfair when she'd been up half the night cleaning tack and had spent so long grooming her horse. When we arrived the instructor roared with laugher and said, 'I didn't know you had a grey pony, Perry.' She rather gave up after that.

After the ride, I flopped back into bed trying to eradicate these painful memories and rest before the next onslaught – Alastair Fothergill.

'So good looking,' Mum sighed. He arrived looking a bit battered, I thought, having spent the windiest week of the year learning to sail on the north Norfolk coast.

'Nothing to stop the wind between me and the Urals.' It always happens to him; he went to film puffins nesting in the Outer Hebrides once. Night filming on 22nd June, the longest day of the year. Poor Al found he only had about three hours of darkness and battled to get everything finished. However, not one to be suppressed by natural phenomena, he's now full of excitement about the new series on Antarctica, which he wants to call *Life in the Freezer*. (I think it's a silly title.) 'Alastair, how exactly is the great British housewife going to react?' I said disparagingly. 'You'll give them nightmares about penguins zooming out of their chest freezers at seventy miles an hour.'

'Well, it might make them appreciate just how cushy their own lives are.'

Alastair loves the prospect of going on an expedition. The great explorer. He showed us a funny promotional video of the ship they're going to hire in order to make the series. It even has a wood-burning stove on board. (I wonder how much wood they take with them?) I agreed that it's without doubt the best-equipped and most amazing boat they could wish for. (Alastair will have such fun breaking all the gadgets.)

I'm glad Al has got a new series to produce. He's been working on *The Really Wild Show* for yonks. (I thought up that title, which was clever of me, only he won't let me take the credit.) We walked down the valley to see the horses. Alastair doesn't like them much. He makes nature programmes but I think domestic animals unnerve him. His most stressful moment in years of making wildlife films was when he lost his neighbour's pussycat. There was an awful fuss about that and all we could think of doing was to sellotape *Lost* notices to lampposts. He'd borrowed the cat to feature in an outside broadcast for the *BBC* called *The Great, Great Tit Show*. Honestly, only Alastair could get away with calling a television programme that. He's irrepressible. He stayed for supper, which he much enjoyed, eating what he described as 'bosom pudding': pears in jelly.

21st June ~ I was tired, very tired. It was a lovely balmy day but I lay in bed, glued to my book, until the evening when I felt better and walked down the valley to see the wild orchids, which are tall and purple now. I've been given all I need. I needed this time.

I went downstairs in search of supper but couldn't find anyone around, not even the dog. My parents, it transpired, were at the pub down the valley. 'Oh, did you have fun?' I asked when they returned.

'No, we did not.' Mum said sinking down in an armchair. 'We spent the whole time sweeping up glass and apologising to people, having to buy them all new drinks.' It was Jake. The dog. He's been waltzing off to the pub every lunchtime with the builders who are working on the property just up the hill. They slow down when they reach our gate and he jumps on the back of the truck. The landlord said he used to give him a bowl of water but he's on stronger stuff now and things have gone too far. Tonight he had a bit of a brawl with what mum described as 'a creature with a blue rinse perm' (a standard poodle) and the owner was not happy, to say the least. Jake looks tremendously pleased with himself.

James rang. He said he thought that Alastair's programme was called *The Great, Great Tit Watch*, part of a series he was producing on garden birds. They'd filmed blue tits at the nest but had to advertise for someone who had a nesting box which great tits were using. 'Alastair had imagined a suburban scene with young children playing on the lawn but the only reply came from a black guy in Park Town who owned a night club.' His nesting box proved perfect. After the filming he invited the crew back to his trendy club. A party of three men and one *BBC* lady clad in water-proof filming clothes descended into the darkened basement, music throbbing. A number of gorgeous black girls in short skirts and very high heels were drinking at the bar. 'It took Alastair a while but he eventually plucked up the courage to ask one of these girls to dance,' James went on. 'Apparently she looked him up and down, took a swig of lager and said, "I don't come here to meet white trash like you."' I'm so glad James loves a good gossip.

22nd June ~ I think the doves started to fly into my bedroom at 4 o'clock in the morning, as soon as it was light anyhow. Somehow I found the oomph to yell at them and go back to sleep. I dreamt I was directing a film with the most difficult children, five standard poodles and a bull-terrier. Perry was meant to be in it but arrived late on set because she'd been buying attachments for her vacuum cleaner. It brought back to me all the aggravation of work and the effort used up in seeming calm when all you want to do is scream and yell at everyone in sheer frustration. Directing can be like pulling a camel along by a thread.

I was speaking to Pippa on the phone yesterday. She works as a make-up artist and has been away filming, working on a big costume drama sixteen hours a day for weeks on end. If you visit a film set in the middle of the day, you tend to see the make-up girls and costume team sitting around on little stools. 'It just looks like there's a lot of hanging around to me,' Rose said when she came to watch us making *The Diary of Anne Frank*. No one is there to watch Pippa frantically chopping hair at 6.00am or setting wigs late into the night.

'There are a lot of moustaches on this production.'

'Big ones?'

'No, little ones, that's the problem. I stuck one on an actor first thing in the morning and when I checked him after lunch it wasn't there. He said, "Oh, I think I must have eaten it." He'd thought it was a bit of pork crackling.' Pippa had to quickly make another one.

I once worked on *My Family and Other Animals*, an adaptation of Gerald Durrell's book, which we spent four months making on the Greek island of Corfu. I'd say most days were heavy, starting at 6.00am, but I wouldn't have missed it for the world. I loved bumbling round Corfu with Brian Blessed and thirty tortoises in my car. That was the time when I first met the *BBC* doctor. Everyone became so ill that he had to come out for a whole week. He said he could remember me running about, dealing with one crisis after another, thinking, 'Yes, but that girl has energy.'

I've decided that what I miss about being on location is the comradeship, pulling together against the odds in order to do something well. I miss leading the team. But is it worth all the aggro? Working in television is fun, but not exactly tranquil. We had another *BBC* doctor observing us on set once. 'What in particular are you studying?'

'I'm looking at how you all handle stress.' I laughed. That day had been awful. We were in Brittany, busy trying to liberate France for a series called *Bluebell*. The unit coach containing all the actors had got lost and then became impaled on a dry stone wall. I had no choice but to persuade everybody to get out and walk to the location, which took forever. The Production Manager was at that moment screeching into her walkie-talkie, rattling away like a machine gun and crackling with angst.

'What are your findings?' I asked the doctor.

'Oh, I think you all absolutely thrive on stress.'

23rd June ~ Nicola had made her husband, Doug, bring me round her copy of Jilly Cooper's book *Polo* on his way to work. 'Oh, Goody. Have you read it?'

'Trash, absolute trash,' Doug mumbled, hurrying off. I could tell he'd enjoyed it. I settled down with the novel for a day in bed but while Mum and Dad went out to lunch I had an enormous number of visitors. It was pouring with rain again. Perry, Robert and Atalanta arrived under a huge green and white striped umbrella. Perry was amused to see what I was reading. I don't know how she recognised it as it's actually been read so much that it has lost its questionable cover. I have to say that the last book I produced for the *BBC* sold 200,000 copies without having a man's crotch on the front. Mind you, it was a reading book for seven to nine-year-olds.

Much later Grizelda arrived with her children, her husband Dane and an Australian nanny called Wendy. It was 2.30pm. They had meant to come for lunch but had a puncture.

Griz had bought picnic food especially so I would not have to cook, and so we all sat at the end of the sitting room with the children and ate it while it rained. I began to feel quite faint.

I don't think Robert can begin to understand what is wrong with me but Wendy did. Her mother had chronic fatigue for seven years and her sister has had it for four. Unbelievable.

Perry and Robert left early in order not to upset Atalanta's routine, but Griz and Dane stayed and went walking in the rain. I insisted they come in afterwards for tea, but collapsed in a heap when they left. They had only been here for three hours. I think Mum was a bit cross when she got back to see me so tired, but it was my own fault. When Diana rang from London, Mum gave her a fifteen-minute lecture on not tiring me out before she could speak to me.

We had asparagus, then strawberries and cream for supper, which was delicious, only Mum gave me some prawns that had been in the 'fridge since Wednesday, and I think they've given me a funny tummy. All I need.

24th June ~ Another day spent almost entirely in bed. It rained. Jilly Cooper had my exclusive attention, which can't be healthy but I love reading about the horses and have decided I'll just have to become a champion polo player one day.

I sat facing a bowl of gooseberries for lunch. They're from the vegetable garden and promise to be good for me but they're hard to eat without sugar. I mushed them up with honey instead, which gave them a nice smoky taste, but then couldn't resist eating Mum's meringues, which are mostly, let's face it, white sugar. I'm going to have to be more self-disciplined. So is the dog. Jake's still wandering off. Mum will have him castrated if he doesn't change his ways. It's a good thing I don't have a teenage brother.

When Granny rang, I asked how things are going in the shop but she got confused and handed me over to Hermione. Apparently the technique of ramming sweaters over people's heads works as a sales ploy if the sweater then won't come off. I don't suppose this would happen in a normal shop, but these Aran garments are handmade locally and are slightly idiosyncratic. It seems that an American lady arrived and was entranced by the whole scene; the craft shop in Hermione's Georgian house, the python, the jam, Granny in her tweeds and regimental brooch. Not actually being able to get out of the sweater seemed to delight her. Hermione was terribly embarrassed, but needed the cash, so she ushered the tourist into her drawing room and sat down to alter the neck there and then while Granny poured sherry. Now, Hermione designs and commissions these garments but she's not exactly an expert knitter herself. She said it took her ages to do, hours. After three (hours) the New Yorker went rather quiet, but finally it was complete, and came on and off OK. 'Gee, lady!' said the tourist. 'That sure is a hard way to make a dime.'

25th June ~ Constant rain; stayed in bed until I went for acupuncture at 5 o'clock. Let me tell you, those needles hurt.

Apparently they have to if they're to have any effect at all. One went in right beside my nose. I can't believe I'm paying for this torture. Jeremy said I'd changed and he's right. My tongue is better, and I'm in less pain... (apart from the needles) but I still have this fatigue and that's for sure. I don't think I have the co-ordination to drive yet. I kept giving myself terrible frights and drove the whole way back with the handbrake on. Stupid girl. I haven't done that for years.

My producer rang from work terribly concerned about my health. At least I could say I was getting treatment. She told me that they were now in rehearsal for the studio. It was sweet of her to ring. I couldn't help feeling that I was missing out on a tremendous opportunity to extend my experience as a director. I have only ever directed a studio on the training course and this should have been my first project and a big break. 'You have taken me so far in my training Lord, and now I'm losing momentum... is this in your plan?'

26th June ~

'Put your chin on there, take a deep breath in and hold it.' She never told me when to breathe out; I nearly popped. Chest X-ray, Stroud General. It seemed everyone working at the hospital had only just about clean hair and wore dismal white nylon overalls over laddered tights. Decaying posters hung everywhere. I can only suppose they were to amuse children but I could have done without X-ray Ted. There was another poster of a bulbous doll having its chest X-rayed. She'd obviously taken her instructions literally and passed out.

I sat in the empty reception area while an odious child ran around screaming. It somehow managed to do this with a dummy in place. Just when I thought my brain would explode, the excruciating noise stopped. Two New Age travellers had walked in, their bedraggled hair and filthy clothes drenched in blood.

I went home and flopped, grateful that I don't work for the National Health Service. I wish I'd asked what had happened to the New Agers though; been kinder. I packed to go to Tamzin's and we drove off under dark grey skies. Mum is taking me to her cottage, then Tamzin, just back from a week in Corfu, will drive me on to see Dr. Loveday in Farnham. My family is so good to me and I'm such a snappy old bat.

We found Tamzin looking tanned but stomping about in her 'mud boots' and ancient riding clothes. Frankly, she looks a bit gungy in this mode of dress, but it's a direct consequence of working with animals. The creatures themselves all look immaculate.

27th June ~ My sister has bought a cockerel called Ernest. It's a noisy birthday present for her friend Raddy. She assured me that Raddy does want one. Tamzin has always been good with chickens. She persuaded a hen we had once to ride on the handlebars of her bike; they'd go for miles. 'Do you know, I think I looked like a chicken in my wedding dress,' Tamzin said. 'It was all frothy white bum and bustle.'

'You looked lovely.' I can remember her walking up the aisle. Mary-Dieu was behind her in pink bridesmaid mode, Perry was in the pew beside me looking terribly smart but in floods of tears, and a massive flower arrangement fell on top of James. Mum, who was in a floaty, green number looking like a wobbly lettuce, was making 'nothing has gone wrong' sort of scowls but it was too late. I'd seen the sight of James submerged in flowers, arms waving hopelessly and had dissolved in uncontrollable hysteria, which grabbed me repeatedly throughout the service.

Perry and Robert were met outside our village church and transported to their wedding breakfast in Chitty-Chitty Bang-Bang (the real car; you can hire it), but Tamzin was married in London so had a 1930s double-decker bus with an open top. I went upstairs, to the top deck with the newly wed chicken and had great fun waving at the passers-by. After a while I realised I was waving to the same bemused tourists for the third time. The bus driver (who was really a veteran car enthusiast Dad knew) got lost and couldn't find his way around the one-way system in the City. Johnty's mother, who was down below in a wide-brimmed hat, found the whole experience quite jarring. By the time we arrived at the reception all the guests were already there – and they had walked. Rose had led the way by scattering rose petals. This was Mum's romantic idea. In reality, she was followed by a rather too keen City of London street sweeper whom Alastair ended up having to waylay.

28th June ~ Armed with a list of symptoms and this diary of my ills, we set off for Farnham and got lost. Being late always makes me feel embarrassed but Dr. Loveday, as Charlotte said, was sweet. She explained (when quizzed) that she was a general physician who took an holistic approach. Having been an allergist she now specialises in neurology and has had a lot of experience with M.E.

Dr. Loveday used what appeared to be an electronic resistor manufactured in Germany and a series of glass phials containing minerals, or derivatives of minerals in solution. A phial would be placed in the resistor and a low electric current was passed through my body, from an electrode held in my hand to a little prodder, which was pressed into my other palm. A dial on the machine indicated whether or not I was short of the mineral in the phial. It registered 80 points when I was normal. But time and again the dial would read 15 or even 10. It seems I'm short of zinc, potassium, magnesium, selenium.... and goodness knows what.

She said that if a virus gets into your liver, your whole system will simply shut down. I could have one lodged in my pancreas. Unfortunately there's no medical test available to investigate this. Whatever happened, the lurgi I caught at Easter time must have seriously impaired my immune system, and since I'd returned to work and extended myself physically whilst on antibiotics, my natural immunity was unable to get my body back into working order. She thought that various allergies were occupying about 45% of the immune system's effort. As a result, my poor body was only managing to exist. It was as if I was running on low batteries, which drain to zero easily. That makes sense. Gordon says that when we can't forgive we can only operate on a low level spiritually because it effectively obstructs God from forgiving us. I expect this is the reason most people are wandering around on low spiritual batteries.

For some reason, maybe because my stomach isn't digesting food properly, I'm not absorbing minerals efficiently. I know I'm lacking in something; I'm like a sheep with the staggers. Dr. Loveday's going to send me vitamin supplements, which take about three weeks to take effect. So Griz was right. Likewise, you need a boost of love in order to be healed from the hurt at the root of unforgiveness.

I also need to be tested for allergies. Mary Loveday said that if I felt better living away from home, I'm probably allergic to something there and should move away. I was given a 'flu jab and an injection of vitamin B complex. (I'm longing to tell Dad that he was right about the Bob Martins.) She also said I must rest.

Although I firmly accept this, Tamzin and I proceeded to have what I considered quite an energetic time wandering around Farnham. 'This is what normal girls do, Sophie, they shop.' I went into a bank and cashed money for the first time in ten weeks. It felt strange. I then did an optimistic thing. We went into a saddler's and I was measured up for a pair of chaps ~ leggings for riding horses. Am I mad or is this what they call 'A step of faith', believing that I'll recover? They were lovely, soft, brown ones. £45. I would never dream of having suede trousers made. One bank, two shops, tea at a café and I was frazzled. Normal girls wouldn't find this exceedingly energetic would they?

29th June ~ I was dragged along to Tamzin's local Conservative Party car boot sale. The fact that it was in aid of the Conservatives was not advertised but we went to give Ernest to Raddy. This was not easy as she was giving children rides in her pony trap. I had to walk round holding the cockerel, which was difficult, as I wanted to buy a cake. I managed to handle a cherry one, which turned out to have been made by Raddy, or rather her nanny. It pleased her enormously that I'd bought it in ignorance of its origin. Her little boy was so sweet. I gave him 10p to spend and he went off and chose 60p worth of rock cakes for his mummy.

I bought my mummy a cake too. She was thrilled to see Tamzin, who had driven me home, and had cooked roast lamb with asparagus then raspberries and cream for lunch. We sat outside in the sunshine with Albert who had brought some rather potent cider friends of his had made. The label called it *Lyne Down Cider*. Too right. Then we all tried Dad's new elderflower cordial. The elixir of summertime. Summertime bottled. It's no wonder we get so much sugar.

30th June ~ Matthew Persson's ordination, the unmissable event to which I was determined to go, took place this day, MCMXXICXCI? AD. Mikie was late coming to fetch me but we sped off to Wells in his whizzy, black BMW. I thus arrived, quite terrified, at a completely deserted cathedral green to find not a soul there except Rose, with my godson Augustus wailing in her arms. Everyone else was inside. I don't think Mikie was expecting Rose to look so beautiful. He loves pretty girls and could fully appreciate that she was wearing *Jasper Conran*.

The Cathedral was full to bursting. The Church of England, alive and well after all. There were easily two thousand people there, but because Mikie was in his wheelchair we were whisked straight up to the front. We sat right alongside the twelve ordinands and watched Matthew's father, who is a Bishop, lay hands on them all in apostolic fashion. It was very moving. Rose had communion with Matthew and then kissed him in the side aisle, which made Mikie smile.

Diana came rushing over after the service and admired my suit, but couldn't resist complaining loudly to the Archdeacon about one of the choirboys wearing an earring. It was rather large. Everyone else thought it alarming too, but didn't dare say a thing. Diana was kind though and took my bags, making the Archdeacon carry the heaviest one, as she led us off to lunch. This was in a medieval hall filled with all Matthew's disreputable friends and a group of very organised ladies from a completely different church. I gave Matthew a 15th century book of sermons, all about 'man and his ƒufferings' (s written as ƒ). I don't know why, but it came from the Dumfries Mechanics' Institute.

Mikie had to go off to a race meeting so I sat quietly with Augustus, who was now fast asleep. I couldn't help observing that while the good ladies had neat sandwiches, all our friends had brought extraordinarily inappropriate food. Robin, who was still dressed in purple and now clashing with the bishop, had bought a picnic of cold lamb chops and squidgey bananas. Diana produced a pineapple and Matthew's old house-mate, the naughtiest man in the whole world, brought strawberry yoghurt. Without spoons. Do you know what happens when you eat yoghurt at church picnics without a teaspoon? It falls all over your French girlfriend's thighs. This isn't too disastrous as, of course, she's wearing a short skirt. You can lick it off. Rose's parents didn't seem to mind, the Bishop is used to his son's behaviour so this was nothing, Diana thought it quite sensible, but the old ladies...

Afterwards we walked, as one does at such times, laden with flowers and baskets, fruit and baby things to The London Rubber Company car. Diana, who is also a godmother, drove us back in the condom car to Rose and Matthew's new house, the Curate's Residence in Quilton-on-Trim, which as it happens, is called Rose Cottage. It's Georgian, has pretty diamond pane windows and lies below an exceptionally tough council estate. We fed Augustus and all conked out.

JULY ~ Unhealing healing for ultimate healing

1st July ~

I love Matthew. He went and gave communion to some 'ailing cancer victims' at a hospice and then disappeared to re-license his shotgun and find a garage in which to hide his open top Mercedes. 'People can't bear to see a wealthy vicar with a glamorous wife,' Diana said as she disappeared.

Why is this? God certainly wants us to be wealthy. Look at Abraham. He had enormous wealth and his wife was so beautiful he was worried the Egyptians would career off with her. I'd love to be rich. 'How does one do it Lord?'

'Give.'

'Really?'

'Give, and it will be given unto you; good measure, pressed down, and shaken together, and running over...'[ix] I gave Augustus a nice clean nappy and tried to amuse him so that Rose could unpack. I wasn't much good at it. He wouldn't stop crying, so we all walked up through the council estate instead, past the houses where Matthew will be having tea. I entered a competition to win a year's supply of Carling Black Label ~ some strong British beer ~ so that he can give them a good evangelical bash. Rose thought this would be a fine idea. 'He's been instructed not to go to tea with people unaccompanied. And when people come to see him I have to be around.'

'Why?'

'Oh, Sophie, I've been advised to sit at my desk in the passage outside his office so that he can't be falsely accused of molesting the parishioners.' She isn't paid for this of course.

'There's absolutely no way I could molest any of the parishioners,' Matthew said striding into the room. 'None of them possess pertaining attributes required to motivate any such action by anybody at all.'

Matthew went to tell me that he thinks I'm a raving hypochondriac. Not exactly compassionate words from an ordained man of God, but why do I need any sympathy? And God doesn't want any. He wants no nonsense men. (With shotguns?)

'You look normal to me.'

'Darling, she looks like I do after the baby has kept me up all night,' Rose objected.

'The *BBC* doctor said I would know that I was better when I started playing tennis non-stop.' I explained. I'm not sure that I could manage a game today but will resolve to get Mum on a court as soon as I return. She loves tennis.

2nd July ~ Rose drove me all the way home.

'Do you think it matters if you aren't naturally sympathetic?' I asked.

'Well, the church should be like a body with different parts,' Rose replied. 'I think we have to do what we are good at. You can't be brilliant at everything. The challenge is working together without bickering.'

'Do you think everyone should specialise?'

'Yes and no. We have to use our strengths and work on our weaknesses.' We climbed the hill out of Bath and suddenly found ourselves driving through green countryside. 'We just have to try to be like Jesus,' Rose said. (Isn't that a song?).

I sang *Old McDonald had a Farm* in order to win Augustus' admiration at tea but he preferred Daisy's playpen to me. He liked the parrots. Rose didn't stay long and I soon collapsed, animal noises whizzing round in my head.

When I asked Mum later if she would play tennis, she looked at me as if I was completely mad. She said it was a ridiculous idea, that I should never have gone to Bath and that what I needed was to get some decent rest. E ~ I ~ E ~ I ~ O.

3rd July ~ 'Do you want a shock?' Mum said coming into my room. 'It's Mary-Dieu. I've had a message relayed from the hospital, telling me to get over there immediately.' Big panic. Real panic. We've been terrified for ages now that she'll top herself.

'Oh Mum, do you want me to come to Gloucester with you?'

'Do you want to commit suicide too?'

I know what's happened. Life isn't living up to the ideals portrayed in women's magazines; the romance of restaurants and roses. In reality her boyfriend has decided to go to college in Enfield, or somewhere the other side of the country. 'Oh, Lord help her, help Mum.'

It turned out that Mary-Dieu was causing a drama in the maternity wing. 'Some woman' had bashed into her parked car and wouldn't pay for the repairs. Mary-Dieu knew 'the culprit' was expecting a baby any minute. Determined to nail her down, she rang the hospital and asked politely if she could sit with 'her friend'. They were charming and agreed, having no idea that their patient was then intimidated into paying for car repairs while she was actually in the labour ward. 'I made her go down to the cash-point machine between contractions,' Mum was told. Perhaps Mary-Dieu should apply for that debt-collecting job advertised in the paper.

4th July ~ Mum says, 'Definitely no tennis.'

I thank God for Diana. A wonderful funny letter has arrived from the Grand Hotel in Baglioni with two pieces of thin paper on which she has written:

"Bomboloni ~ spezialite di Bologna!"

I hope she doesn't mean lavatory paper.

And Rebecca has written, on the eve of seeing her neurosurgeon. She's so utterly practical and unemotional about her predicament. And everything else. She always has been. 'I think you're suffering,' she says, 'from T.M.J.' I turned the page. 'Too Much James. If the doctors knew him, they'd ban him for six months.' I don't think I've seen him since he had to leave Miss Lear's.

5th July ~ Tennis out of the question. My parents are on the River Thames anyway. They take a lot of food and a chainsaw.

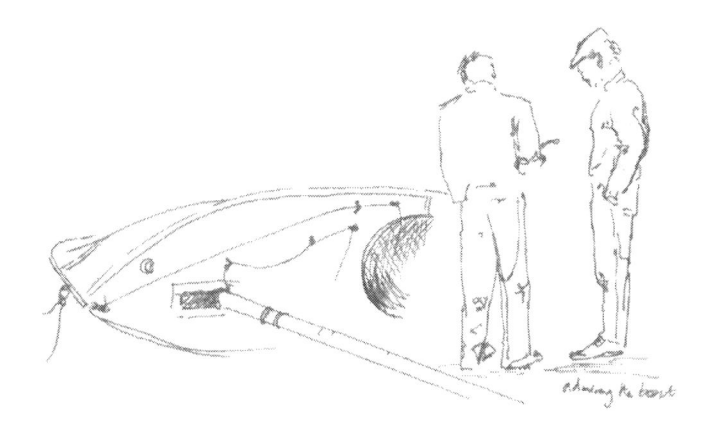

Dad has a 1902 steamboat called *Daffodil* and powers it by asking farmers if he can make use of their fallen trees. He chops them up and chucks the wood into his boiler. There's a lovely steam kettle on the side of this and you get to drink a great deal of tea. Mum quite likes it all but won't let on. She did once comment that it's the only boat Dad's ever had with a fire on board. She hates getting cold feet.

6th July ~ James brought Rebecca over to stay. She can't drive herself because she's taking drugs to suppress the possibility of epileptic fits, which can be triggered by head injuries. Her skull looked much better but she did arrive with a terribly swollen bottom lip. A lot of strange noises came out of her mouth as she tried to explain what had happened. 'She's been bitten by a wasp,' James said impatiently. I couldn't work out her reply so she wrote down,

'*How did he get a degree in zoology?*'

'?'

'It was a *bee* and it *stung* me.' They've both noticed that my speech is not coming out right ~ proper ~ properly either.

James said he doesn't want to talk about insects. He was meant to be filming a sequence about the large blue butterfly that has an intimate and symbiotic relationship with a certain ant. He'd been off to Spain to find them.

'I was assured that hundreds and thousands of these butterflies emerge at once, on the same day, every year,' he said in a grumbly kind of way. 'They don't. Well they didn't for us. We went for three days and nothing happened, so I hung around with the cameraman for another whole week. We saw… six.'

'Oh, but James, we have them here.' There's a field behind the pub covered in anthills, which I remember from when we were little. Tamzin fell off her pony and landed on top of one. She said it was soft like a cushion, but leapt up, covered in ants. James tottered off to inspect the location while Rebecca and I looked at the array of supplements that have arrived from Dr. Loveday:

- Vitamin B Complex: 2 x 5ml daily. This tonic comes in a huge bottle. (Apparently the easiest way of absorbing is in liquid form.)
- Magnesium phosphate: up to 6 tablets daily. (That's interesting. I was given this as a teenager.)
- I have to take 50mg of zinc, with my supper.
- And no less than five other capsules three times a day. (That'll keep me busy.)

7th July ~ Rebecca is much improved and has taken to teasing me about my Yuppie 'flu. As she points out, I do look remarkably well. My hair is growing at an incredible rate and has never looked better. But because Rebecca has just been so debilitated herself, she does appreciate what being grounded is like. It's difficult for others to imagine how I feel and I'm only grateful that they try to. I've experienced such kindness, even from sceptics like Matthew.

The big problem with M.E. has been that because its symptoms are invisible, its victims aren't accepted as being ill. Some patients won't accept they're sick themselves and push on until they end up in wheelchairs unable to even stagger to the loo. Others, who do rest, are seen as shirkers, and have been stigmatised by employers and colleagues. I haven't been but do get irritated. 'It must be worse in other countries. Imagine being a Japanese person, having to go around explaining that you have 'low natural killer cell syndrome', which is what it's called there.'

'Perhaps it sounds OK in characters.'

'Maybe. In America, you have to tell everyone you have C.F.I.D.S.'

'As in *Day of the Triffids*?' Rebecca said, with an arch look.

'As in Chronic F-I-D-S. But you have to have had it for six months before it can be labelled 'chronic'.'

'What do you have before then?'

'Just a bug.'

'Fids?'

'Aphids.' Soon James will be able to include me in his documentary.

It's only because a medical test hasn't been found for the virus or whatever it is. It would certainly be easier if I could say that I had glandular fever. My symptoms are similar. It would save a lot of explaining. Healthy people can be so self-righteous.

'Until they realise,' Rebecca pointed out, 'how easily they could be in your shoes.'

8th July ~ Heavy rain. Definitely no tennis.

How can doves possibly symbolise peace? This lot is driving me barmy. There are twenty-eight here now. The place is covered in guano. They're nothing but stupid, mucky albino pigeons. Dad reckons they keep the buzzard fed through the winter, but not to tell Mum this. Rebecca gave him a look.

My Aunt Hermione rang, inviting me to stay in Scotland some time. She said a funny thing happened today at the craft shop. A woman came in, looked around at all the Scottish curios and then shouted, 'Yes! Just what I need.' She held up a pair of tartan souvenir knickers. Then, to Hermione's amazement, she put them straight on declaring that her own had got wet out on the loch. Granny wasn't a bit shocked.

'Very sensible,' she said as she took the money. Mind you Granny always made me wear two pairs of underpants when I went to school. It's a Scotch thing; I had normal ones and then great big woolly over-knickers to keep me warm. It was always embarrassing admitting to this when I changed for games. She probably still wears two pairs herself.

Rebecca said that her sister was a bottom shuffler and had to wear the same sort of thick woolly pants when she was a baby. 'What is a bottom shuffler?'

'Oh, some babies refuse to crawl; they bottom shuffle instead.'

'How long for?'

'My sister shuffled for months. Mum said she wore out several pairs of gym knickers becoming an expert and managed to get up quite a speed. Once she shuffled out into the middle of the main road in front of our house.'

'Golly.'

'Yes, luckily a woman motorist saw her there and picked her up.'

Rebecca wants to visit these relations of mine in Scotland. 'I think we'd better wait until you're a little more robust.' She still can't taste or smell. Dad had read that sniffing beetroot juice can heal this. He plodded back from the vegetable garden with a handful and boiled them up. Do you know what sniffing beetroot juice does to you? It gives you red nostrils. Fuchsia pink, to be exact.

9th July ~ An amazing, sunny day. We occupied ourselves cleaning Solomon's tack in the sun. It was beginning to go a bit mildewy. I got out a great big concordance and looked up what it says about bridles in the Bible:

'Do not be like a senseless horse or mule

That needs a bit and bridle to keep it under control.

Many sorrows come to the wicked,

But unfailing love surrounds those who trust in the Lord.'

~ from *Psalm 32*

My Granny loves me unfailingly, and prays for me. She also rings up every single day and it's hard to know what to talk about. She says she is concerned about my speech. I spoke to her about the knickers. 'I didn't wear any on my wedding day.'

'Didn't you, Granny?'

'No, it was the 'thirties and my dress was cut on the cross; they'd have shown through.'

'Did Great-granny know?'

'She noticed when I was half way up the aisle, I heard her gasp.' Oh dear; she was very fierce. Granny was married in Arusha in 1934, twelve days after her twenty-first birthday. They had ordered special champagne from France, only my Great-grandfather was an alcoholic and spoilt things. He left the service early, drove back to the farm and had all the champagne buried under the coffee bushes. The guests had to drink the toasts with cups of tea. What was even sadder was that Granny's father had been so drunk he couldn't remember where all the bottles were buried. They're probably still digging them up today. I told Robin who said, 'What a shame. Champagne doesn't keep you know.'

10th July ~ I found my old school report from when I was ten. It said, 'Very good; though she still needs to guard her tongue sometimes from making silly remarks.' Rebecca says I haven't changed, I'm just having problems articulating clearly. Her father came to collect her and I suddenly felt very little. Then I read in the paper that I'm the same age as the *E-type Jaguar*, *Amnesty International* and the *Sindy* doll. The plastic ones. (Ha.) I wonder if God is concerned with my age? 'God is passionately concerned with every detail of our lives.'[2] Of course. I still make silly remarks.

'The Pang worked well.'

'What?'

'Those straw bales in the River Pang,' James shouted loudly down the phone, 'they were doing some very interesting experiments there and I got some decent footage at last.' I couldn't think what he was talking about. 'You told me go and film freshwater molluscs there.'

'Did I?' I must be going completely dotty. I know nothing about molluscs. Neither do I want to much.

'It must be old age creeping in,' said James. 'You said you'd read about it in the newspaper.'

'Oh, yes.'

11th July ~ Acupuncture: into the torture chamber once more I go. I'm still not sure about submitting myself to this treatment. Jeremy is very sweet but he did let it slip that he's glad so many people have M.E. because he's going to make lots of money out of them. I'm afraid I wasn't very impressed. Umm. I've been reading articles and letters from M.E. patients who say that in general they've been very disappointed by alternative medicine especially when the cost of it has impoverished them. They recommend asking a lot of questions. What about Aromatherapy?

Definition of Aromatherapy found in *The Tatler:* 'The use of natural oils which are absorbed by the skin as lipsosalvants, to promote healing by detoxicating the body and oxygenating and hydrating the skin.'

I reckon I can accept natural oils and herbs used in medicine, alternative, complementary, integral or otherwise. (All natural chemicals, as Granny says.) They never stop using oil in the New Testament. (And wine.) The M.E. association say it's 'the most helpful therapy in alleviating... symptoms' but that it's not a cure in itself. They add the same disclaimer as they do for all alternative therapies. It boils down to a need for discernment when choosing a therapist.

Just brilliant: I found my old flute with a pile of music from the shows. It was such fun. I sang away into the night, *Westside Story*, *Gigi* and *My Fair Lady*, something I haven't done for years. I felt so refreshed. I reckon that God will indeed take care of every detail of my life. It's just that it's up to me to jolly well do what he says.

12th July ~ Another day in bed. I was woken by a furious Mary-Dieu on the phone. She just said, 'Take her.' We seem to have to do everything Mary-Dieu says.

Mum is in Soho, auditioning to play the part of a fat lady, so Dad had to go to Gloucester. I feel I'm moving at the speed of a bottom shuffler, or some sort of strange deep-water fish living on the ocean floor under huge pressure.

13th July ~ Mum and Dad went off to Henley with Daisy in *Daffodil*. Their steamboat. I stayed in bed. It would have been too much for me to go. I do nothing. Say nothing. My thoughts are dull and don't travel far. I still find it difficult to concentrate for long. I'm fed up with not being able to fall asleep, or stay asleep at night and yet I doze away my days.

A card has come from Rebecca, thanking me for her stay and begging me not to drive. She says, 'I remember that when you were driving me I was TERRIFIED. It's ironic that while I'm legally not allowed to drive but would be perfectly safe to do so, you're legally allowed to, but totally incapable.' (Oh, dear.)

14th July ~ It transpires that Mum persuaded Tamzin and Johnty to come along and help Dad crew the boat yesterday. It was a disaster because their bull-terrier, Maud, did not like being on board one little bit. Then everyone forgot about Johnty and left him closing a lock. He had to run miles up the towpath to catch them.

I'm not feeling that animated myself but since the *Action for M.E.* Newsletter recommends writing poetry I'm having a go. Thanks to my pill popping all I can think of is ♪*A spoon full of sugar makes the medicine go down.*♪ Perry is staying while Robert is off on exercise. Just like Mary Poppins, she's 'practically perfect in every way.' It can be quite irritating. Nothing Perry does ever goes wrong. She manages to look immaculate, cook delicious meals, clean the house and schedule time to get a suntan while looking after two babies effortlessly. 'Childcare is not something I find particularly stressful,' she told me. She put each little girl in a shallow washtub of water and they were happy for hours.

Atalanta is very concerned with her appearance for such a small creature. Her idea of heaven is to spend the morning in a shoe shop, and she's only fifteen months old. Daisy is more interested in digging up worms. We are all so individual. 'You're rather good at looking after children, Sophie, because you give them independence.'

'Oh, thanks.' It's actually all I can give them right now. I think Perry is tactfully making allowances for the fact that I let them get filthy dirty.

Dad returned from Henley covered in blood; cross because he'd cut off the ends of his fingers. Mum didn't get the part of the fat lady. Now she's cross about being too thin. Tamzin is cross with both of them for leaving Johnty on the canal bank, and says Maud is still cross too. 'What am I meant to do about any of this, Lord?'

'Listen. Be a listener.'

Oh golly, that is just what I've been demanding of everyone else. I must 'Do as you would be done by', as Diana says.[8]

15th July ~
Lord forgive. The Lord forgave,
So I must forgive as well.
And now I know that I must grow
From what you didn't mean to show.

Does that make any sense at all?

16th July ~
The light on the hills is golden,
And the light in the valley is green.
I sit and watch, absorbing it
While it's still here to be seen.

17th July ~

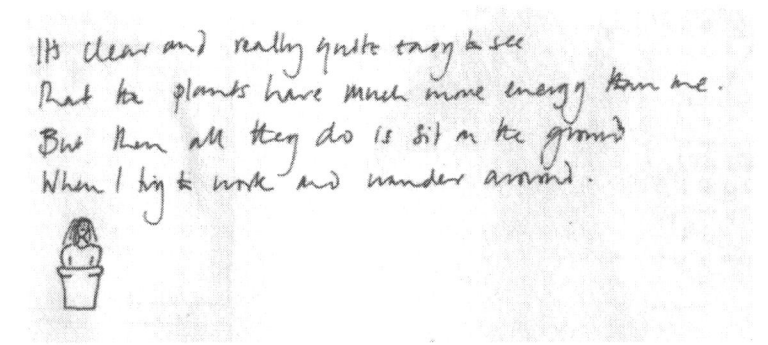

It's clear and really quite easy to see that the plants have much more energy than me. But then all they do is sit in the ground when I try to work and wander around.

I think I'd better forget the idea of writing poetry. I'm in the garden with Daisy. She's good at chasing doves.

18th July ~ Acupuncture. I bought some bands to wear round my wrists that are excellent in preventing seasickness. They have white plastic bobbles attached to the inside, which very simply exert pressure at a certain point on the inner arm. They've been clinically tried, tested and approved, especially for staving off morning sickness in pregnant women who can't take tablets. They're much more appropriate than seasick pills –

which I tend to sick up. Jeremy showed me how rubbing the small of the back can relieve period pain and how massaging the base of the thumb can ease stomach-ache. You just have to keep rubbing. Interesting. It must be to do with everything in the body being interconnected.

Dad says he gets acupuncture naturally and for free whenever he clears brambles or pulls up thistles. But I think he's referring to *dry-needling*. I suppose hunter-gatherers get pricked and stung all them time, picking berries and raiding bee's nests.

19th July ~ I just seem to be deteriorating, getting tireder and tireder. Like a child, I live in a selfish world of my own and cry easily. I feel so frustrated. I can do nothing and my brain feels as if it's gliding sideways.

Why, why, why? All the tests show nothing wrong: chest x-ray: normal, blood count: normal, liver: normal, thyroid: normal, glandular fever: none, anaemia: none.

I've been reading a book by David Watson written when he was ill. He says: Don't ask Why, ask What? 'What are you doing with my life God? What are you saying to me? What do you want me to do?' The most important thing is knowing God's will and doing it. It is far more important than having the question of 'Why do I suffer?' or 'Why pain?' answered.

20th July ~ Rose rang. She said that she had to give a talk to a youth group on *The power of God in our lives.* I suggested likening the power to the wind. You can't see it but you can feel the effects. It's there for us to use; we just need to hoist our sails. You need to learn how to sail too, how to use the power of the Holy Spirit. What can be difficult to understand is that at times we are sitting in the boat, sails set, hand on the tiller and although the air is all around us there's no wind. We just have to wait for it to come. That wait can be difficult.

21st July ~
But those who hope in the Lord
Will renew their strength.
They will soar on wings like eagles;
They will run and not grow weary,
They will walk and not be faint.
 Not my poetry but from *The Book of Isaiah.*

Gordon sent it to me. He wrote: 'When it comes to alternative or complementary medicine do make sure that your practitioner is operating from an entirely clinical basis, and is not into psychic healing.' He says the Ch'i spirit, Yin and Yang energies; the Taoist roots of acupuncture aren't exactly 'scientifically proven entities.' I feel he has a point. From the beginning the small voice inside me, akin to my conscience, was urging me not to go down this path. I was just impatient and desperate to try anything to get well. Although all my doctors have endorsed it I'm not sure that acupuncture is helping me anyway. 'Ask *what* not why.'

22nd July ~ I didn't have any more needles stuck in me. And I asked about the concept underlying the treatment. Jeremy gave me a clear clinical explanation of how his aim is to activate the immune system. He said that the 'Yin and Yang' theory behind acupuncture just helps you apply the science... but I'm not convinced. I was thinking, 'There is a way that seems right to a man, but in the end it leads to death,'[x] when he declared that acupuncture doesn't really help people with M.E. much. I've had six sessions. Why didn't he tell me that in the first place? Instead he suggested I 'take a break from the therapy indefinitely.'

23rd July ~ What now? About turn. I'm setting my sails to harness the wind. If the doctors can't get anywhere I obviously need a miracle; I'm going to seek proper ministry and the power of God. Why have I waited so long? People have been praying for my health constantly; Rose, Mum, Granny. Gordon is getting the whole church to pray. I'm sure this has helped enormously, and staved off the clinical depression that I've read in the medical journals is a symptom of M.E., but I need complete healing.

It says here in my Bible, 'Are there any among you sick? They should call for the elders of the church and have them pray over them, anointing them with oil in the name of the Lord. And their prayer offered in faith will heal the sick, and the Lord will make them well.' It was written by James, Jesus' brother[xi].

I'll go for that. Our village church doesn't have a ministry team up and running, so I rang the Christian Healing Mission in London. The experts. They'll be able to help me if there's a psychological cause to this in my childhood or something. The earliest appointment they could give me was for 15th August. Ages away!

I phoned Gordon to thank him for a book he'd sent and let him know my plans. He suggested I contact a Christian healing centre in Gloucestershire. There's one in a village called Harnhill, close to Perry's house. I rang and hope to go to a service on Friday morning.

24th July ~ Mum returned Daisy to Gloucester with trepidation but found Daisy's father was there, mild mannered as usual despite the stormy atmosphere. The next thing was that Mary-Dieu rang to say that her boyfriend had gone off with Daisy and could Mum find out if he'd taken her to Essex? How was she going to do that? Mum said she found herself coming out of the supermarket in floods of tears, wheeling the trolley round and round the car park looking for her silver car. She couldn't find it anywhere; eventually she remembered that she'd driven there in Dad's blue one.

25th July ~ Poor Mum probably needs a good game of tennis just as an outlet for her emotions but I still can't play. In the book I'm reading, Adrian Plass says, 'It's not what we do but who we are that matters most in life ~ not what we endure but how we endure it.' I'm not much help, but at least I'm here. And I can use a telephone. I rang Mary-Dieu and found her boyfriend had only popped out to hire a video.

I discovered two earwigs in my hair today. I don't know what they think they're doing there. Tamzin said they make very good parents. I asked Alastair who declared them to be predators: 'cheetahs of the insect world.' And they were doing things on my head.

26th July ~ I went to the Harnhill Centre for Christian Healing. They had a service in the ancient little parish church where a friend of mine was once married. It was full and I was late. The chaplain gave a very good sermon. He stressed that we were healed by Jesus and for him, not for ourselves. A small team prayed for me and asked that I would be healed.

I drove on to stay with Perry taking a copy of *The Screwtape Letters*. My brother-in-law might find it amusing. He's a soldier after all.

Atalanta is a funny girl. In the mornings, she sits beside her mother at the dressing table and plays. She pulls out all Perry's knickers and puts them on her head. She then puts all Perry's bras around her neck and then she puts on Robert's British Army identity card, which has his name, rank and photograph laminated in plastic. His little smiley face peers out from behind the underwear. Enough to daunt any demon.

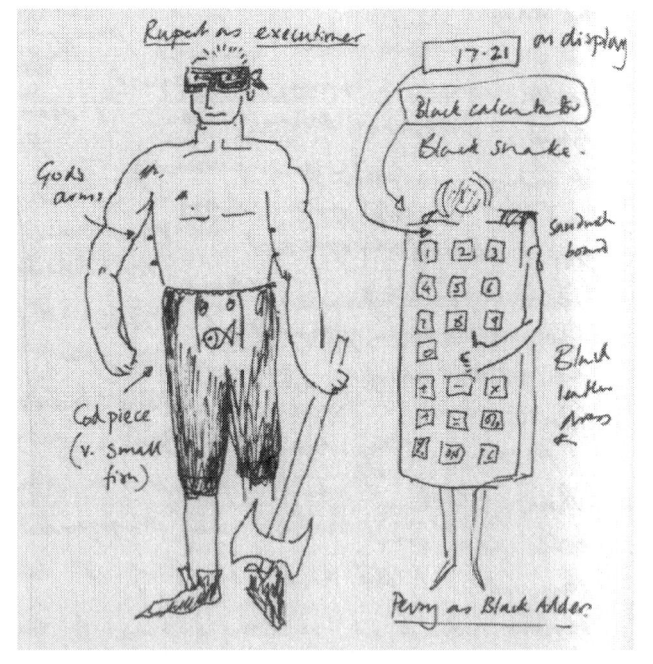

They're off to the last regimental ball of the *17th/21st Lancers* before amalgamation. Perry is busy making the costumes. It's a *Blackadder* Ball. The invitation says, 'All ancestors and friends are requested to attend in cunning disguise.' Robert is going as an executioner. Perry is going as a black calculator, with 17.21 written on the display. It took me rather a long time to work out why. Sad, my brain must be deteriorating. But is it odd to have a fraction for a name. They're becoming the *Queen's Royal Lancers*. I wonder why? They don't fight with lances anymore. They have tanks.

27th July ~ Perry has just caused shockwaves of disbelief and amazement in the AA Insurance office by giving her full name to the female clerk. 'She couldn't accept that my real name is Peronelle. Then she asked for Robert's.'(Oh dear.)

'Did you have to spell it?'

'No. I thought she couldn't be that dim. I said, "It's Wolf. Wolf like an animal." His first name is Wolf.' (If they have a boy then he must also be called Wolf: 'To Peronelle and Wolf, a cub...')

28th July ~ Quite interesting. I got home to find a letter had arrived from *Action for M.E.* I'd asked them about acupuncture. The man just said that he knew of forty-nine sufferers who had treatment but that it didn't benefit any of them for more than a day-and-a-half. If I add my name to the list it would make fifty non-benefitters.

My father has been planning to take *Tulip*, the dinghy he built in the spring, up to Lake Windermere where the Steamboat Association is holding a rally. *Tulip* only runs under sail or outboard motor but he says he can't take his *Daffodil*, as she's just too delicate. Mum thinks that, even though I'm rather more delicate than a twenty-four foot steamboat, I ought to go too, pointing out that I could get good mountain air while sitting on a velvet cushion all day. It won't cost a thing.

I found myself being driven north and we are now staying in the most beautiful clubhouse overlooking the lake. It was designed by Vosey in 1899 but looks incredibly modern with terraced gardens full of roses and startling views. I feel like an Edwardian convalescent taken off to a hotel in Switzerland for revival.

29th July ~ A sparkling, sunny morning and a lovely, warm hazy day. Daddy launched his little dinghy and sailed off down the lake despite the fact that there seemed to be lack of wind. The steamboat enthusiasts made rather scathing comments but he managed to get half way to the end before we caught him up.

I was taken out by a distinguished engineer called Arthur Podmore who, sure enough, seated me on plush velvet in his small but opulent steamboat. I did nothing at all but watch the sunlight on the water and gaze at the towering mountains around us. We had a picnic lunch in an Edwardian boathouse and I spent the afternoon in a steam launch called *Shamrock* from which a chap called Roger produced iced buns and endless cups of tea. He had an exquisite steam kettle made when he was caught in a storm off the Shetland Isles. It had handles that looked like rope but were made out of seven braising rods twisted together since he'd run out of brass. A good-looking man from *The Daily Telegraph* stood precariously on *Tulip's* tiny aft deck and took photographs of the fleet lashed together at teatime in Merganizer Bay. He nearly fell in.

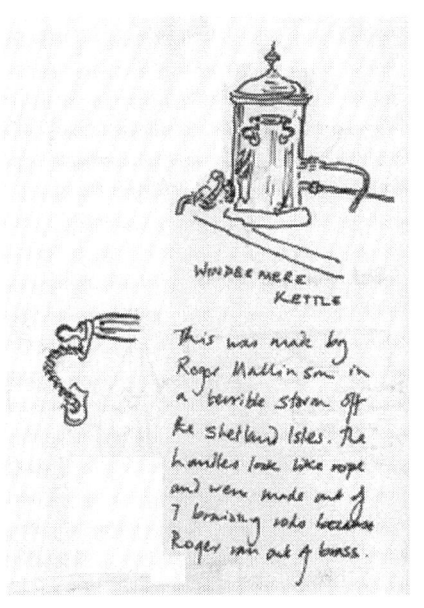

Windermere Kettle

This was made by Roger Mallinson in a terrible storm off the Shetland Isles. The handles look like rope and were made out of 7 braising rods [welded?] Roger ran out of brass.

Later, Dad and I ate alone in the Vosey dining room, looking out over the lake towards the setting sun. We had delicious steaks and then raspberries and cream in tall pink German glasses that glowed in the slanty light.

30th July ~ This trip is one huge meal: we all had breakfast together at a large round table at the club; massive helpings aimed at taking you up mountains. I love the Lake District. No one minded when I had black pudding.

I ordered black pudding when Mikie took me out to dinner once. Perry was horrified and said I must be very careful what I choose when I'm out on a date.

'Because, Sophie:

(a) It's not sexy to eat dried blood.

(b) You get black bits in your teeth.

No.....It's NOT funny.'

Steamboats are very quiet, and are usually beautifully designed along classic lines. They seem to glide across the water leaving no wake. However, on Windermere there are speedboats. One tore past us, coming so close it created a wave that plopped neatly onto my head. I was drenched. I know the speedboat driver saw what happened but he stared straight ahead, looking self-important.

We made our way up to the *Steamboat Museum* in Bowness for lunch. I sat very quietly, trying to dry off in the sun while the enthusiasts around me enthused loudly. Their excitement over engineering and the potential for steam is quite contagious.

I assumed all steamboat fanatics must be engineers but one turned out to be an eminent paediatrician. We chatted about how rushed National Health schedules and an increasing reliance on drugs are forcing us to lose the *art* of healing in the west.

'I feel that seeing your GP for twenty minutes once a month just isn't enough if you have a long-term illness to cope with,' Dad said, 'even if your doctor is brilliant and you're getting the best medical tests free of charge. You need additional attention.'

'I worry that people are going in for alternative medicine *instead* of going to their GP, since they might require surgery,' the paediatrician insisted. 'It happens. I found one mother had been receiving treatment from a homoeopath for a year when she needed a cyst the size of a pineapple removed from her womb. And this wasn't in Hong Kong, she was from Hampshire.'

Things always go wrong at home when Dad goes away. Mum rang to say that Robert's mother has had a heart attack at a hotel in Reading. She managed to pull through but it just shows you. Our lives are so fragile. She'd been playing bridge.

31st July ~ Conversation between steamboat children:
'What's your house like?'
'It's semi-detached.'
'No, I mean steam?'
'The garage?'
'Yes.'
'Oh, the garage is like a workshop full of lathes and stuff...we've got a railway line going round the garden.'
'So have we. What gauge?' he asked, sounding resigned rather than keen.
'Two-and-a-half inches. Have you got bits of engine all over your house too?'

'Gran has a standing engine on display in the hall.'

'My mother has to have a steam engine four foot long in her bedroom and a model boat on top of the wardrobe, but my room is a steam-free zone.'

Our steamboat *Daffodil* sat in the garden for as long as I can remember but my father had other adorations too. When I was little we had a massive open-topped fire engine with a Rolls Royce engine, which my parents would pack with friends. We'd drive a mile down the road and it would promptly break down, blocking the lane for hours while my father fixed the clutch. There was a 1914 car with wooden wheels like a cart and an enormous 1927 Norton motorcycle with a sidecar. When Dad stripped the modern paint off the petrol tank he found the initials C.J.P.D. scratched on it: Charlie Dodson, racing driver super-star of the day had raced it in the Isle of Man T.T., which he'd won two years running. He was my mother's uncle.

AUGUST ~ Anything is possible

1st August ~

I actually spent yesterday in bed, but my batteries felt slightly stronger this morning and I joined the others. We sailed up to Pull Wyke Bay at the northern end of Windermere. It was lovely going up towards the mountains, not so nice at the Langdale Chase Hotel. A pretentious man, in a rather too-open shirt, got unnecessarily annoyed about us blocking in his hideous speedboat when everyone had rafted their boats together for a brew up. 'That's the miserable creature who drenched my seats,' said Arthur Podmore, sucking on his pipe and staring meaningfully at the man who strode off into the hotel in an unreasonable cloud of hatred.

'And me, Mr. Podmore.' The waiters, also infected by the man's nastiness became so fraught I had to walk away and lie on the lawn by the lake eating my own sandwiches. I've just read that, 'there are people in this world who cause trouble because it makes them feel important.' I suppose they're so ineffective in their own lives they want power over others. It seems to be the key to understanding all the bullies I have known.

Why do we let bitterness and resentment rule our lives? I should feel sorry for that poor man but of course I don't feel like it at all because he's been so brutish and rude. I have to look past my emotions to the facts and, in this case, pray that the man is released from the ugly things he's let in that are eating away at him like maggots. What a waste when he could so easily have made a joke of it or asked for a cup of tea. It made me determined to spread enthusiasm in my life. That's what I've learnt during my time in the sunshine with these ebullient steamboat people.

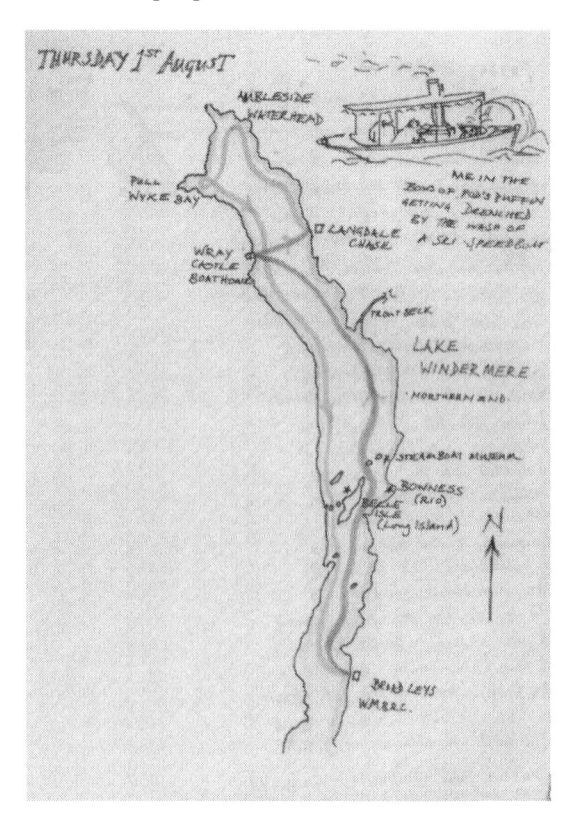

2nd August ~ We left the crowded waters of Windermere and drove through rain to Coniston Water. It was peaceful and still and wild. We drove up the eastern side. The oak woods clinging to the hillside and flowing down to the shore took me reeling back to my childhood. 'Here we are, intrepid explorers, making the first ever voyage into uncharted waters. What mysteries will they hold for us? What dark secrets will be revealed?'

Long ago I appeared in the feature film of Arthur Ransome's book *Swallows and Amazons*. I played Titty, or rather I was Titty for a while wearing thick blue gym knickers, which the crew referred to as passion killers. The book was written in 1929 and although the film adaptation was made in the early 'seventies it had an ageless quality and was repeated on television at Christmas time year after year, between Rock Hudson and Doris Day. I was once handed a copy of the TV billings in the *Radio Times*. On one page I was credited as producing a documentary for teachers that I'd just spent six months pouring myself into. Above it was a huge colour picture of myself as a gawky looking child, described as the star of *Swallows and Amazons*. My life travelling in circles. Our Head of Department caught me in the lift. 'Do you think I could have a VHS tape of your programme?'

'Oh, yes,' I said, thrilled that he was interested in my series. 'But I haven't finished dubbing the music yet. Do you mind having a copy with the timecode on?'

'Ah, er. No. It was actually a copy of *Swallows and Amazons* that I wanted; my sons are longing to see it.' And off he rushed.

My father tipped his boat off the trailer and we motored over to Peel Island where we'd made the film. Wild Cat Island. It was slightly less over-grown but had hardly changed in the eighteen years since I'd last been there. It still had just the one old fireplace where I'd cooked potato cakes with Virginia McKenna and talked about very savage savages. Arthur Ransome had us call self-important men in open necked shirts 'natives' then, so I suppose it's not surprising that Granny, who was a real child in the 1920s, still does.

I walked down to the secret harbour where I captured the Amazon, up to the oak tree that I climbed 'for fear of ravenous beasts' and on to the place where we had gutted fish. It's a wonderful island. I'd love my children to be able to go and camp there. Not that I did in reality, I was only ever there with an eighty-strong film crew. I'd worked hard, even then as a child. It was often cold and we would have to hang around for what seemed like hours, waiting for lights to be set or clouds to pass. As I walked out over the same rocks I began to feel the emptiness of not having enough to do. Strangely enough, filming is an incredibly boring occupation for children who find it difficult to endure the hanging around. It's a restrictive discipline; I hadn't been allowed to go off exploring or even walk around the headland then. Now I don't have the stamina.

Although I never wanted to be an actress I started working at the age of ten, when I was in a dramatisation of *Cider with Rosie*. I had to accompany Laurie Lee on the piano and plodded through *Oh, Danny Boy* at an agonising pace. 'Do you think you could play just a little faster?' the director asked.

'No,' I said, flatly. 'These are crotchets, they don't go any faster.' Bossy aged ten. However Claude Whatham, who was directing, thought it quite funny and must have remembered this, for he cast me as Titty; that was how I got the part.

People ask what effect the feature film had on my life. It's an odd thing to happen to a child. It made me neither rich or famous, but helped professionally. I took the lead in another feature film when I was fifteen, and paid much of my own way through university by working as a film extra. All this gave me enough production experience to cope when I entered the *BBC* as a researcher in 1982. After three months there, I started casting children for a series based on the Arthur Ransome books set on the Norfolk Broads, *Coot Club* and *The Big Six*. I remember that was stressful. I couldn't find a boy to play Tom Dudgeon, the most important character, who needed to be able to sail well. I dredged school after school, meeting literally hundreds of children. We were getting very close to the deadline and I was almost in despair when I (prayed and) took Olivia, who was thirteen then, off to see a musical in the West End as a treat. During the interval I turned round and saw a boy, perfect for the part of Tom, sitting in the seats behind me with his sisters so I started chatting to them. 'Do you by any chance sail?' I asked.

'Oh, yes. We've got a cabin cruiser in Devon and I often take the helm.' I went to meet the boy's parents and found myself blushing violently, looking up at David Dimbleby, inviting his son to come and audition at the *BBC*. That was a bit daunting.

Dad and I motored back and ate supper by the lake before driving on south through the night. The motorway is unbearable otherwise if you're towing a boat. I crawled into my bed at 2.00am but slept well for the first time in weeks.

3rd August ~ I feel devastated again, seemingly unable to turn away from gloom and defenceless against the onslaught of despond.

'Always turn your face to the sunshine and the shadows will fall behind you.'

~ Geoffrey Tregloun

What I have turned my face to is a letter from the Clinical Director of Research at *The Royal London Homoeopathic Hospital* saying they don't often use acupuncture for chronic fatigue. Apparently it's good if you're into pain management, for treating nausea, allergic disorders and withdrawal symptoms but patients do have to keep going for treatment. It's not a cure and doesn't offer patients a long-term solution. Neither does it heal the source of pain.

A leaflet had also arrived from *The British Medical Acupuncture Society.*[2] They report that acupuncture works by way of stimulating nerves in the skin and muscle and thereby increasing the body's release of natural painkillers, namely endorphin and serotonin. In response to my questions they wrote:

Dear Sophie,

Chi, meridians, energy balance etc are all traditional concepts developed by Chinese physicians 2,000 or more years ago. The BMAS is a group of contemporary medical doctors who use modern methods of diagnosis and treatments involving a full range of available therapies. Acupuncture is one therapy we use. We tend to apply this therapy based on modern ideas of how the nervous system works in relation to the rest of the body. Most of us do not use the ancient concepts of life force and balance of chi in applying acupuncture therapy.

Acupuncture may help some patients with ME, mostly in pain control, but improves well-being only in a small percentage.

Best wishes,
Mike.
Dr. T Mike Cummings
Editor AIM, Medical Director BMAS

They stress, repeatedly, that it's vital that the practitioner is a qualified medical doctor, accountable to the General Medical

Council. They sent me a list of their accredited members. Jeremy was not on it.

4th August ~ Why am I suddenly prone to depression? I've heard it can be caused by exposure to leaky gas appliances or central heating boilers, but we don't have gas. Our boiler is brand new and in a shed outside. Anyway it's August. Is this depression a clinical symptom of M.E.? It's probably because I've run out of vitamin B, which is designed to stave it off. I'm so enervated that I feel disinclined to do anything at all, let alone work out what to do about this, but managed to order some more vitamins. Mum thinks I must be a step or two forward in other respects but my right eye tics when I do more than a little reading, which is annoying.

Although it seems as if none of my prayers are being answered, I'm determined to keep thanking God for all the good things, and indeed the things that seem bad. You never know the ramifications. Tamzin had a friend who slipped on a grape in the greengrocer's and fell down so hard she was whipped off to Casualty. They found she had a cancerous growth on her spine. She had an operation and it was neatly removed before becoming malignant. If it hadn't been for the grape she would have probably died; I mean, when was the last time you had your bottom X-rayed?

We have to go deeper than questions. David Watson's book is a great guide. He says that 'Saviour' means Healer and that

'Salvation' means Wholeness, with God's authority and rule affecting every area of our lives. Through Christ, and through his death on the cross, our bodies, our relationship with God and our relationships with one another can be healed. Restored. That's quite something. It means that no matter what happens, no matter how often we muck things up, no matter what the enemy tears apart, we can claim restoration. It's been paid for; we just have to put in the claim.

It's clear Jesus healed a whole load of people. And you can see the healing wasn't just a gift he kept for himself but a ministry that he wanted to extend to all his disciples. Rose and I lived with a girl who, due to a skiing injury, had a steel plate keeping her leg straight. After someone prayed for her she bent her knee and started walking around normally. Disco dancing. Miracles do still happen.

I've been reading about the London Christian Healing Mission. Amazing things have happened there and many, many people have been miraculously healed. They keep records and statistics. About 50% of those who come asking for prayer suffer from depression. Only about one in twenty-five people prayed for experience instantaneous and dramatic healing. Most of it's gradual.

5th August ~ While I was sitting up in bed reading, Mum decided to go swimming in the lake ~ with Bee. She got all hot after the otter's walk and decided to strip off and jump in. It's normally quiet here during the week and the water is so murky no one passing could tell what you were wearing. Only this time Mum was unlucky. She got caught by an otter fanatic; well, not physically caught but kept chatting for ages. She couldn't get rid of him. 'He didn't seem to appreciate that I might be getting cold. He kept asking stupid questions.'

'Like what?'

'Like, "Do otters eat vegetables?" and then Bee decided that she wanted to get out.' Mum absolutely had to catch her before she ran down the lane, as otters have zero traffic sense, but of course she couldn't get out with nothing on in front of the creepy man.

'What did you do?'

'Well, I told him he'd have to look the other way.' On realising why he scarpered.

6th August ~ I cannot help feeling antsy, as the Americans say. Although I love being at home, I think I must take the specialist's advice and move again, so I've asked Tamzin if I can stay with her. Whatever I do I must get rid of this gloomy foreboding, these negative thoughts. They're isolating and will only make me increasingly despondent. This is depression, not an emotion but a physical mood. It's not a moany-ness. It has no relation to how I relate to other people.

7th August ~ I can't bear it. Mum has let her parrot out to give it some freedom: it flew straight through the kitchen and landed on the edge of the frying pan.

Mum and I ended up having a major row. She doesn't seem to accept that all these doves and captive birds can spread the most disgusting disease. We aren't allowed near a public lavatory for fear of catching something heinous, but does it matter if a parrot lands on the sausages? No.

'You're making a fuss about nothing.'

'That parrot is a liability.'

'You're just getting paranoid about disease.' I stomped off to bed, cross with Mum and cross with everything, then sat there saying, 'I refuse to pander to anxiety and confusion,' over and over again. Even though I think I'm useless I can still ask God to use me. It should be easy.

8th August ~ I'm at Tamzin's house. They have terribly sad news. Johnty's dear little niece has died in a car accident on the motorway. She was nearly three years old. Her mother, who was driving, is badly hurt with a cracked sternum and can't remember what happened. The vehicle ended upside down on the embankment and their spaniel, who had been thrown right through the dog-guard, was found wandering around on the motorway. The medics tried their very best to save the little girl but after seven hours had to turn off the life-support machines. Her poor parents. The only good thing was that their son had just been left with his granny. We all cried. How different this great sadness is to clinical depression.

9th August ~ Johnty went up to London to see his brother. I was glad that I was able to be with Tamzin. Shakespeare said we must 'give sorrow words'. 'Oh Lord, help me share your promises.'

In his book *Fear no Evil* David Watson says, 'Nothing is more important than our relationships...first and foremost our relationship with God, but also our relationships with others, especially our family. In our busy Western society we put too much emphasis on work, achievements, money and success, invariably at the expense of our relationships.' But later he admits that his own work for the church in York was so demanding that he and his wife literally burnt out. Although advised to take a sabbatical they never got round to it. They ended up having to because of his extreme ill health. David was dying of cancer when he wrote the book. He was fifty.

10th August ~ Tamzin and I went riding, I on her massive hunter Bod wearing my new chaps, she in sleek jodhpurs on Raddy's tiny orange pony. It was a day of days; a beautiful midsummer morning. Bod looked wonderful but was half-asleep the whole time. Unlike when last I rode him. This was at a Hunter Trials when he would only go sideways. 'Yes,' Tamzin said, 'life is quite different when he gets excited. I went hunting in a snaffle once; harum scarum. There was nothing I could do but knot the reins, hold on tight and lean back.' After that the Field Marshall, Raddy's father, lent her a stronger bit. 'They call this one a gag,' Tamzin explained, showing me the device, which puts pressure on the top of his enormous head. 'I use it very gently. It has these moving pieces called cherry-rollers so the horse can't hold the bit between his teeth.' Serious braking gear. I made her look for meteorites while we rode along, so she trotted the pony round in circles while I clomped on ahead.

Maud has so much energy it tires me out to watch her, but I have to say she takes frequent rests. She's remarkably secure and sure of herself. I shall take a few notes.

Lessons to be learnt from a bull-terrier:
- Never forget to enjoy your life.
- Have confidence in the way you look.
- Always make yourself as comfortable as possible.
- Rest whenever you can.
- Eat with great enthusiasm.
- No matter how many times you get screamed at, always look innocent and appealing.

- Do not bear a grudge; it won't do you any good.
- It can be to your advantage to be obedient.
- If you stare at someone long enough you will eventually get what you want.
- If what you want is buried, keep digging until you find it.
- Let people know when they have invaded your territory.
- Always give people a wonderful, friendly greeting.
- Never give up the opportunity to go for a walk.
- Be loyal; commitment is always rewarded.

Tamzin says that this is an exact portrayal of Mum. Except the grudge bit.

Johnty has a huge sense of commitment and works far too hard, easily doing twelve-hour days. His company moved offices to a converted barn recently. It had been sprayed extensively with something to treat woodworm. We all think that inhaling the residual chemicals day after day is doing him in. Although he won't complain, he's admitted to not being at all well. His whole body aches constantly. He won't stop working and is strong enough to keep going despite the pain. Tamzin said that it's driving her batty. To our amazement he readily agreed to go and see Dr. Loveday. He says running down canal towpaths has nothing to do with it but I think he might have M.E. too.

11th August ~ I feel the nature of my illness is changing. Although still constantly and inexplicably fatigued, I no longer find driving so daunting. Really; it's OK. I just take things slowly and keep taking small rests. I made it to Tamzin's cottage without being a liability and feel fine about driving alone now.

As it turned out, I broke up my next journey by going to lunch with Griz and Dane on my way through to Perry's house. It was a dog day. Everyone seemed to have one. Alastair was there, with an extraordinary looking, floppy dog called Dogger. It belongs to his new girlfriend.

For some reason he convinced Paddy, who is not a baby anymore, but three and a half, that there was a dog up the chimney. Everyone kept looking up it. We walked to the village church to look at their medieval wooden effigies. There was a little carved dog at the knight's feet. I know why; to keep them warm.

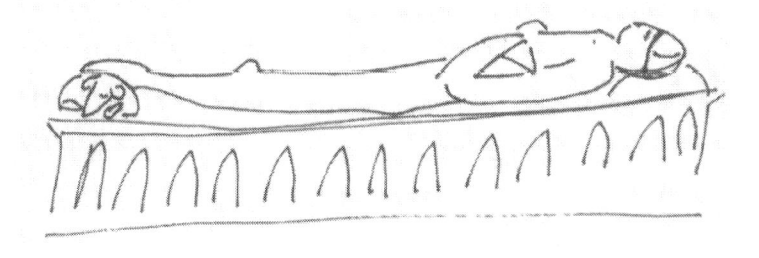

On my way back I stopped and walked on the Berkshire Downs in the golden evening light. I sat where you're not allowed to, above the head of the ancient horse cut in the chalk, and looked out over the endless vale below. Being ill is certainly changing my perspective on life, or rather giving me a chance to look at it from afar. We all ought to do this from time to time.

12th August ~ Atalanta was pushed by her glum aunt (me) past all the parked up tanks on the Army base. They look like the epitome of depression; dark, massive and seemingly immovable. The information on M.E. said cheerfully that you couldn't die from chronic fatigue. The only known fatalities are suicides. That's why depression has to be taken seriously; it's quite dangerous. Robert told me, while Perry cut his hair in the kitchen, that they have a number of suicides in the Army. He was sitting without a shirt in his emerald green tracksuit bottoms looking like a muscley Ninja Turtle. Is all this suicide from a rampant spirit of death? I shall turn my back on it and go looking for meteorites instead.

13th August ~ Perry said that her mother-in-law has completely recovered from her heart attack and is back playing bridge. 'She calls it her *Dangerous Sports Club*.' I tried to help with the ironing but flaked out. 'It's a real pain having to iron all these khaki shirts of Robert's,' Perry agreed. 'They're such a dismal colour. In the winter I just do the collar and cuffs, telling him not to take his jumper off.' Efficiency incarnate. 'Note, please, that I do not use chemical cleaning agents or air fresheners and all clothes are thoroughly aired when they come back from the dry cleaners.' It's probably why I feel so much better in her house.

I told her about the horse. Not the white one in the hill, but Tamzin's hunter. 'Do you know the Field Marshall?'

'Not personally. Is he unstoppable too?'

'He pinched Mum's bottom at a dance of Raddy's once, she's still indignant about it.'

'Rubbish,' Perry said, unloading the washing machine. 'Mum loves getting attention from senior Army officers.' She did fall for the C.O. of the local regiment once. He was called Patrick so we called him Pat Pat on account of his tactile tendencies. Dad coped with the situation by inviting him to spend a weekend on the boat. He had to share a tent with Mary-Dieu, who was nine, and she was sick all over him in the night.

14th August ~ Drove eighty miles from Perry's to London. Collapsed. I remembered when I'd met the Field Marshall. I was driving through Reading once, following signs to *All Routes* and trying to cope with a bad bout of hayfever. I sneezed, my car jerked forward and I bumped into the car in front. I could see I hadn't done any harm but it was awfully embarrassing; I had to 'draw up to stop and examine the damage with the other motorist.' This turned out to be the General, who emerged from his Renault Five in full Army uniform. I was terrified. He glanced at his bumper, came up to me and said, "Young lady, if you do that again I'll be obliged to marry you."

15th August ~ The first thing I read when I arrived at the Christian Healing Mission in London was a poster saying, 'We mustn't come seeing what we could receive from the Lord, but asking what we could do for Him.' I had an appointment with a lady called Barbara there that afternoon. She politely asked me upstairs and I walked straight into an old fashioned bathroom. We burst out laughing. She opened the door into the sitting room, which should have been obvious, as it was right in front of me. As soon as she recovered her breath, we sat down and she prayed, thanking God for bringing me there and thanking Him for me. It was quite a welcome. We talked for a while about my problem.

Barbara said that when the intercessors had been praying for me that morning one of them had had a clear picture in their mind's eye of a rainbow. She asked me if I knew anyone in the New Age movement, so I told her about Jeremy. She said that I'd better renounce that treatment and we prayed for everyone I'd been to see for healing. An interesting thing happened to me *physically*. When I prayed for Dr. Loveday I felt full of joy and overflowing with thanks. But when I prayed for Jeremy I became incredibly scrunched up and bowed. It was a pronounced physical reaction. Barbara advised me: 'Be on your guard; do not let your mind(s) be captured by hollow and delusive speculations based on traditions of man-made teaching and centred on the elemental spirits of the universe and not on Christ.' – quoting a letter Paul wrote to the Colossians when he was in prison in Rome. She laid hands on me like an apostle and prayed for the fatigue, for the healing of my body and mind. She then read me *Psalm 144*. It spoke of making my fingers and hands strong to do the Lord's work.

So, I accepted healing and was delivered from any harm from any treatment I'd accepted. I was commissioned and anointed with oil, just like in Bible times. I felt Jesus speaking to me through Barbara. He spoke to me firmly and directly, as if I was a child, telling me that he loved me, and that I must let him look after my family and my friends. I wish I could remember all the words but it was all about love and trust. My eyes filled with tears. I felt very privileged.

16th August ~ I drove all the way back from London feeling completely normal, looked after both babies today and Alastair who came for supper. No pain, no sore throat. Great, should be able to go back to work soon.

Rose rang from Quilton to ask if I could pray for Matthew. He hasn't been had up for accosting parishioners yet but is being checked out by two heavies: men in leather jackets with hard expressions on their faces. The father of one of the girls in his Youth Group is a big time crook and it seems he wants to make sure Matthew is OK. The minders follow him everywhere.

Alastair arrived saying he can't believe Matthew is being employed as 'a vicar', especially in such a rough area, but he seems to have got to know most of the people on the council estate already and they think he's great; he gives them lifts in the soft-top Mercedes. Alastair went to sleep in Mary-Dieu's old room so he could drive back in his own open car in the morning. It's rather an ancient and unreliable one.

17th August ~ Feel grim, really ill, as bad as ever. Oh dear, am I not healed after all or is this just going to take time? I wonder if Diana would think all this barmy? Barbara assured me that our prayers for healing are answered, it's just that sometimes the packages travel rather slowly as if posted from Australia by surface mail. Why? It could be lack of faith but not always. Is it because our character and our closeness to God, which are more important than our physical state, still need to grow? '...For when your faith is tested, your endurance has a chance to grow. So let it grow, for when your endurance is fully developed, you will be strong in character and ready for anything.'[xii] God wants us healthy *and* complete. I probably need the inner healing before I can receive the outward, physical body back in working order.

Mikie has had many prayers for healing and yet he's still in a wheelchair. Why? Is it because God can use him more effectively? Because the Lord loves him and knows that without rigorous constrictions Mikie would destroy himself? As things are he certainly makes an impact in the world of racing. A visual impact apart from anything else. Diana doesn't think he's barmy. I think she admires him for his determination and optimism.

18th August ~ Here we are, I'm reading a book called *Beyond Healing* by Jennifer Rees-Larcomb who was very ill for a long time with acute encephalitis. She's obviously full of faith and was prayed for by a series of experienced ministers, all reliable instruments of God, but she didn't receive healing for ages. In the end, having been wheelchair-bound for years she was completely healed when a very shy seventeen-year old girl asked if she could pray for her after a service. She said that she really didn't think this prayer was going to have any effect, yet it did. She literally stood up, walked off and started bossing her family around. What is evident from her books is that Jennifer learnt a great deal during the time when she was ill. While the illness took her away from physically looking after her six children, it gave her time to write and time to pray. She hung on to the belief that, 'God knows exactly what He's going to do and how He's going to do it. You have committed all your worries to Him; now, by an act of the will you must leave Him to take care of them. These days we often demand instant healing from God, like instant coffee or mashed potato, but God's timing is perfect and He sees us from the other side of eternity where only the soul endures.'

I don't believe it. Rose was nearly squashed flat by a tree in the supermarket car park. She'd finished shopping and was sitting in her parked car, reading the newspaper before meeting a friend for lunch. 'I can't think why,' she said, 'but I decided to get something out of the boot. As I opened it I heard a loud crack above me. I just left the car and ran.'

A massive branch fell off the tree. Rose was caught by the twigs and leaves but escaped being hurt by the heavier branches. Some old ladies rushed up to see if she was all right and one of them scurried off to get the manager. When he saw the fallen tree he said, 'Wow, it's a good thing no one had parked underneath it.'

'Oh, but they did, dear,' said the old lady taking twigs out of Rose's hair. When he peered through the leaves he saw, to his horror, Rose's soft-top Mercedes. Had she been sitting inside, the branch that had gone straight through the roof would have hit her on the head.

'And, Sophie, if Augustus had been there, strapped in his car seat, I would never have run away from the car.'

19th August ~ Robin said he once found his Morris Traveller bashed in a supermarket car park. He went to ask if the video cameras had recorded who had done it. The manager said they were rather more worried about a man who had just reversed his car and squashed his wife against the wall. She was quite dead.

Things aren't as they seem in Quilton-on-Trim. The master criminal wasn't worried about Matthew, he wanted to know what 'the Vicar' thought of his daughter's boyfriend but couldn't find the right chance to ask. Matthew was chuffed that he'd gained his respect but the ensuing parochial visit entailed walking between two chained up bull-mastiffs, which leapt up at him, barking maniacally, as he made his way to the front door. The boyfriend had advised him that if you kept your wits about you and walked up the path in a very straight line, they couldn't reach you. The chains just weren't long enough. Matthew said it was all rather unnerving but he did receive great sympathy for the Merc (which is only a bit squashed). He's certainly earned street-cred in Quilton, where all the locals noticed the henchmen following him into the pub.

Matthew reckons this criminal, the girl's father, was involved in a seriously big armed robbery. They couldn't pin him down in court. He employed a top barrister who got him off, but now he's into a scam involving timeshare investment. His company's been getting names and addresses from what they claim to be the respectable electoral register, but isn't. They persuade people to come to presentations by telling them they've won cruises in the Caribbean. The embarrassing thing is that I might just have gone along if I hadn't been so ill.

20th August ~ My General Practitioner doesn't know what to do with me. She suggested anti-depressants again because the chemical effect does help, but I said, 'No, thanks.' I don't want to find that I have problems coming off them. I'm not in danger of committing suicide. We agreed that without stretching myself too far I must set goals and keep them to avoid accepting illness as the norm. She wrote me off work until the end of September. When I've been ill for six months I will, apparently, be labelled 'chronic'. This qualifies me for an appointment with a Dr. Prior, the National Health Specialist for M.E. I wish he'd been able to see me a little bit earlier.

'Am I really impatient, Lord, or is it that I loathe wasting time?' I hate to see wasted lives, or rather talented, able people doing the wrong thing with their lives. So many of my friends have become sucked into the British financial system that they're enslaved by their own jobs. They've been lured into such a materialistic orientation with high mortgages, company cars, insurance policies and private health schemes that there's no escape. It seems fine when their work is fulfilling, but what will happen if the once-invigorating challenges consume them? What happens if they lose their health? What happens if they reach the age of sixty-five and think, 'If only... I wish I'd done that'? I passionately want people to realise their full potential, but hate it when this is achieved at a sacrifice to their family life or even to their way of living.

'Sophie, you are a crack-pot, they do it for their kids, to give them a decent education and a bit of stability,' Diana said when I put this to her.

Umm. But not everyone has children. There were a number of very capable women working for the *BBC* in London who never married and devoted their whole lives to their job before dying at the age of fifty or so from a condition I now dare to attribute to overwork. The cause of death might have been cancer, but what caused that? Mind you they worked devastatingly long hours, not simply because they needed to or wanted the overtime payments, but because their social life dwindled until they had little else to live for. I could so easily have followed them.

21st August ~ The fatigue is back. Badly. 'Why am I not being healed?' I ask again. The question is, can God's power be blocked? Well, yes. Our sin blocks it of course; pride and idolatry, unforgiveness – behaving like the man in the open-necked shirt on Windermere; he must be blocking God from his life. Getting all legalistic and religious can also block it. Fear and doubt, getting involved with anything that isn't of Christ, can deny him and can block prayer.[xiii] Simple really. The answer is to repent and forge ahead, not be wimpy.

And I must look at the facts. What do my doctors say? What is my goal? I must get away again, as soon as I can. I definitely feel better elsewhere; whether it's the environment or the stimulation I don't know, perhaps both.

Mum's been irate about her J.P. work and it makes me feel I can't cope. No wonder she's tired. She sat in court all morning, then drove thirty miles to Gloucester to see Mary-Dieu and Daisy to collect all their washing. Piles and piles of it. At least five washing machine loads. Then she comes home, climbs into her swimsuit, eats lunch, puts the washing on and cleans the entire house. Then she has complete heebi-geebies because the parrot escapes. She's still running around in her bathing costume although she hasn't yet been swimming. I wish she'd resign from being a J.P. and that Mary-Dieu would do her own washing.

Must focus on my own goal of escape.

Dad returned from the vegetable garden. I'd wondered where he was. He probably went down there to escape Mum's physical expression of emotional turmoil. Sometimes there's nothing one can do or say. Dad also likes to be fairly self-sufficient. He has a water turbine generating power from the river to heat our hot water. We had a goat once so that we would have our own milk. She was called Snowy and had enormously long horns. Slight problem; Mum let her escape. Tamzin and I trudged over the hills for miles but couldn't find her so Mum alerted the local newspaper and asked if they could help. They ran a front cover story: 'Snowy is Adrift...'

Snowy was found, early one Sunday morning, in a graveyard. We went over to find the goat surrounded by very excited children. She wasn't dead. Oh no. She looked up, saw us and charged straight at Dad. He hadn't put his contact lenses in and couldn't see to catch her. She ran right between his legs and was never seen again.

22nd August ~ My parents have had an aviary built ~ a massive green birdcage cemented into the terrace outside the kitchen. After years and years the birds are out of the house. We were almost driven to distraction by their screechings, which have stopped since they've been permanently moved outside. I hope it is permanent. Having commissioned the thing (which was made especially for us by two art students sweating away with a welding torch for days), Mum has now decided the birds will get wet. I think they like the rain. They have barrels where they can retreat to when it gets cold but they won't use them. Instead of waiting until they do, my father has been made to buy a green plastic tarpaulin, which now hangs off the top and encases the whole structure. I found the arguments over getting this green thing up the most tiring episode of my life.

Today we let Henry out and put him in the cherry tree next to the cage. It poured with rain. He refused to come down, despite Mum calling endlessly from beneath. I looked out of my bedroom window later and saw him just below me, drenched but looking very cheerful. 'Hello Henry,' he said to me.

'Hello Henry.' I don't think he minds being wet at all.

Josey, Ovril + Henry in their new environment.

A postcard arrived from Alastair thanking us for supper eight weeks ago. He must have sent it from the southern seas. It was of brown boobeys. They're birds. Seabirds. There are also blue-footed boobeys, but Al says that all the girls he knows want brown boobeys. What are we girls going to do with him? At least Diana will enjoy the joke. She's always comparing browns with her sister. I mean comparing suntans. I don't. Tan.

23rd August ~ Mum and Dad in Wales with otters. I have to stay here to feed the parrots. Goal withdrawn.

I've been tossing and turning an idea about. My thought is that expectation is more central to healing than faith. I don't think all those hordes in Galilee had a mature faith in Jesus, because they really didn't know him.[xiv] But they were expectant and confident he would heal them. Expectation is hope. I've never considered hope as being very powerful but I suppose it is. Empires are built on hope. Great parrot cages are, and that's for sure.

24th August ~ It came yesterday and nothing, by means of logic or reason, could do away with my gloom. I felt so physically weak that I couldn't work
   or walk it off,
   and being with people didn't help much either.
   I tried reading,
   eating,
   drinking pints of water.

By nighttime I felt as if I was sitting in a dark cold forest surrounded by demons. And they're all my own worries and fears. One is the fear of never ever getting better. I couldn't help listening. They whispered all the time, mocking me until I was quite wound up. The ideas they planted became so real and threatening I started to cry. I began to feel out of control but

I've been taught what to do and I did it. Like hurling a burning stick at the wolves I named each fear, and told it to go in the name of Jesus. It was surprisingly difficult to get the words out. The worst fear hiding in the shadows behind me, pretending to be little and nameless and insignificant was the leader of the whole gang, Self-pity. As soon as I'd got rid of him, I felt totally peaceful and calm. The lies had been evicted. I fell asleep feeling I'd won a battle.

25th August ~ The USSR's communist party has ceased to exist and I've won a prize. Two Jilly Cooper novels published about ten years ago. I've already read them.

Nicola and Doug came to lunch. We ate outside in the sunshine with the dogs milling about. I made some salads out of all the lovely things Dad has been growing: tomatoes with basil from the greenhouse and lettuce with courgettes, beans, and cucumber from the vegetable garden with a herb and mustard-seed dressing. Perry would have been very proud of me.

We made Doug (Nicola spells his name Dug) swim in the lake before allowing him inside to watch the athletics. He didn't get the joke about brown boobies at all. Nicola is beginning to look pretty fat, but she would do, her baby arrives in a few weeks time. I must make her a mobile. I asked her if she would like the novels I'd won to take into hospital but she has read them too. She was trying very hard not to talk about nappies.

Doug makes walking sticks. Thousands of them. He bought the factory from Dad. They supply the National Health Service, who give them away to people who do stupid things like break their bones slipping on the ice. It's true. The sales always go up in January. Dad used to hope for a hard winter.

A letter arrived from the Healing Mission saying that they're still praying for me. Good, I'm feeling sad. I think he meant it as a joke, but Doug has upset me. He called M.E. 'The Scrounger's Disease'.

26th August ~ The demise of Communism in the Soviet Union ~ the great coup and excitements in Moscow have passed me by. I'm too weak to even read about it. I feel depressed beyond all measure.

Rebecca rang to say that, despite knowing of my misgivings, she has been going for acupuncture in an attempt to regain her sense of smell, and that something quite interesting happened today. She said the lady practitioner asked her to take off all her clothes and stood looking at her from behind. 'Hang on, I'm just going to get my husband,' she said. Rebecca said she felt rather unnerved at first, as they stood gazing at her naked form. It transpired that the acupuncturist's husband was an osteopath. He could see that her head was totally out of alignment, in relation to her spine.

'Oh, yes,' Rebecca told them. 'Every specialist, at the various hospitals I've been to since the accident has said that this is a permanent result of my injuries and that absolutely nothing can be done about it.' The osteopath put her right there and then. Click, click, crunch. She's thrilled, and rather indignant that she'd been written off as incurably damaged by the experts of conventional medicine.

27th August ~

Calvin Coolidge, once President of America, wrote: 'Nothing in the world can take the place of persistence. Talent will not: nothing is more common than unsuccessful men with talent. Genius will not: unrewarded genius is almost a proverb. Education will not: the world is full of educated derelicts. Persistence and determination alone are omnipotent. The watchword 'press on' has solved and always will solve the problems of the human race.'

I would add, Mr. Coolidge, sir, that if we find ourselves getting nowhere, no matter how hard we persist, we need to try out different strategies. I have a very persistent wasp trying to get through my bedroom windowpane, but unless it tries another window it will never get out. In fact it's annoying me so much I might first squash it flat.

How am I going to get out? What windows are open in my life? At least there's no one here who has to put up with my grumbles. This illness isn't logical. I'm not putting on weight. Where does the energy derived from my food go? It's as if I'm leaking. I feel as if I'm literally about to disappear down the plughole.

28th August ~ Mum and Dad still in Wales. Goal: eat lunch. Depression with a suitcase keeps coming and threatening to stay. 'Go away, you're not welcome here.' I've never felt like this before, not for so long anyway. I refuse to feed the gloominess by thinking about it. Being ill is so B O R I N G.

29th August ~ Viral infection/influenza. Bad night, bad day.

30th August ~ Very unwell. Fighting hopelessness.

31st August ~ Sick. Mustn't focus on self. Must look up.
Goal: stay alive. Someone once asked me: 'If you died, and found yourself standing at the pearly gates with St. Peter holding a clipboard and asking how you qualified for entrance into heaven, what would you say?'

'I don't know.' How could I possibly justify myself? Nothing that I've done has been vaguely good enough to warrant entrance to heaven, into the brilliance of God's presence. Even if spent my life saving starving babies I'd fall short of the mark. But... 'Jesus took responsibility for all my sin when he died on the cross.' If I can hold on to that and walk away from selfishness and filth, I'll able to pass through the gates. Even though I don't deserve to.

SEPTEMBER ~ He will direct your paths

1st September ~
Bad. How does one fight insomnia? My eyes are all bulgy; I must be getting myxomatosis. They say, 'Don't face depression in isolation,' but there's no one else here. 'Oh God, do you want me to be ill? Why do you want me to be ill?'

2nd September ~ Goal: not die. Must pull myself together. I'm not going to die. Others have faced far worse than this and have made it through. Simply feeling good isn't a number one priority in my life anyway.

'Life will only work out one way to our complete satisfaction and that is by following the pathway of God's will. It's no use putting an apple pie in the washing machine or the washing in the oven. God has made us for himself and our hearts are restless until they find their rest in Him.' *Dr. Leslie D. Weatherhead*

Umm, I know, I tried to put a packet of bacon in the dishwasher this morning. I think it's called cognitive dysfunction though, loss of intellectual ability. I cannot retain new information.

I feel I ought to find out more about M.E. but it's very difficult trying to research an un-researched condition when you're ill.

3rd September ~ Feeling bleak but my determined stand against depression continues.

Whilst I accept that we have to endure the blows of the sculptor's hammer, I reckon it'll do us good to fight persecution and suffering if we can.

I was bullied at school when I was ten. I hated it, but fought relentlessly. Tooth and nail.

The boy who bullied me used to hide up trees and jump on top of me as I walked past. Once after school, while we were waiting to be collected, he took a bicycle chain and came towards me swinging it around my head. I had to catch the chain before it sliced across my face.

I should have told my parents of course and let them deal with the wretch, but I didn't. I knew that standing up to him was the making of me as a person. In doing so I lost a great deal of shyness and gained a resolve and strength of character that's stood me in good stead.

I've got to get tougher right now, get a grip on this illusive mood and refuse to entertain it.

These last few days I've just been clenching my teeth and saying, 'I'm not going down that road.'

Campaign to beat Syndrome cont...
- Reduce all stress, relaxing physically and intellectually.
- Pace myself carefully, resting after every activity.
- No stimulants: alcohol, tea, coffee, fizzy drinks.
- Fill myself with immune system boosters: Efamol, zinc, garlic, ginseng.
- Keep swigging vitamin B complex. Vitamin B12, I'm informed, enables you to think more clearly by increasing the oxygen-carrying capacity of blood and helps to detoxify the liver.
- Continue with magnesium and other supplements.

I read that these are technically referred to as 'coping strategies'.

Mum rang from Wales where she has been 'raising awareness', i.e. the otters have been delighting crowds at the Welsh Show. Sixty thousand people came to see them. It seems an awful lot. 'Jims is so sweet. If he gets a bit shy he just disappears down the front of my T-shirt and wriggles around.'

Dad came on the line and said that a small child saw this and said, 'Look Mam, a woman with moving insides.'

4th September ~ Feeling better. The 'flu has lifted.

Looked after Perry's dog, Tadpole, and Atalanta so she could go filming in Bristol where her episode of *Casualty* is being recorded. Dog proved far more of a handful than child. Had no energy so solved problem of canine hyperactivity by tying lead of dog to pushchair and we all, effectively, got towed down the lane. It was very nearly disastrous.

I found Perry had forgotten to pack any spare baby-grows. And I thought her efficiency knew no bounds. I had fun dressing Atalanta up in some old clothes of ours that Granny had once made. She loved trying them all on; we had a great laugh. Mum used to dress all of us alike; three little blonde girls in rosebud dresses. When Mary-Dieu came along she ended up inheriting a lot of bridesmaid dresses and three of everything else in different sizes. Poor child. At least she was spared the embarrassment I suffered of being dressed in exactly the same way as my little sisters until I was *fifteen*. Mum used to make us go to church in matching grey tweed coats and red bunny fur hats that did up under the chin.

Perry arrived back intrigued to find us still busy dressing up and thrilled to find a stock of clothes to keep Atalanta clad for the next ten years. She said she'd spent the day wearing a peculiar thing to make her look pregnant. 'It amounted to being an extremely effective device for contraception,' she said. 'Most off-putting. I told the Costume Designer, who spent the rest of the afternoon giggling.' He remembered Perry from when she was in the *Onedin Line*. We'd all been extras in it when we were children. Mary-Dieu asked the Costume Designer, "Are you Head Thing of the dressing-up things?"

Mum was mortified, but he'd thought it so amusing he had the statement printed on a T-shirt that afternoon.

5th September ~ Perry's dog was far more difficult than ten children today. Infuriating. It was Mum who offered to do the babysitting and yet I get lumbered with it. I was thinking, 'I'm either about to turn into a dog lead or a doormat,' when a girl I hardly know sent me a packet of crayons and this:

It's between you and God ~ by Mother Teresa
People are often unreasonable, illogical and self-centred; forgive them anyway.

If you are kind, people may accuse you of selfish, ulterior motives; be kind anyway.

If you are successful, you will win some false friends and some true enemies; succeed anyway.

If you are honest and frank, people may cheat you; be honest and frank anyway.

What you spend years building, someone could destroy overnight; build anyway.

If you find serenity and happiness they may be jealous; be happy anyway.

The good you do today, people will often forget tomorrow; do good anyway.

Give the world the best you have, it may never be enough; give the world the best you've got anyway.

You see in the final analysis, it's between you and God;
It never was between you and them anyway.

It's Rebecca's birthday soon and she has invited me over. I feel as if I should be able to make it and I might be of some help. It would be a goal, an event to aim for. And she's insistent that I come.

6th September ~ Determined to start winning real goals. I'm off on tour again, aiming to rock myself out of this condition. Stayed with Perry. She's the most amazing wife on earth. I am in awe and wonder. 'What's your secret?'

'Afternoon rests.'

7th September ~ Robert is the most amazing husband on earth. He certainly extends grace to his peculiar female relations. Me. My health must completely mystify him. He has never, ever, ever been sick. 'What's your secret?'

'Playing rugger.'

I got into awful trouble with Robert this morning. He came downstairs looking very frightening. Atalanta and Perry looked up at him and then followed his gaze. 'Sophie,' Perry said, breaking the terrible silence. 'What have you done?'

I couldn't think. Robert didn't say anything at all. Then it came back to me: I'd used his razor to shave my legs.

8th September ~ The weather was glorious for Rebecca's party. I wasn't feeling quite as brilliant, but thought, 'I must achieve this goal, then I'll rest.' I left Perry and Robert's house wondering if I'd ever make it, but drove along slowly and carefully, getting to West Sussex in time for lunch. And it was a lovely, lovely lunch party by the swimming pool ~ very relaxed with lots of old friends and *no* babies. I felt replenished.

In the late afternoon everyone went climbing on huge round straw bales and pulled me up on top. You'd think you could make them roll by walking round on top; don't try.

9th September ~ Rebecca has two aunts. One is called Blottie; the other is called Rotter. They call her mother Doppy. I call her Mrs. Hunter. She's currently looking for her trowel.

10th September ~ Rebecca's actual, real birthday. She went off to spend the money she'd been given on books and had the last in her course of acupuncture. It hasn't been able to bring back her sense of smell but she's pleased she met the osteopath, as being out of alignment would have caused huge problems for the rest of her life.

The family is celebrating all over again. We had delicious prawns cooked in garlic butter with crusty bread for lunch and there was champagne, only Rebecca wasn't allowed any because she's still on drugs. She said she felt a bit like Granny must have done at her own wedding. I tried to help but Mrs.

Hunter insisted that I shouldn't take on any demands at all. They're being very good to me.

'What I give out in teacups comes back in buckets,' as they say in the north of England. I came to help and I've ended up receiving more than I could imagine; staying here is like receiving a gift. The house is called Heath Farm but Rebecca's friends call it The Health Farm and indeed I feel as if I'm on holiday.

Perhaps it's time to have a holiday from being ill. I'm still owed two weeks' paid leave from last year anyway.

11th September ~ Rebecca is very keen on becoming a hot-air balloon pilot and has great plans to set up balloon safaris in Africa some time. She certainly has a big dream.

It's all James' fault. He's been flying hot-air balloons for years and I know exactly what his motive was. He wanted to attract pretty girls, because all young ladies are keen to go ballooning. Once. He used to dress up as Phileas Fogg and was hoping for American heiresses as crew but ended up with me.

I fell for the ploy but I didn't fall for James. Instead I fell on top of him when we crashed into the Marlborough Downs. It was quite jarring, but at least I was on top and he's soft. I ended up having to walk miles and miles across the endless chalk country, desperately looking for his father in the 'support car'. It got darker and darker until in the end I was walking by starlight. James' father was on a bumpy track, about to give up, when he saw two hands and a pair of skinny white legs walking towards him. Since I was wearing a navy blue shirt and shorts, my arms and legs were all he could see of me. He said the image has been indelibly etched onto his memory.

*Rebecca's birthday
Balloon jumper!*

12th September ~ Rebecca, James and I once went on a ballooning trip to Ireland. We had no support vehicle at all which was crazy as there were huge expanses of water and we could, conceivably, have come down in a lough or been blown out to sea. Instead I remember James landed in a very small field bordered by not only dry stone walls and telegraph lines but overhead power cables. He yelled a lot coming down. A dear little old Irish dairy farmer ran up to us smiling and waving his stick. 'Did you have an experience?' he asked.

Later in the holiday, when I'd left them to go and see Perry, Rebecca said they took about an hour to cross over one lake as the wind dropped half way, which must have been scary. When they eventually came down on dry land and were busy deflating the balloon, another little old farmer came along. He asked if they were going to fly back.

13th September ~ Various people arrived with their newborn babies for us to worship. It's compulsory. At least I'm gaining parenting experience. In fact there's no escape. Rebecca says that she would like six children: three sets of twins. She makes it sound like having a litter. I'm rather alarmed at the thought of this, but am quite likely to produce twins as my grandfather was one. Dad's father. He was an artist. His twin died young from tuberculosis; I have his *Daylight* book.

14th September ~ Walked through Petworth. Very nice. Followed by a trip to Billingshurst; we totter off like pensioners on an outing. But I'm having such a good time I feel guilty about not working. 'Sophie, don't. Relax. When are you going to see the specialist?'

'Day after tomorrow.'

'Well shut up.'

Rebecca wrote to Sarah-Jane saying she was nearly ready to return to work at the horse safari camp in South Africa. Wish I could go too. Rebecca says she thinks that I shouldn't actually be driving yet.

15th September ~ Drove to Tamzin's cottage on my way home for an appointment with the specialist. She has found a meteorite in her field. Not the specialist ~ Tamzin. It isn't a big one but is incredibly heavy for its size. All her friends came over to look. We stood around not knowing what to do with it. 'If you ask me,' Raddy said, 'It looks exactly like a man's thingy and should be put away.'

16th September ~ I feel quite frightened now. I'm sure it's silly but I think I have cancer. I went along for my appointment at the hospital to see Dr. Prior, the National Health Specialist for M.E. While examining my tummy he suddenly looked up and said, 'Your liver is very soft. Sophie, I'd like you to come into hospital for tests as soon as possible.' He looked grim. 'You'll need to be in for four or five days, staying overnight.' Why on earth do I have to be there so long? He explained that they need to take scans of my innards.

I lay in bed later feeling like a meteorite falling through space, thinking, 'I'm thirty. It's awfully young to die,' and got in such a state imagining that I had an incurable liver cancer that I ended up *having* to pray. I desperately wanted God to speak to me. He did. An instruction to 'Read *Proverbs* ~ chapter four' entered my fuddled mind. It's quite strict, *Proverbs 4*, just what I needed and talks about long life and radiant health, so I must not worry.

17th September ~ I gather I'm not prone to having twins; Tamzin says traits like that go down the female line, but I'm going to have to wait two or three weeks before I can go into hospital. I've decided to continue following Dr. Loveday's advice and move away from home. Grizelda has kindly asked me to stay in their big farmhouse. She said she would like the company while her husband is abroad as she gets frightened staying there by herself with the little children. It seems we all have to cope with some sort of fear. I'm determined to ignore this fear of cancer. It is, as yet, ungrounded.

I assured Griz that I would not be much good as a security guard but she was insistent. I think that while she probably would appreciate the companionship, she's being very kind in making it easier for me to accept the invitation. I found a bedroom had been re-decorated especially for me.

18th September ~ It's much harder to get gloomy here. Griz keeps coming up with the most extraordinary stories. She's insisting that I drink sheep's milk. She claims that, originally, everyone in England drank it and cows were never milked at all. Then the Black Death came along. It killed sixty million people. Although rats spread plague, the blame was put on sheep and they started milking cows instead. At least I don't have the Black Death.

I want to tell Griz that I'm worried about cancer but I can't. I don't know why. Instead I've made a decision not to fret until I have the facts before me and have been reading all her *Anne of Green Gables* books to keep my mind off the subject.

Well, Anne of Green Gables' acquaintances seem to die of pneumonia the whole time. It was quite a respectable way to go. Pneumonia and typhoid. I suppose it was the downside to living on Prince Edward Island at the turn of the century. Perhaps cancer is the trade-off, as the Americans say, for living in our day and age. But Anne says: '…don't let's ever be afraid of things. It's such dreadful slavery. Let's be daring and adventurous and expectant. Let's dance to meet life and all it can bring us, even if it brings scats of trouble and typhoid and twins!'[10]

19th September ~ On with Grizelda's health regime. An *avocateur* of good food and exercise, she's putting me on a diet of solely organic food. No chemical will be allowed entry to my body. She says I need lots of enzymes and nutrients to oxygenate my brain and get my little neurotransmitters functioning effectively. Some herb called gingko biloba is meant to increase blood flow to the brain and thereby improve your memory, but she didn't have any on her. I took some ginseng[11] instead with my ginger tea. I think it does more or less the same thing. I would rather take it than antidepressants, which might cause my blood pressure to drop still lower.

We juiced apples, picked hazelnuts and walked around a ploughed field. 'Perhaps we ought to go fishing and eat raw trout like Jeeves in P.G. Woodhouse.'

'Why?'

'He claimed fish was brain food.'

'I don't think he ate them raw.'

'No, but I like raw fish. We could get a lemon and make our own sushi.'

'Well, I worry about the presence of flukes,' Griz said. 'Parasites can wreak havoc in your system and give you terrible sleepless nights, not to mention fatigue. Make sure you've been wormed and didn't catch bilhartzia in Africa. The reason why most babies can't sleep at night is because they catch worms off domestic pets.'

Griz also says that one should not underestimate the strength of a virus. She thinks that she caught the same bug as I had in January and then again at Easter. 'If it was just influenza it was a particularly vicious variety. It laid us all flat for two whole weeks and I could do nothing for ages afterwards. Mind you, we were all so rundown and knackered we fell like ninepins. We'd have gone down with anything; parents of small children are often ill.'

Dad once told me that when he was young and tuberculosis was still a risk, any bug was taken very seriously. You were kept away from school if you had a cold and not sent back until you had been completely better for days. Perhaps we just don't take convalescence seriously enough anymore. Before the war, people thought home nursing important and were very good at it. The big houses would even have a special sick room where blinds were kept drawn. Griz pointed out that this was because there were no antibiotics around then. She believes that these are now prescribed too easily and that this could let human beings down in the long run.

What concerns and fascinates Grizelda is how nutrition can affect children's behaviour. She says small boys with blonde hair and blue eyes are particularly susceptible to becoming hyperactive if they eat preservatives, colourants, artificial sweeteners or certain foods. The natural silicates in tomatoes and citrus fruit can drive them up the curtains. Mikie says his racehorses are incredibly responsive to what they're fed. Different grains have a pronounced influence on temperament as well as their weight gain.

Paddy, Griz's little boy, is rather more keen on cars. He can identify any model on the road and he's only three-and-a-half. 'Vauxhall Cavalier,' he said as one whizzed past. I was looking at the person inside. It was Mrs. Shalgoski, my old art teacher from school. She happens to live in their village.

20th September ~

'We're trying to persuade Sophie to start painting seriously,' Griz told her at the kitchen table.

'You always had the technical ability,' Mrs. Shalgoski said taking a swig of coffee.

'Did I?'

'Well if I can remember your work from what, fifteen years back, then I'm quite sure. Yes.' Goodness. Perhaps I ought to keep sketching after all. Then Mrs. Shalgosky told us that the Romans drank cows' milk.

We took Mrs Shalgoski (I can't adapt to calling her Sheila) to see the hats. Griz makes hats. She's a hatter, a milliner. She has a room full of silks and feathers and heads, wooden ones that expand to size. Bizarre. I used a little piece of her red velvet and some gold braid to make Tamzin a meteorite holder for her birthday; a cushion for it to sit upon.

21st September ~ Truly organic food can take a long time to prepare. We went blackberry picking, cooked and sieved them, mushing away, getting everything covered in purple and all to make one tiny little jelly eaten in a trice. It was delicious but I had to have a lie-down afterwards. I gazed at the ceiling thinking that although one can get addicted to ultimately poisonous substances, on the whole our bodies do tell us what they need. I need Marmite and radishes, bananas and fillet steak. I do not need cheese but can't stop eating it once I start.

I know one thing: I really hate traffic. I can't stand being in the fumes. Pollutants and the smell of chemical substances repel my whole being. I feel I have to live out in the country. Mind you, outside the door of this farmhouse the barns are stacked with huge containers of fertiliser and chemical sprays and I know there is a 'fridge full of vaccines and antibiotics for the cattle.

Griz's husband, Dane, returned from Washington. We talked about National Insurance payments and private pensions. The 1988 Social Security Statistics state, 'There's a one in six risk that you will be incapacitated for longer than six months at some time in your life.' They must be including people over the age of eighty. Or are they? No, I think they mean during your working life. A bit nerve racking if you're a daddy. Dane says you can insure your salary, but he hasn't.

22nd September ~ We went up onto the Berkshire downs and I shot a video of the children. Some people trotted by on horses. 'It doesn't look as if there's much to it,' Dane declared. No. I wish I could ride to the ends of the earth right now.

23rd September ~ Instead I flew to Glasgow, clutching a packet of organic bananas and accompanied by Rebecca, off to stay with my Aunt Hermione. Granny, who is back in Bedford, was very concerned about how we were going to get the twenty miles from the airport to the house. 'There are a lot of roundabouts and it's very confusing.' It wasn't in reality; my uncle Shuggie came to collect us in his Honda. My married-to-my-aunt-uncle. There isn't a term for him in English is there? Aunt's husband. Anyway, I caught Rebecca telling him not to let me drive. Humm.

Rebecca was dying to see the python in the hall. Hermione assured us that Great-granny had stuffed it herself. She had to skin it while the muscle was still moving, before rigor mortis set in. Apparently she was very skilled at this task and was the only person Great-grandfather would allow to do the job. The python is nearly twenty foot long. It must have taken ages and smelled revolting. 'Oh, skinning crocodiles was much worse,' Hermione said cheerfully. 'They smell to merry heaven but the skins were terribly valuable when I was little and we used to eat the tail meat. It tastes a bit like lobster.'

It transpired that Rebecca had skinned a Mozambique spitting cobra in South Africa (after someone else had killed it with a panga). 'I wanted to chop the snake up and feed it to the baby herons as I reckoned they needed some real meat,' she explained. 'We turned the skin inside-out and rubbed it with salt and sand,' she went on. 'I thought that if I left it in the sun I could cure it but it got too dry and broke up.' I'm horrified.

Shuggie was thrilled that she was so interested and enthusiastically took us on a tour of all the other odd things made out of game trophies that they salvaged from Great-granny's bungalow in Ayrshire. As well as being the British Representative in Tanzania and a coffee farmer my great-grandfather had been a big game hunter. The snake and crocodiles, shot for being dangerous pests, were only part of the scene. When he wasn't burying bottles of champagne he must have shot everything in sight. He had specimens of every different species stuffed and mounted, and exported back to Scotland, even a giant rat.

'My most embarrassing moment,' Granny once said, 'was driving through London in a taxi with the head of a stuffed giraffe sticking out of the window.'

'What was the house in Ayr like?' I asked.

'The bungalow? Colonial to the letter. Every single thing in it was made from African animals. Even table lights were made out of stuffed egrets. The bird would be holding a cord with a light hanging down from its bill.'

'Where did he hang the giant rat?'

'Oh, he got fed up about that. It shrank.'

There are two feet that once belonged to a black rhino, which are now wastepaper baskets. It's gross. 'Well,' Granny said, 'a wastepaper basket is the most important piece of furniture in a room.'

The bizarre artefacts go on and on. One was supposed to use the pad of an elephant's foot as a salver for letters. There are leopard skins, wildebeest-tail fly-whisks, a washbag made from a buffalo's scrotum, and one rather bald warthog's tail, mounted on a plinth and just sticking up. For no apparent reason at all. The rest of the stuff was so moth-eaten and disintegrated it had to be burnt; but Tamzin has a photograph frame made from the forelegs of an antelope. A picture of Granny as a girl is suspended between them. She was a great beauty and the hooves are polished.

24th September ~ My Aunt has bought a yacht. She has spent all her knitting money on an elegant dark blue Swedish vessel; thirty-two foot long and moored on the Clyde. It's about seventeen years old and came at a good price because it's very spartan inside. It looks brand new and quite perfect to me. We drove down the glen to see it at the marina.

'I didn't mean to buy a boat at all,' Hermione said. 'I went to trade-in my car for a rather newer one. The salesman at the garage offered me such a low price for my two-year-old Ford Sierra that I was going to have to find another £8,000 just to buy a horrid demonstration model that smelt of orange drops. "I think you're giving me a rotten deal," I told him.

"Tell you what," he said. "You send round the boss and we'll see what we can do."

"I'm the boss of my company."

"Och no, I mean your husband."'

Hermione was furious. Livid. In such a rage she could hardly drive. She's no longer the meek little Army wife she once was, but fast becoming a tycoon and, as far as she's concerned, her company car has nothing to do with Shuggie. 'It's so irritating being talked down to. I had to stop the car and walk along the Clyde to calm down.' When someone sailed past she asked him where he was going. 'He called back, saying that he was off to Venezuela and wouldn't I like to come too? I said, "Yes, please," and nearly went off to get my passport. But of course I didn't. I walked on thinking, 'what's wrong with the Sierra anyway, it takes the hay and it takes the dogs. It takes the yarn, takes the jumpers.' Then I saw this boat for sale. They were asking the same price as I was going to have to pay for the 'demo model'. I thought, 'Fine, I'll keep my old car and buy this boat.'' And she did. My uncle is going to have to do it up of course.

25th September ~ Shuggie told me at breakfast that the chap who sold Hermione the boat was, in fact, a car dealer; a very clever one. When they tried it out he ignored my uncle, gave Hermione the helm and was totally dismissive about the galley. She was thrilled to buy the yacht and thrilled about keeping the car. 'I knew it was worth far more than the garage on the Clyde had been offering. Olivia wrote it off after sailing in Argyll two weeks later and even the insurance valuer gave me twice the price.'

We walked in the sunshine alongside Loch Lomond, stopping to gaze up at the mountains. It was a beautifully clear day with the leaves just beginning to change colour. I think Hermione is right to buy a boat. Granny is disgusted, thinking it a terrible waste of money, but I think we should invest in our dreams. She'll sail to Venezuela one day.

Jamie, my cousin and Olivia's brother, is in Madagascar right now, saving the rainforest and living in his dream. I would love to join him there one day.

'Don't go,' Granny said. 'Olivia went and had to eat a toad.' She didn't; she went to a French restaurant and had frogs' legs, but Jamie does live off dried fish, rice and malaria tablets so I don't think I'll go just yet. Rebecca says she's longing to and has started to make plans to fly on to Madagascar from Johannesburg some time.

26th September ~ Big excitement as Hermione's boat arrived on a low-loader. They only managed to squeeze it past the house because Shuggie took down the chimney-breast but he says he wants it outside the back door so that he can work away on it through the winter. He needs an electrical supply, water and everything. Rebecca, who is a great sailor, was most interested and is encouraging him to install a deep-freeze so they can sail to remote places. I'd better not tell Granny.

The epicentre of Hermione's knitting enterprise ~ her empire ~ is now situated in the old stables beyond the house. Hand-knitted garments arrive in the post from outworkers and balls of wool for the next mohair cardi are sent back with a cheque for the labour. Rebecca and I tried to help by weighing balls of wool and sewing in labels but just got in the way. (Got shouted at.)

I think most of the mohair garments are hideous but Hermione couldn't care less. There are piles of them in baby pink and powder blue. 'If they sell in Japan, it's just fine.' And sell they do. All over the world. Well, Tokyo ~ New York ~ Paris. I think it sounds really swish. Shuggie says it's sheer hard work.

'How did you manage to start exporting to America?' I asked.

'Oh, that "Gee lady, that's a hard way to make a dime" woman who couldn't get out of the jersey turned out to be the Separates Buyer for Bloomingdales.'

The cashmere jerseys are stunning. You just want to stroke them forever. I'm amazed; they get bundled up, shoved in the washing machine and hung up to dry on the pulley in the kitchen. Cashmere is tough stuff. Hermione designs lovely long jerseys knitted in cable stitch so they hang beautifully and look good while keeping you warm.

27th September ~ Rebecca's mother rang with the news that her cousin had given birth to a baby in her car on the pavement outside the hospital. I had a phone call too. My Departmental Manager rang from London. I got that awful sinking feeling. She asked me about my plans for the future. I explained that it was hard to make any because I was still waiting to go into hospital for tests. She then explained that, due to a Government directive, the *BBC* was radically cutting departmental budgets and that she was being obliged to reduce staff posts. The simplest way she could see of doing this was not to renew annual contracts once they expired, and as I was ill and not in the middle of a series I didn't currently play a vital role in the working of the Department or its output. Although I'd originally been a permanent *BBC* employee, I'd given up the security of my old post and moved onto contract so I could stay in her department two years ago.

28th September ~ I'm feeling a bit shattered. I'm beginning to digest the fact that I think I've lost my job. It's been more than a job; more than a career. It was my life. Only the *BBC*, it seems, can fire you without telling you that you're fired.

What about me? I've nothing else I can do. Except go on being ill, but what about when I recover, which I hope will be soon. Hermione said jokingly that I could buy her business and then she can sail off round the world with Shuggie, but I couldn't begin to sell mohair to the Japanese.

If I don't regain my full health, what work can I do? I couldn't possibly take on a business. But neither can I make films.

29th September ~ We flew back to Heathrow and took the Underground into London. There was a party of animated young German businessmen on board. None of them had been to England before and they started asking us what they could do. All they learnt was what not to do.

When we reached my station I was dithering with my suitcase for so long the automatic doors began to shut before I could get out of the train. One German kindly reached out to stop the doors closing but they did, trapping his hand, which was holding a didi-bag containing all his valuables. He stood there gasping with his hand stuck outside the train doors.

There was a ghastly moment of panic as the train moved off. It jerked forward, stopped, and we all held our breath. The doors sprung open, the hand came in and Rebecca and I fell out onto the platform with our bags, roaring with laughter and relief.

30th September ~ I felt so much better in Scotland and although I've taken things gently and in stages I completely dissolved when I reached home.

I have yet another throat infection. Now I'm all frustrated and churned up. I feel like tearing my hair out. I can't stand it, why can't I just recover like normal people do the whole time?

Rebecca is as fit as anything now. I know she still can't smell and hasn't started working but at least she could climb Ben Lomond if she wanted to. I'm looking at the possibility that I might well have cancer. It's so common. 'Oh Lord, no. I don't want to die yet.' I really don't want to die. I want to live. I want to ride across African plains and swim in turquoise seas. I want to get married and have children and live in the country and be normal. I want my life to make a difference.

I was doing well in my career and loved it. I was producing innovative stuff and could have made a difference there. I felt that making programmes was what I was made to do; that I was flying. But at what personal cost?

I worked above the post office in Shepherds Bush Green half my time, in particularly seedy, ill equipped offices. When I went off filming it was great, but I never saw my family and I hardly ever saw my friends. I only just made it to Tamzin's wedding and Augustus' christening. I was fully committed, almost married to the Corporation. Although I lived frugally, I never made enough money to go my own way.

But I did gain invaluable experience, a tremendously good training and had a great deal of fun. I feel I mustn't forget this or waste what I've learnt.

'Oh Lord, are you behind this door that is closing? Do you want me to go and do something else? Should I look at making myself a new life?'

Our lives are terribly long. Television isn't the be all and end all. There's time for all sorts of different careers and exciting things. I don't want to live in London slogging away forever. I want to travel. I would love to live in Africa. I always thought that if I were a man, I would be a game warden and combat rhino poaching.

Why on earth do I think, 'if I were a man'? If I had my *health* I could become a game ranger. Why not? It would be wonderful. I'd love to work outside all day long, to live in the wilderness observing wild animals and be able to do something for conservation. I've always wanted to work with horses in wide, open country.

And, I've always wanted to spend part of my life as an artist; a painter. I thought it would be impossible to make this financially viable in England, but perhaps I could find a way.

Me.

OCTOBER ~ More of your grace

1st October ~

Which way am I going to find a way?

My doctor told me today that I must stay off work for another two months. (Heck, I won't have any work to go to in another two months.) She said that even then, only a very gradual return would be recommended. Her compassion flowed into the room and made me feel like bursting into tears.

I must keep calm and hold fast even if things seem to keep sliding past. I'm sure I only got my last job because I prayed about it. I can remember standing in a loo at Elstree Studios before going into an interview for (the sergeant major's) post of a production manager and praying fervently because I didn't want promotion at all; I wanted to be a drama director. I failed the interview (which made me furious) and was sent off to *BBC Training* to assist on the Film Director's Course of all things. I was allowed to sit in on all the lectures. Within six months I found myself in *BBC Education* directing my own dramas, having a wonderful time saying, 'Action', 'Cut', and bossing the poor technicians about.

God opened the door. None of my contemporaries in the drama department started directing until they had done hard time on the studio floor. Yes, God certainly opened that door. He gave me my heart's desire. But was I busy fulfilling my own dream just for me? That is a futile and a fragile thing, easily lost.

2nd October ~ Standby to go to hospital.
Have heard from God: 'Prove by the way you live that you have really turned from your sins and turned to God.' It's from Matthew. Not Matthew, Rose's husband, the *Gospel of Matthew. Chapter three.* I'd decided it would be constructive to read through the New Testament and underline every sentence that is relevant to my situation right now. This one wasn't what I was expecting, or what I was longing to hear, but it's probably what I need.

We should of course concentrate on how we live day by day; it's the big challenge. I still have to work on my attitudes towards strangers. I'm still judgmental and critical. In fact I'm not a very good Christian at all. I need to learn the skill of being able to live well with others, especially my parents who I'm absolutely commanded to honour.

Dad arrived home looking very grey. He'd been asked to talk about otter conservation at an agricultural show. The organisers had gone to no end of trouble fencing a small lake so the otters would be happy, but although known as aquatic mammals, otters don't actually live in water. Well Californian sea otters might, but not ours; they're dead spoilt. After swimming around for a bit Jims decided it would be fun to climb out and escape into the big wide world beyond. Poor Dad, he ran for miles desperately trying to catch Jims as he scampered past all the trade stalls. Then he completely lost him. 'Oh, but I felt sick with worry.' You do; the final scene of *Ring of Bright Water* is on constant re-play in your mind when you lose an otter.

'What did you do?'

'Well, I kept asking people if they'd seen him but they just looked at me with complete incomprehension.' Eventually a great scream emanated from the Sheep Improvement Stand. Jims was there, rolling around delightedly on a big, fluffy, white sheepskin.

Rebecca rang and said she'll buy Jims his own sheepskin. She wanted to ask if I'd seen an unusual number of daddy longlegs. I don't think I've noticed more about than usual. 'The London Underground is infested with them. Didn't you notice?'

'All I noticed was an article in the paper about fare dodgers.'

'Perhaps there's a correlation; I'll write a letter to *The Times* about it,' she declared. 'I'm sure the daddy longlegs are not paying for their journeys.'

I'm beginning to think sick people with not enough to do can end up making a real nuisance of themselves.

3rd October ~ '...And he healed the people who had every kind of sickness and disease.' from *Matthew chapter 4 verse 23*. That's what I underlined today.

I feel elated but have no stamina. A letter has arrived from a 'fellow sufferer' asking my advice on acupuncture. She seemed to think that I'd gone to Shanghai for treatment. There must be confusion. And did I believe in homeopathy? She is taking tablets that are apparently very strong because they have incredibly small amounts of zinc and magnesium in them. Doesn't make any sense scientifically, if you ask me. 'It's good to be able to write to you,' she went on, 'because you're one of the few who know what it actually feels like. People sympathise but haven't a clue what you're going through, especially since I put on 'a face' to try to cover up my true feelings and to seem a bit more interesting.' She'd been an international swimmer.

I've been reading a book called *Miss Buncle Married*, written in the 1930s by D.L. Stevenson. The heroine has just gone off to visit a lady who has been ill for years, expecting to find 'a querulous invalid.' Not a bit:

'Mrs. Thane was a woman who had seen a great deal of trouble; she was disciplined to suffering; she was calm and patient; she bore her semi-invalid life and occasional pain with cheerfulness and fortitude. It was not the life she would have chosen (for she had an active mind and was intensely interested in People and Things), but she made the best of it and created a little world of her own. She could not go out into the world, but she created an atmosphere around her, and the world came to her.'

I thought this was a wonderful portrait, and decided to copy it out for the sweet girl who had written to me, because I think she's right to put on a big smile for visitors. I wanted desperately to encourage her, ended up writing reams and exhausted myself in the process.

I've been eating toast and marmalade in bed. The leaves on the cherry tree are golden now. They're being bullied by the winds. The crows seem as restless as ever, unnerving the doves. Henry yells at them.

4th October ~ Augustus' First Birthday. Felt hyper, my throat burning. 'God blesses those who realise their need for him...' *Matthew 5 v 3*

Alastair says that daddy longlegs have exceptionally venomous poison. Their bite is lethal, but only if you're another insect as the quantity is so minuscule. So much for homeopathy. Ahh, but what if 100,000 daddy longlegses ganged up and came at you at once? I keep thinking about the concept of being mobbed by a whole load on the tube although it's hardly likely. I don't use it. The London Underground System. OK, I did when we came back from Scotland, but Rebecca was with me and she would have fended them off.

Dr. Prior called me in. I was nervous but he just asked if I would be prepared to try a course of magnesium injections. This wasn't what I was expecting but it seems an answer to prayer. I've been reading in *The Lancet* that massive intramuscular doses of this mineral are, for some reason, having a beneficial effect on M.E. sufferers and was hoping it would be available. Dr. Prior said he'd no idea why this should be effective as it seems unlikely that having such high volume of a mineral rammed into your body could be beneficial but, if I was willing, we could give it a go. I'm going to be one of the first patients to receive this treatment. Wow. I made the brave decision and cheerfully agreed to a course of six injections.

Then I saw the size of the syringe. It looked like something you would only ever use on horses. An injection has never lasted so long. Homeopathy began to look like an attractive option. I couldn't sit down afterwards and had to drive home at an angle.

5th October ~ Tired, day in bed. Had to lie on stomach. 'Keep on asking, and you will be given what you ask for. Keep on looking, and you will find. Keep on knocking, and the door will be opened.' *Matthew 7 v 7*

I keep on asking for my health of course but am due to go into hospital on Monday. The specialist said that I'm going to have to eat a barium meal. I'm not sure what this consists of but

Tamzin says it's the vilest thing in the universe. You have to eat barium so they can x-ray your gut.

One problem about going into hospital is that Mum is convinced that they're very dangerous places. Lethal. She's paranoid about germs and is sure that you can catch diseases of all descriptions just by stepping through the door.[12] The mere idea of hospital lavatories crucifies her. Perry has kindly said that I can go to her house for de-contamination when the hospital finally ejects me.

'Jesus called his twelve disciples to him and gave them authority to cast out evil spirits and heal every kind of disease and illness.' *Matthew 10 v 1*

Oh, Glory – I hope I haven't let in a wretched spirit of infirmity. I asked Robin who came by on his way back from Scotland. 'Well, cast it away, just in case.'

He'd been casting for trout, staying with Rose's family who have a lodge in Perthshire and was glowing from walking up grouse on the high moor all week. (Alastair calls this method of shooting birds 'blasting', but it's well managed blasting.) 'I went for a long walk up into the Cairngorms with Matthew,' Robin told me. 'We'd just settled down by a loch, literally in the middle of nowhere, when two terrifying men with torn clothes and wild hair came running down towards us. I thought we were going to be attacked but Matthew just smiled, stood up and said, "Hi there, how are you doing?"' Robin went on, eyes rolling; 'I was just thinking he was handling a dangerous situation rather well, that he was quite a good actor, when one of the men said,

"What you doing here then, Vicar?"

"Oh I'm on my holidays, what about you?" It transpired that the men were tramps who Matthew knew from Bath. They used to go to the soup kitchen for the homeless that he set up in the winter and were chuffed to see him again. They had come up to Scotland for their holidays too.

6th October ~ A brochure for adult art classes has arrived in the post. I couldn't think why or where it was from, but judging by the postmark, I think that Mrs. Shalgoski has sent it to encourage me.

Daisy came, which was wonderful, but my mind felt like a shattered light bulb and I didn't want her to tread on the pieces. 'If you cling to your life, you will lose it, but if you give it up for me, you will find it.' *Matthew 10 v 39*

7th October ~ 'We can make our plans, but the Lord determines our steps.' *Proverbs 16 v 9*

Mine go straight into *Acute Medical* Ward 12 at Gloucester Royal Infirmary. I've never been to hospital before; only as a visitor.

'Is it time for me to go to the toilet?'

'Well, I really don't know.'

'Where is it then?'

'It's just outside on the right, Doris,' I told her.

'Is it?'

'Doris, you've been a dozen times today.'

'Have I?'

'Yes.'

'Where is it then?'

At least this dialogue cheered up the girl in the corner, who was now crying with laughter rather than pain. Doris seems to be entirely incontinent anyway, so the conversation is useless. She's eighty-two and, I'm afraid, quite dotty. All I can say is that she's immensely cheerful about having zero recall. Later on she asked me when she was going back to hospital.

'No, Doris, you're in hospital.'

'Am I?'

'Yes, that's your bed.'

'Oh, right oh, me cherry oh!' she laughed, plopping down happily on mine.

The other women on the ward are very sweet to her. I'm not nearly so tolerant. She keeps on trying to sit on my bed and I would rather she did not. She has a nasty stain on the back of her dressing gown. The smell is terrible.

Doris is not the only batty one. An anæmic lady in the bed opposite, called Mrs. Hawkins, spent all morning refusing to have her operation. 'I've got me iron tablets at 'ome, they'll do me.'

'But you need this operation, dear.'

'I won't have it,' Mrs. Hawkins snapped back, her mad eyes glinting through her thick, oval, black-rimmed glasses. 'They say I'm mental an' I'm not surprised. I wana go 'ome. I'm bored to tears in here, bored t' tears, bored t' tears, bored t' tears, bored t' tears...'

The nurses told me that she has been in the local mental institution for most of her adult life and not to lend her any money. She must be over fifty. She's diabetic and for some reason had fallen into an insulin coma and been admitted to the *Acute Medical* ward.

'But why is Doris here?' I asked the nurse.

'Oh, apart from having a drop of Alzheimer's and being incontinent she's perfectly healthy; there's just no room in *Geriatric* at the moment.'

Mrs. Hawkins spent hour after hour repeating the fact that she was bored until the rest of us were starting to go insane too. Try as I might, I couldn't feel sorry for her. She probably can't help being selfish but there are critically ill people on this ward and they need to sleep. I would have lent her my magazine but I don't think that *Elle* would have had much relevance to her life, especially seeing as it had 'Madonna reveals all' written on the front cover. I didn't want it to act as a catalyst; her behaviour could be described as 'unpredictable at best' as it is. Fortunately there was a sachet of scent inside the magazine. I normally can't stand them but it was better than the smell emanating from Doris' bed. I asked the nurses about it twice but they seemed distinctly reluctant to do anything about it.

There was a big disturbance in the ward after lunch. ''Ere, what's that black wriggly thing over there?'

'What's wrong?'

'That black wriggly thing up 'er arm?' Doris was shrieking now (but I think she knew she was being amusing.)

'Is this what you mean?' asked the nurse holding up a blood pressure gauge.

'I don't want to look,' Doris said emphatically, hiding under the bedclothes. But she couldn't resist a little peep. 'Do those things bite or what?' (By now we were all clutching our sheets with suppressed laughter.)

'No, it's quite harmless, honestly.'

'Well, keep it away from me, you hear?' But then a student doctor came over to examine me, bringing his own blood pressure gauge with him. 'Oh lor, there's two of them now.'

Mrs. Hawkins rather enjoyed all the attention. After this episode she became more animated, muttering and groaning; whingeing about food.

'You're obsessed with food, Doreen,' said the nurse. 'Do try to think of something else.'

'I know,' she said, looking pleased. 'I be obsessed with insulin too... And sometimes I'm violent,' she muttered, her eyes glinting strangely.

8th October ~ Doris made sleep virtually impossible. It was mainly the smell, but later her snoring. It was like listening to a creaky barn door. At 4.00am she was up and staggering around naked. The poor woman at the end of the ward, who was seriously ill with heart disease, had Doris on her bed for a frightening time before she ran off to the men's ward. Then the shouting really started and it wasn't coming from her. She'd tried to get into bed with an elderly man.

Apart from Doris, the insane Mrs. Hawkins and the two acutely ill ladies there was also a painter/decorator installed in our ward with his tabloids, dirty overalls and appalling jokes. And we were all in our nighties. He wasn't working. He was a visitor. The nurses chased him away at night but otherwise he was pretty permanently fixed to the eighteen-year old girl busy haemorrhaging in the corner. He offered her absolutely no sympathy, but whenever she had the strength would start snogging and giving her such physical attention that I had to draw my curtains in revolt.

I resolved to insure myself for private health treatment. Any Christian thoughts of understanding and mercy dropped to zero.

It's hard to find the resilience when you're feeling grotty and don't get any sleep at night. 'Oh God, show me what I can do, how to cope.'

Trying to escape from the ward was futile. There was nowhere to go. The Day Room was a fug of cigarette smoke. I couldn't stand in the corridors all day; they were hung with more depressing posters. This time there was a drooping picture of the pancreas and notices on fluids, which I'm afraid, were somewhat lacking, certainly in the field of graphic design. Desperate handwritten signs about 'Learning to speak again' and 'Deb's leaving do', stuck up defiantly with yellowing tape, screamed at me from every wall. Whenever I tried to converse with the nurses in their cubicle, they made me go back to my bed in case I missed being inspected by the posse of doctors galloping through. They didn't even want to let me take a bath.

Then I found a seventeen-year-old girl lying, crying in a private room. She'd collapsed on a hockey field in an insulin coma and had to be in under observation for a few more days. 'I'm so lonely. I wish I could have a bed on a ward.' I chatted away, assuring her she was much better off where she was, and gave her my magazine.

9th October ~

'They've put me on rat poison.' This lady wasn't mad at all but explaining that she was being prescribed Warfarin to thin her blood. I think she was finding it all a bit hard to digest, mentally that is, so I tried to encourage her to talk about her medication and condition. I felt truly sorry for her. The details of her previous internment were appalling. She said that the ward had been consistently full of people's visitors and their screaming children.

I still can't find the compassion for Mrs. Hawkins. I should; she's mentally ill, certified insane, but I can't manage to look past her huge selfishness; she seems to delight in making life unbearable for everybody else. Perhaps if she received loving attention she would stop making a nuisance of herself. 'Lord, give me grace.'

Doris finally put her hat on to go to the loo. It was a tweed hat with a feather in it. Off she went, making comments about the weather. Mrs. Hawkins started shrieking with laughter. On and on and on. The nurses took absolutely no notice. I began to feel annoyed on behalf of the terribly sick people on the ward, especially the poor woman on rat poison. I don't think this hospital environment is conducive to healing. I went and begged the matron to see to Doris' transferral.

'I woke to the sound of running water late last night,' I explained. 'Doris was sitting on the side of someone else's bed, peeing onto the floor. In the morning,' I said, ploughing on, 'I discovered the reason for the smell. She has been stuffing her wet incontinence pads down the back of her locker, which happens to be nearest my bed. None of your staff seem prepared to do anything about this.' I gave her a 'this is too much' look. The matron nodded in agreement.

While all this was going on, I was being monitored and observed. Dr. Prior ran a whole series of examinations and tests on me. They looked at my throat, took spit and blood. I was given another injection of magnesium sulphate. Then I had more tests. I'm truly grateful they're so thorough. The State must be spending a fortune on me. 'What is this one for?' I'd ask the student doctor.

'Oh, they're testing you for a series of rare blood diseases, I'm not sure which. Can I examine your chest?'

'Weather permitting,' said Doris.

Then, without forewarning or explanation, I was taken by wheelchair down endless subterranean corridors to a shabby waiting room where I was told to drink two glasses of what seemed to be washing-up liquid. It was vile. I'm ashamed to say it took me fifteen minutes to get it down.

I was led into a small, bare room, required to undress and put on a wrap. The silence and absence of peeling posters struck me. A very sweet girl directed me into another white, windowless chamber with nothing in it except a huge scanning machine. I had to lie motionless on a thing like an ironing board, which passed backwards and forwards through the very bright light of a circular scanner. I found it an alien experience, a nightmare in white; just like being in a photocopier. How would they ever manage to get a character like Mrs. Hawkins in there?

10th October ~ Out of hospital. Huge relief. The only person to come to see me there was Mary-Dieu. Her visit was a complete surprise. She was very cheerful and sweetly brought me some dried flowers. She's been admitted for major orthopaedic operations a number of times in an attempt to rectify the ravages of polio and assured me she understands how endless and smelly it can be.

After I returned from my scan yesterday I found Doris had gone. It was rather sad; I'd never said Goodbye. In her place was a jovial creature I can only describe as 'a lady of the street', a determined and vocal extrovert who seemed extremely pleased to be in a bed so close to mine. She had long, grey, matted hair and satanic tattoos decorating her ancient skin, of which there was a great deal on display. She was surrounded by antiquated, deteriorating and overfull carrier bags. If anyone touched one they were screamed at for an extended period of time. A tactile male visitor of similar ilk, who seemed quite at home with the smell, sat beside her bed which gave him an excellent view of me in my night clothes. Me, sitting amid the smell of bodies never washed.

Test of faith: to love the unlovely when you don't feel like it.

I'm afraid I discharged myself.

11th October ~ From the decontamination zone: I'm staying in Perry's house. It smells clean and wonderful. No one is dying here. No one is remotely mad. I suppose the Army base might still be a target for Saddam Hussein, but I don't care.

12th October ~ Nicola's had her baby; a sweet little girl called Rosie.
I went to see them in Malmesbury Cottage Hospital. It was very old fashioned, full of lilies and smelt glorious. Nicola's ward must have been built in 1890 and felt exactly the same as one of our dormitories at school. There were five other young mothers there, all pretty and quiet with gentle, considerate husbands. I would have happily crawled into one of the other beds. Nicola and I could have lain there chatting away as we did all our years at school.

13th October ~ I'm feeling low again, much worse than I would ever let anyone know. Although attacked regularly in the last few days by feeling ill and depressed, I forgot how truly bad it could be.
I'm assured by the medics that depression is common in all chronic illnesses, but it's different today. I can't help but feel rejected. I know this one, it's an old opponent, just another lie, just one more weapon set against me, but it's real: REJECTION. I have to go into the office, see my bosses and collect my stuff.

'I know the experiences of our lives, when we let God use them, become the mysterious and perfect preparation for the work He will give us to do... So many times we wonder why God has certain things happen to us. We try to understand the circumstances of our lives, and we are left wondering. But God's foolishness is so much wiser than our wisdom. From generation to generation, from small beginnings and little lessons, He has a purpose for those who know and trust Him. God has no problems ~ just plans!' Corrie ten Boom

I'm still reading Matthew's Gospel; Jesus is being so cool about facing his death sentence. Goodness knows how rejected he felt. It says that when he was in the Garden of Gethsemane he bled from every pore. This is a documented medical condition and recognised as a symptom of extreme stress. I don't think he let on how bad things were.

14th October ~ Excitement of excitements; I went to Stroud General Hospital for another magnesium injection. I can't grumble. It's my birthday tomorrow and I have lots to do.

7.00pm ~ I've passed all my hospital tests. Nothing's wrong with me. What a huge mercy. I do not have cancer.

15th October ~ I had a brilliant birthday. I woke to presents in bed at home and later went up to London with a fruitcake Mum had made for me and a lovely bottle of champagne from Dad's special store in the playroom. I drove through

Cirencester and Bibury. All the beech woods are golden now and the Cotswold hills were bathed in autumn light. Once in London there was time for a lovely deep, hot bath before my friends came round. Rebecca arrived early and ended up cutting Robin's hair in the kitchen while we ate the cake. Diana arrived, Robin left, Tamzin arrived, Diana left, Perry and Robert came at the same time as Alastair and James who had staggered up from Bristol with a huge present. Pippa arrived with lots of food, made salad and ordered pizzas, which we ate with the very good champagne. Perry made me wear a blue velvet hat that she bought me and a huge, rainbow striped jumper that Mum had thought would cheer me up. Well, yes and no. It makes me look like a *Play-Away* presenter.

I did feel ill but was so cheered and so enjoyed myself that the feeling felt quite removed. Sadly, not every day can be like this.

16th October ~ Cleared up after the party and paid for yesterday's exertions by being in bed all afternoon. I lay thinking about tomorrow. I must try not to interpret losing my job as rejection or take it personally. I must concentrate on the facts. They have to cut three posts and mine is an obvious choice, determined purely by my state of health. I could try to persuade them to take me back two days a week, but I hate that sort of compromise. And I find I still can't even watch television.

Rebecca gave me a paintbox yesterday; it's a very good one with a whole range of artist quality watercolours. It was very generous of her. I unwrapped the cellophane from all the little pans and thought about what I could do with them.

17th October ~ Went to work. I felt OK when I was there, functioning on Dextrose energy, but it was draining and I was shattered later. My former producer met me and I was shown around the space-agey White City building, which my department had moved to. I couldn't help feeling that she was edgy, worried that her over-scheduling had caused my illness. The thing is, that all that time ago I'd been so flattered that they had wanted me to direct a second series that I allowed myself to let them. We found the boxes full of my files and tapes were being stored in an office known as *World Christianity*. I stood there for a while wondering if I'd been lined up to work on this series.

I saw the Manager and my Head of Department about the fact that they would not be renewing my annual contract when it expires in November. I think it was more awkward for them than for me. I made light of it, said I wanted a break and would rather get well and maybe do some travelling than stagger back to work part time. It's what I would like to do and I didn't want to make them feel guilty. It was only afterwards that I thought, 'Heck, they've sacked me just because I'm sick and I've been working fulltime for them all these years.' It never occurred to me to ask whether I was due redundancy payment.

When I was in the office, I met the man who had taken over my project. He'd pulled on his waterproof trousers and started with about two hours' notice. 'I can't tell you what a relief it was,' he said. 'I have to say how grateful I am that you were ill.' He'd left the *BBC*, aged about fifty-five and started his own production company, only the work just didn't come in. 'I'd literally been praying for a job. I was about to have to sell my house.'

18th October ~ Crisis: 'Mary-Dieu has been arrested and is on a charge of attempted murder.'

It transpired that Mary-Dieu had got so annoyed with her boyfriend that she ended up chasing him around the park with a carving knife in her hand. I don't think she could have killed him because she can't run very fast, but of course it looked very dramatic and the passers-by dialled 999. Well they would. And the authorities called my parents.

Mum scooped up Daisy, whom she was looking after, and hurried off to Gloucester Police Station. 'I thought it might help if I arrived with a baby but it didn't,' she told me on the phone. 'The Police weren't very pleased.' (It was ten o'clock at night.) 'I had to leave the carrycot at the main desk with the constable on duty.' (Oh dear) Mum then declared she was a J.P. and made her way down to the Charge Room. (The Police thought she was a G.P. and since Mum looks acutely Anglo Saxon and Mary-Dieu is half Vietnamese they had no idea she was her mother.)

'Mum! What was it like?' (I used to work on a detective series and always wanted to know what a real Police Station would be like.)

'There was a smell of wee-wee and terrible swearing was coming from the cells.'

It transpired that Mary-Dieu was the one using metaphorical language. All the other prisoners were telling her to shut up. 'She is amazing,' Mum said. 'I went in to see her and all she was wearing, and in this terribly cold weather, was a black mini-skirt and a purple bra.' (It's actually an Indian halter-neck top but Mum's right, Mary-Dieu is extraordinary.) So is she; she managed to get Mary-Dieu 'Off on Domestic' (domestic violence.)

19th October ~ The immediate problem is that Mum thinks that we ought to look after Daisy for a few weeks. This is not easy when I'm in London and my parents are in the middle of a contract to work on a film.

I felt bad about not being at home for my family, but too ill to drive down until late in the afternoon. When I did get to Gloucestershire I couldn't find the child-minder's house. Mum had given me the wrong directions, or I hadn't taken in the right ones. Everyone I asked was terribly sympathetic but hadn't a clue where the nursery was. I got all panicky, more stressed than I've been all summer and was shaking uncontrollably by the time I found the place. Dear little Daisy was sitting in the sunshine smiling up at me. She was very quiet and good all evening.

Mary-Dieu rang. In fact she just yelled at me down the phone for a long time. It was quite discouraging. 'Hey,' I said, changing tack. 'What was it like being in the Charge Room?'

'What?'

'What was it like being underneath the Police Station?'

'Oh, yeah, well. I had a panic attack and was sick all down my shirt, so I whipped it off.'

'What did the coppers do?' (She does have an impressive bust.)

Mary-Dieu burst out laughing. 'They all turned round, except the policewoman who rushed off and came back with a tea towel.'

'What did you do with it?'

'I said, "That's not going to cover much, is it?" Stupid woman.' Apparently the policewoman came back with a blanket and they put her in a cell.

'Did they give you anything to eat?'

'Sophie, I was pissed out of my mind, I didn't want anything to eat.'

'Why are you so angry?' I asked.

'You all look down on me,' she said sulkily.

'That is not true,' I said.

'I'm twenty now and you all treat me as if I'm still a child.'

'You can't run around waving knives at people,' I implored.

'You can't blame anyone else any more just because it makes you feel better for five minutes.' Was this a stupid thing to say? It certainly was not what she wanted to hear. She didn't want to stop screaming at me, but she didn't want to listen either.

'You're the end,' I said, exasperated.

'No I'm not,' she replied, quick as a flash. 'I'm just the beginning.'

Mum returned from work and calmly took the receiver from me, making arrangements to meet Mary-Dieu in Gloucester. I then had to give my parents the news that my file at the *BBC* has been put neatly into the round filing cabinet. The most useful piece of furniture in the room; the wastepaper bin. I feel as if it's I who am becoming the problem child.

20th October ~ Mary-Dieu has threatened to kill Mum now. Mum is not a bit worried, 'Oh, no, I'm indestructible; far too fat. The knife wouldn't get through my rolls. Don't tell the Police, she'll only lose her Council accommodation. Pass me that blade for the liquidizer.' She isn't concerned, she's busy mushing up carrots, intent on creating a supplementary diet for her otters. They eat fresh trout from the trout farm and day-old chicks from the falconry centre, but Mum is determined they should have more vitamin C and is intently mixing porridge oats and this boiled carrot with raw beef into what she calls 'patty-pies'. (And this is someone who's been cynical about my vitamins.)

I thought Mary-Dieu would be amused about the concept of the otters now eating vegetables but she's still shrieking. 'Why don't you ever listen to me?'

'Tell me what the problem is.'

'You don't understand,' she screamed.

'Please let me try,' I said sitting down. 'I love you.'

'You don't care. Anyway, you're just mean to me,' she said not listening.

'I care about you very much.'

'No you don't. You only care about yourself.'

It's true, I'm a rotter. It's Mum who is amazing. She goes on and on. Her love for Mary-Dieu can only be described as unconditional. Oscar Wilde describes this as being able 'to give and not expect return.' He went on to say, 'It's not the perfect, but the imperfect that is in need of love.' But none of us are perfect and we all need it.

21st October ~ Terribly depressed emotionally now. Bed.

'Most people have, at some time or other, to stand alone and suffer, and their final shape is determined by their response to their probation; they emerge either as slaves of circumstance or in some sense captains of their souls.' Charles E. Raven in *A Wanderer's Way*

It seems we have this choice, Mary-Dieu and I, but no chance of sharing the pain. Oh, Gracious, being a human being can be tough. This time on earth must be to forge our characters, to teach us about communication, to increase our understanding; I just don't feel up to it at the moment.

Mum went off to raise money for *Mencap* with the otters. I'm not sure what the connection is, but never mind... They go off to the most extraordinary places. She took them down in a submarine once. Well, the submarine didn't go underwater but Mum somehow managed to climb down inside, (down the conning tower, Dad says it's called,) with an otter on each shoulder. Jims got off onto the iron ladder and started exploring the submarine all by himself. One of the ratings shouted, 'Who the flipping heck (or similar such words) allowed an otter on this sub?'

'The First Sea Lord,' replied my mother.

22nd October ~ Cold and rainy; stayed in bed all day long. Mum has been advised, asked by the medics and social workers, to take Daisy back to Gloucester. Of course. Mary-Dieu's need is to love and be loved.

'I was *invited* to visit the submarine because it was called *HMS Otter*.' I suppose that is not unreasonable. 'The otters had a lovely time playing uckers with the sailors.'

'Did you meet the First Sea Lord?'

'Oh the Admiral's a great fan. He sent me a poem once:

"Mad was the miller's daughter who lived beside the mill. There was otters in the water, but she was 'otter still." Hilarious.' Yes, Mum.

The latest hoo-ha with the otters is that the government has decided they're Classifiable. As DANGEROUS WILD ANIMALS. We now have to be licensed to handle them and their enclosure has to be inspected and passed by all sorts of worthy bodies including the local fire inspector. I can't think of anything in their lives that could possibly ignite. It's all mad; I'm off to organise my own life.

23rd October ~ Drove to London in the rain, went to cinema with Pippa, car towed away.

24th October ~ Felt weak. It rained all day long.

25th October ~ A letter has arrived from Sarah-Jane in South Africa. This is a miracle, as she never writes. She has invited me out to stay for as long as I like, saying emphatically that I'll get better there. It would be wonderful to get away from all this rain. She said the horses were well and that she still has some of the herons they found abandoned as babies in the spring. When the brood was old enough, she released them but Ron and another called Hero remained, hanging around the camp. 'He was named Hero because he was particularly good at catching mice in the kitchen rondavel.'

Gordon rang to ask how I was. He said I must try to get to church and I will.

26th October ~ Appointment at 126 Harley Street. It was quite exciting to walk down the legendary street, knock on the big front door and sit in the gigantic waiting room. Mary Loveday had attic rooms on the very top floor. They looked more like a series of small white labs than consulting rooms. There were a lot of glass phials standing in holders and a smell of the sea from saline solution in which the allergens were suspended. Here her nurse systematically tested me for allergies.

Good news. Diana's sister Amanda is to be married, or so it has been announced in *The Times,* to a Mr. James Radclyffe Brewster. I was able to make it to their engagement party in Twickenham. Amanda was wearing an amusing, black, elasticated, raffia mini skirt. 'It's a size 8,' she said triumphantly, 'and it fits perfectly. I'm normally a size 14.' (She is nearly six foot tall.) 'The shop girls explained why ~ it's meant to be a dress.'

27th October

Lunch with my friends Charlie, Jane and their newborn. Another babe to inspect. I have to say that this child has incredible eyes. Charlie says admiration is mandatory; they need the encouragement to wade through piles of laundry and cope with the endless wailing nights. The trouble is that diplomacy can force you to lie if you're not careful. And I'm far too forthright. I told one friend that their baby looked like a Vervet monkey. It was true, she did, newborn babies do, but I've never lived this down. Dad gets away with all sorts of comments about babies somehow. He went to see his chiropodist once and peered at the hideous infant lying in a carrycot in the surgery. 'It looks just like a bull-terrier,' he said.

'You're the only honest man who has come through here,' said the chiropodist, pleased as punch, and it was his baby.

Jane explained that a person's sense of humour fails them when they suddenly turn into a parent and are tired out all the time. She then looked up at me and burst out laughing. She's thrilled, despite the hard work; they had been longing for a baby for ages.

Church on Sunday evening: A talk from John Irvine, Gordon's boss: 'Faith is being sure of what we hope for and certain of what we do not see. It's a willingness to let God work His purpose in our lives. Trust; let Him do the impossible.' In that case one could say that faith is taking on what God says and hanging on in there, despite the odds.

28th October ~ John said, 'We cannot produce faith, it comes by God's grace; all we have to do is accept God.'

Health update: Times of normal activity are interrupted by periods of fatigue when all the usual symptoms flood back and my speech gets muddled. I find I have good days when I feel almost 'hyper' or whizzy and tend to take on far too much, gabbling as I talk, but I easily overdo things and my throat flares up. What I cannot, cannot handle is any form of stress. Getting lost in the car reduces me to tears and I find it hard to think my way out of difficult situations. Example:

I had the most dreadful afternoon. All I had on was an appointment with Mary Loveday in Farnham but managed to get very stressed in the process. I stupidly took a screwdriver to try and tighten my front door lock before I left my flat. I'm not technically incompetent but just couldn't fix the Yale mechanism. With the lock in pieces, I couldn't leave with the door open to the London street. After one hour I gave up in frustration and persuaded a builder to come down off the roof opposite to help me. But he couldn't fix the thing either.

Now, being much later than I ever expected, I drove straight into rush-hour traffic and sat in it all the way to Surrey. Then, discovering I had no map, (why? why? why? I always have maps.) I lost my way to Dr. Loveday's house. I stopped to phone from a pub, but it was so noisy I couldn't hear. I went over the road to the phone boxes and discovered I had no coins. Got change; couldn't get Directory Enquiries. Found number from phonebook in pub. Crossed road back to phone boxes. Was nearly run over by a reversing car. Rang up in tears. The doctor's husband calmly gave me directions... from the wrong pub. Got lost. Drove incredibly badly. Took ridiculous risks. Prayed.

Found house. Neurotic patient faces neurologist. Neurologist provides cup of tea. She showed me all the tapestries she does to relax after work. They were all so neat on the back that you could see the design from either side.

Dr. Loveday had the results back from my tests and declared that I'm allergic to mould and fungi floating around in the atmosphere, not too violently but enough to thoroughly zap my strength. She reckons that about 45% of my immune system's capacity is occupied in fighting the allergy, so it's no wonder I catch every bug going round. There's no escape from the mould either. Not in England. I could go and live in a desert. She gave me some drops to take every day so that my body will gradually build up a resistance to mould. Deary me. She said I must accept all the National Health Service had to offer me, including the magnesium injections.

She ran me through her Vegatest machine[13] again. My readings had gone up substantially from last time; from 20 to 60, from 5 to 40. Wow. She said this was good, that my mineral levels and absorption were up, but it wasn't good enough. I should be reading 80 on the dial. She thought that if viruses had been lodging in my pancreas and liver they've probably gone, but that I was still battling with other problems. She described my body as being like a strong wall with weak cement. I'm to continue with the medicines, especially the vitamin B.

She thought going to southern Africa a good idea because it has such an arid climate, but that I shouldn't go until February.

'Is there anything I shouldn't eat?'

'Eat whatever you feel like,' she assured me.

'And dealing with depression?'

'Keep taking vitamin B complex.'

29th October ~ Drove home for another of Dr. Prior's whacking great magnesium injections. Very tired. Awful smell of dead rat in the house. Mum isn't a bit concerned about the potential risk of harbouring Weil's disease; dead rats are classified in her brain as natural country dirt and not a serious concern. She says she can't smell a thing and that I'm just oversensitive to everything these days. I put a burning log in the basin in my bedroom in an effort to fumigate the place and placed sliced onions all the way up the stairs. Apparently they absorb germs and smells.

Dare I go to South Africa? It seems a better option than hanging about in the dank twilight of another British winter. The entire woodlouse population of Gloucestershire seems to be congregating in my bedroom. I've always been rather fond of woodlice, but I read that they indicate damp, so perhaps I need to get out of here quick.

Mum has just rushed back from court. She'd had to convict a little old man for repeatedly shoplifting. He'd been caught when a box of Oxo cubes fell through a hole in his pocket, rolled down his trouser leg and along the supermarket aisle. 'Then we tried a miserable woman for shoplifting, who claimed innocence on the grounds that she was just scatty and had forgotten to pay, I ask you.'

Knock. Knock. Knock!
'Answer the door,' Mum yelled, 'I'm in a tearing hurry.'
It was the Police. 'I'm terribly sorry officer, but I can't talk now,' she said. 'I'm just zooming off.'
'Madam, the only place you're zooming off to is with me.' Mum had left the court, gone and filled up her car with petrol and had forgotten to pay for it.
'Oh, dear. Let me give you the money to pay the garage.'
'Madam. We will accompany you back there. You must pay in person.'

30th October ~ Nicola brought her new baby for tea. 'What did your doctor say?' she asked while burping Rosie.
'That I'm allergic to mould of all things.'
'Yuck, mouldy cheese?'
'I think airborne mould; fungi spores floating around in the atmosphere.'

'Well, there's black mould on this window frame.' She was right ~ it did have tiny bits of black, dotty bathroom mould around it.

'What a ridiculous thing to be allergic to. All this for that.'

It occurred to me that Jeremy the acupuncturist was sort of right. Mould forms in warm, moist conditions – on bathroom tiles and when water condenses on windows. He said I had a problem with heat and damp.

NOVEMBER ~ Where does the wind come from?

1st November ~

Back in London, running away from the mould. Despite all my treatment at the hands of medical specialists, I'm still incapacitated. I can't help wondering when my prayers for healing will ever be answered.

'Hope is not a feeling or a wish, but a firm understanding of what is to come. The certainty that we'll spend eternity with God will affect how we spend our lives today.' This was from a talk by Gordon speaking in church on *Paul's letter to the Romans*. 'We can rejoice, too, when we run into problems and trials, for we know that they are good for us – they help us to learn to endure. And endurance develops strength of character...'

Well, I have a terrible problem: a blocked loo. It was Diana's fault. She flushed a paper kitchen towel down it. I had to agree that I would have done the same thing, but really. It happened at suppertime when not one plumber in London wanted to answer the phone, so we rang all our friends to ask their advice. In the end I was doubled up with laughter, my ribs aching. Try it: ask everyone you know how to unblock a loo over the phone. But you don't need to as I now know what to do:

HOW TO UNBLOCK A LAVATORY

- Tape a (thick) plastic bag over the end of a mop.
- Hold mop above loo by upright handle. Use mop as you would a plunger.
- Blockage should float to surface.
- Don't try to flush blockage down again; take it out.
- Get friend to wear disposable rubber gloves, otherwise friend will not want to take blockage out.

'Might be useful as a corporate team building exercise,' I thought.

'Don't be silly, Sophie. It's hardly relevant to Public Relations.'

'Oh, really. Isn't it?'

2nd November ~ You would think laughter should improve your health but I feel polished off. Poisoned. I must try to get to grips with this suffering theory:

Trials→ Endurance → Strength of Character→ Confidence → Hope

It makes sense even if you think of it in terms of the business world. Athletes must also need to persevere and train in this way.

If hope is expectation,
And faith a commitment to God,
What is the outcome of expectation + commitment?
= Absorbing what God says and acting upon it: Love extended, love in action.

- Faith x Hope = Love
- Commitment x Expectation + Obedience = God's plans realised.
- If I commit to God, he'll give me Hope and a Future.
- Faith → Hope → Healing

Gordon said most Bible translations talk of suffering rather than trials. 'The word suffering, in Greek, means pressure or stress. It also means pain but it does not refer to illness.' (That's interesting, there seems to be a goodly supply of pressure and stress, problems or trials in most people's lives without the addition of sickness.) Gordon assured us that it would, 'produce perseverance and character.' He added, 'This transformation, this work of God in our lives leads to Hope. This is the work of the Holy Spirit refining us like silver or gold.' In suffering we can achieve more than we can imagine possible.

'Well Lord, watch carefully as you refine me. I feel so melted I might just slip away.'

3rd November ~ Grizelda rang to say that her little boy, Paddy, has broken his femur. It means six weeks in traction. Being only three years old he can't comprehend the pain, the enforced immobility or understand why he has to stay in hospital. The accident threw Griz completely and, now under tremendous strain, she has to spend most of her time in the children's ward with him. While Paddy is longing to be let out, her baby Eliza doesn't like it there much either and her husband is working in New York. I suggested that she gives herself a break right now and schedules friends to be with Paddy every afternoon or evening.

My brain is popping with questions about suffering. Maria Tunstall, while dying of cancer in her early thirties, made this recording:

'When one goes through difficult times, it's very easy to start questioning and doubting God's ways and character and motives. One is tempted to ask: Does God care? Does He know what's happening? Is He still in control? We have found the only way to counteract these doubts and questions is to *fill our minds with what the scriptures say about God's character* and to hold on to the many promises in Scripture that He gives us. We have to remember that *infinite power ruled by infinite love* is the basic Bible description of God's character.'

4th November ~ I went to visit Paddy in the John Radcliffe Hospital. I didn't want to expose my body to possible infection but I had to go. He lay with his leg in traction looking horribly uncomfortable but on the most amazing bed you have ever seen. It had been made into a Police car with a hooter and wing mirrors, lights and a steering wheel. He wanted me to draw the set-up, so I obliged and then tried to encourage him to paint. He seemed extremely healthy and frustrated beyond all measure.

Around him were some very sick children. I felt so sorry for their parents. To have a little child suffering and fatally ill must be the worst thing. Griz says you feel all the pain with none of the comfort.

When I got back to London I lay, wrapped up against the cold, reading one of those little *Daily Bread* books; *Thoughts for the Day*. I looked up the readings for 4th November. Along the bottom of the page was written, 'The best name for God is compassion, which means 'suffering with'.

5th November ~ How do we cope with suffering like this day in and day out? Do we simply have to endure, try to deal with the pain and look beyond it? Like letting go of our worries it's not always easy. Sometimes all you can do is remember it could be worse in Bangladesh and try to see the funny side. Life is always worth living when you can laugh.

Dad had a friend who was suffering from a bad heart. He came to stay in order to relax and find a bit of peace in the country. (I'm beginning to think there's something paradoxical about that particular theory.) Anyway, it was very hot that summer. The chap was about to go swimming in the lake when a huge boxer dog, that belonged to our neighbour, made a bee-line for him, leapt on his back and started to do rude things. Dad was terribly worried because his friend was frail and not up to being mounted by a boxer, but the chap pushed the dog off, looked at Dad and said, 'Don't worry, I'll have the pick of the litter.'

6th November ~ I'm in a soggy, floppy pancake state even though I did nothing yesterday but lie in bed and read. I find it so odd, so lonely being in London and not working. I keep thinking about my department and what everyone's been doing since I fell off the merry-go-round. They're re-cycling my old programmes for Daytime Television, which is good. There was a funny one I made about what eleven-year old girls and boys think of each other that seems to be repeated every week. But, to my horror, I found that between programmes they put up a photograph of me working with the children. I looked so young and energetic. I was.

My Executive Producer never used to ask a person under pressure how they were. Knowing how irritating this would be, and yet wanting both to find out and show concern she'd ask, 'Are you surviving?' It was a cue. You could laugh, and then tell her the worst without sounding moaney. Like my boss, God never promises to save us from suffering but he does promise to be with us. If I were a soldier, I would want my troops to hang on in there and plough on regardless. It's essential that we outlast and withstand the enemy's attack.

What happens when we reach the end of our tether? When we are in complete anguish or crushed with grief? David Watson says, 'Be honest with God. Bring him your anger and bitterness and despair.' I have found that when I've been in emotional turmoil and cried out for help that's when he has indeed taken over. He's responded by sucking away the pain. I've been comforted. 'And the Holy Spirit helps us in our distress. For we don't even know what we should pray for, nor how we should pray. But the Holy Spirit prays for us with groanings that cannot be expressed in words.' *Paul's letter to the Romans cont...*

I don't deserve it; it's God's grace. His comfort poured out at no small cost. Someone once defined this as: **G**od's **R**iches **A**t **C**hrist's **E**xpense. G.R.A.C.E. The outcome of grace is that despite everything we become all that God intended us to be and do all he would have us do.

Mum is staying here at my flat. She has to go to an audition at Television Centre tomorrow to play a dinner-lady with a 'Brummie' accent. She's currently wiping the surfaces in my kitchen avidly, and practising it.

7th November ~ Because Mum has a phobia about dirt on the London Underground, as well as in public lavatories and hospitals, I said I'd drive her down the hill to Wood Lane. It's not far. Even if 'It's disgusting' does sound funny in a Birmingham accent I didn't think she could arrive for an audition shimmering from thoughts of all the germs.

Mum made her way downstairs and before I knew what was happening, blood-curdling screams were coming from the street. I rushed down thinking she was being attacked. She'd found an old man, curled up asleep on the back seat of my car; an ancient tramp in a completely pickled state. He wore a long, dark overcoat and a thick gold earring indicating he was probably a very elderly gypsy. He was wearing the blue velvet hat Perry gave me and had made Mum's rainbow jumper into a pillow.

'Good morning,' I declared brightly. 'Would you like a cup of tea?'

'Give us a drink.'

Mum was horrified by the smell. Quivering with repulsion. It was indeed suffocating; he'd been sick and had peed on my seats. Poor Mum couldn't cope with this at all but I think that sleeping next to Doris had given me greater resilience. Mind you, it's difficult trying to look after someone who doesn't want any help. I found some bananas and a packet of biscuits in my kitchen but, although clearly emaciated, the tramp wasn't interested in food. This probably meant he hadn't eaten for days. The sick had really just been saliva and alcohol. He was quite cold. In the end I put a screw-top jar of sweet tea in his pocket and helped him pull the rainbow jumper down over his coat. He made his way down the street in this colourful garment and the blue velvet hat, which looked oddly appropriate; like a battered topper.

It's incredible what human beings can go through and survive. James says we are an extremely adaptable species; programmed to survive against the odds. 'Well James, I'm very grateful that you were prepared to help me get through this illness,' I told him.

'You've encouraged me in the past. What are we doing here if we aren't here for each other?'

'Well, thank you for sharing the tedium.'

'It wasn't hard. You'll be better soon, and then you'll disappear; muck off somewhere.'

'Do you think?'

When he left, I took my book and read late into the night until it was finished. George Elliot was talking about coping with long-term pain: 'We get accustomed to mental as well as bodily pain, without, for all that, losing our sensibility to it: it becomes a habit of our lives and we cease to imagine a condition of perfect ease as possible for us. Desire is chastened into submission, and we are contented with our day when we have been able to bear our grief in silence and to act as if we were not suffering.'

If so, is this a good thing?

It doesn't sound it. It's a way of surviving but shouldn't we seek a way out? I used to draw on my own self-confidence and resources. Now I know, that apart from anything, it's more effective to simply ask God. I think he enjoys solving problems.

It's no use rebelling. I had asked the tramp where he was going. What a stupid question when his whole life is witness to the fact that he doesn't want to know.

Mary-Dieu is determined that rebelling is the answer and Paddy can't help but rebel. It might be an easy, reactionary response but it isn't a very effective way of overcoming problems and certainly has negative consequences. And, it's an awful strain for other people, particularly parents desperately trying to help. We all tend to rebel in some way. My independence is rebellion, sort of. Silly: I should look for a more creative way out.

8th November ~ Rebecca has found a way. She started writing a series of educational children's storybooks in the summer; they're about the principles of science. Now she's asked me to illustrate it. I thought it generous of her to share her inspiration. The first book is about the force of gravity and involves drawing a lot of vegetables.

Mum wrote a book once. It's called *Bee, a Particular Otter*. She has what she calls a paw-tagraph, one of the otter's footprints reproduced as a rubber stamp, and with this she signs copies. People love it. She's already sold 15,000. Once she made Alastair go and help her.

'I've just had the most embarrassing experience of my entire life.' He made it sound as if it was all my fault. 'Your mother,' (Oh no) 'made me,' (Oh, dear) 'go to a book shop in Burford.'

'But you love book shops in Burford, Alastair.'

'She took her otter,' (Ahh) 'to sign books.' (He had an I-couldn't-believe-it, it's-totally-ridiculous look on his face.) 'I had to look after the otter,' Alastair reported. 'A German tourist walked in, wearing,' he said in a shocked and disgusted voice, 'a mink coat.'

'Oh dear, did Bee get angry?' I gasped.

'No! She...' there was a pause. 'I didn't know what to do.'

'Oh, Alastair ~ what?'

'The otter leapt out of my arms onto the woman's shoulder and started to...'

'What?'

'Make love to the coat.'

'Oh, you know what you say then, you say...'

'I DON'T WANT TO KNOW.'

9th November ~ I've just found that having my car steam-cleaned cost more than it would have done to put the tramp up in an hotel and I'm not feeling very rich. My *BBC* contract has expired and I will no longer receive sick pay. I've had a pretty good innings and I'm not ungrateful. I gather that I am eligible for a small sickness allowance from the Department of Social Security for the next six months... if I remain ill or unemployed.

I have no other source of income and am not sure how I'll manage, but have put my finances in God's hands and myself on a tight budget. Pippa's rent just covers my mortgage, but it looks from here as if I'm going to have to find a way of living on thin air.

They say we learn of God's love for us during times of suffering and loss. It's then that we gain personal revelation. And, 'if we are to share his glory, we must also share his suffering.'[xv] I want him to transform the loss into something positive. I'm walking down this valley with one aim and it's to reach the mountain. It's the way to get there.

10th November ~ 'In the natural world nothing's wasted,' James reminded me. 'Every dead tree, every creature that loses its life is re-cycled, providing a livelihood or home for all sorts of birds, insects or fungi in the process.' The system's perfect; it's only Man that upsets the balance and causes dereliction and pollution.

I can't stand staying in London any longer, and don't feel particularly well here. Off again.

11th November ~ I've just seen the most extraordinary white animal sitting in a box in Tamzin's garage. I couldn't think what it was. Maud was shocked too. She took one look at it and ran.

'It's Thelma.'

'No?' It doesn't look like a cat at all.

'It's awful, Sophie. I'm so upset with Johnty,' Tamzin said, sounding like Fanny Craddock.

'Why?'

'She had skin cancer but Johnty thought I'd be upset if she was put down so he persuaded the vet to amputate her cancery ears instead.' Thelma seems happy enough, but she does look very alarming. An earless cat.

Poor Thelma, what an indignity. I hate it when animals have to suffer. In the natural scheme of things they don't have to endure the ravages of old age. They get taken out by predators and become nourishing meals. If lions or wolves seek and pull down sick animals, disease never gets the chance to spread. I suppose it's a good thing I'm not an antelope or I'd be a goner by now.

Suffering is not something that lingers in the natural world. On the whole predators have to kill so fast that animals are dispatched quickly. People always ask why God allows suffering, especially amongst the innocent, but I don't think it was in his original plan. It's clear that mankind is largely to blame.

Perhaps God should never have given us free choice, but then we would be locked in like the plants. No, unfortunately we have free choice to hurt others. The damage is liable to build up and accumulate not only in our own lives but over centuries.

This poor old world must be like a computer that desperately needs de-fragging.

12th November ~ Another nightmare. I woke up in a terrible sweat. This time no one had ears. It was awful. Human beings look worse earless than cats do. In the dream I kept trying to put on my sunglasses but there was nothing to prop them up. I don't normally think about such things.

Johnty has bought the smartest black car you have ever seen. As he uses a company car for work, Tamzin and Maud are whizzing round in it. They look rather like Dick Dastardly and Mutley from *The Way Out Wacky Races*. 'The people at the newsagents really shift.'

'Inside the shop?'

'Yes, they see me getting out of the motor in my tatty riding clothes with a bull-terrier, and scurry.'

'Why is this?'

'They think I'm a drug dealer.' She's terribly pleased. So is Maud.

I had a meeting (at Tamzin's kitchen table) with Rebecca who approved the ideas and sketches for the book on gravity for seven to eight-year-olds. We kept getting diverted as she was fascinated by the concept of earlessness. I showed her the meteorite, which was sitting on its cushion for all to admire. 'That,' she said, 'is just a lump of iron pyrites. A rude looking one.' Do Tamzin and I have friends with similar mindsets?

Johnty told me that Dr. Loveday had confirmed that his aches and the hung-over feeling are indeed symptoms of intolerance to the chemical woodworm killer. She has told him to keep off wheat and yeasty foods, like mushrooms, and has given him a pile of supplements too. She told him that although M.E. is usually triggered by a virus, notably chicken pox, it seems accidents, immunisations – especially Hepatitis B, unremitting stress and exposure to chemicals like organophosphates can also set it off.

13th November ~ I saw Mikie today. He says that the last six weeks have been the worst of his life. He's coming under a lot of criticism from those looking in on the racing world, condemned for working in an industry fuelled by gambling. I think setting up his yard has been immensely tough. He said he turned a corner though two days ago; saw the way ahead. He's definitely been given the strength and determination to continue and now has new projects planned.

Mikie is working under tremendous strain and pressure. He has become an advert for 'Suffering leads to perseverance, which builds character, which leads to Hope.'

'The amazing thing is that I asked God to use my weaknesses and he does. In actively overcoming the problems I'm being refined and strengthened by all this.'

'Yes, I think you have a new dignity,' I said.

'I've grown up, you mean,' he said, laughing.

'Keep on looking ahead.'

'I do thank God for all this, despite the pain.'

He's hardly in an enviable place yet, but he knows our spiritual lives are a reality. I admire him. I know that on top of everything else he's in agony from his broken back.

I'm beginning to understand how suffering can be the foreshadow of maturity.

14th November ~ Trying on dresses day. Tamzin told me I am too old to be wearing cast-offs then gave me a whole pile of her clothes. I certainly don't look mature. Perry would be horrified.

15th November ~ I've made it to a wedding at last. Guy and Tanya's wedding. Diana and I wove our way through the London rain, under her gold umbrella, to a very smart reception held at Temple. The only thing that went wrong was that the groom had, like Paddy, broken his leg so badly he couldn't walk and had to be pushed about in a wicker bath-chair. The best man had organised a splodge-gun war for Guy's stag weekend and it was just too rigorous. All the same, I have a feeling that what happened was that Guy just fell over a straw bale.

I could hardly walk either. I met a friend, who works on *Newsnight,* who's planning a trip around Namibia. When I said I'd love to come she gave me very sideways looks. But I was thrilled to make the wedding and see all my old university friends. Alastair was looking very red.

'Are you read all over?'

'Yes,' he said shyly.

'Like a newspaper?'

'Yes, I am.'

'What happened?'

'I was having a bath when the Ajax bath scouring stuff fell in. I took out the plastic bottle, so I didn't think it would matter, but it has. I'm stinging all over.' I didn't know what to suggest. Rose thought he'd better sit in a bowl of milk.

16th November ~ Made it to church. I reckon I've had a shortfall in my understanding and appreciation of Holy Communion. '...this is my body, which is *broken* for you.'[xvi] He was physically broken for me and shed blood in mind and body for my sin. We need to accept this and appreciate that it's a victory because it makes the forgiveness of our sins legal and a physical reality. Mikie has helped me see that I too must be broken, must deeply repent in order to be worthy to receive this grace. 'But Lord, are you honoured by our repetitive prayers, by the Anglican liturgy?'

'Yes, the love shines through like light into heaven.'

17th November ~ I woke up this morning thinking, 'I don't know what I can do but I've got to be where God wants me to be.' But, 'What am I going to do with the rest of my life? Where do ideas come from? Where does our insight originate?'

'Don't copy the behaviour and customs of this world, but let God transform you into a new person by changing the way you think. Then you will know what God wants you to do, and you will know how good and pleasing and perfect his will really is.' from *Romans, chapter 12*

I suppose that entails having to dump certain mindsets and draw away from bad influences. I'm beginning to realise just how Satan works. He doesn't do anything. He can only do things through us, by tempting us, sowing ideas in our minds. He operates through little things like criticism, which hardly seem like sins but can end up being bossy and mean, negative to our relationships. It's through us he can abuse others and spread corruption until whole countries are seeped in depravity. But he relies on our action. Or inaction.

Satan must be gambling on us all the time. 'Will she lie? And if she does how far will the deceit spread? How many dominoes will fall?' He must be waiting to see the outcome of the gunk he's invested in us, and all the hurt and rejection we've received at the hands of other people.

So, why doesn't God intervene? Free choice. Because it's our responsibility to stand against the devil. Or tell him to go away, like Jesus did in the wilderness.

Pippa said this is a little too much for her to digest right now, but she'll think about it. She drove me down to

Gloucestershire and is sleeping in the little spare bed in my room. 'Oh good,' she said, pulling back the bedspread. 'I can tell all my friends I've been sleeping with Brian.' He was a character from the *Magic Roundabout* and an icon of our childhood. A snail. He had a red shell and wore a pork pie hat. His smiling, snaily self is printed on the pillowcase.

18th November ~ 'Be glad for all God is planning for you. Be patient in trouble, and always be prayerful.' *Romans, chapter 12 verse 12*

There has been an incident in Quilton-on-Trim. Diana, who was staying with Rose and Matthew after the wedding, was woken up by what sounded terribly like burglars. As they often let tramps sleep in the church meeting rooms below their part of the house, they weren't a bit concerned and told her to go back to bed. 'Well, hang on,' said Diana looking out of Augustus' bedroom window. 'A man's trying to break your front door down with a spade.' Matthew grabbed his shotgun.

'I'm going to shoot him in the leg,' he said, loading cartridges at the top of the stairs and using words curates aren't meant to use.

'No, don't,' Rose pleaded, jumping up and down, frantically hoping that if she made a big stamping noise it would frighten away what now seemed to be a whole gang trying to batter their way in.

'Stand back.' Matthew was just about to fire when the burglar looked up, saw Diana hanging out of the upstairs window and ran.

'He's making a getaway,' she yelled, hurtling down the landing. And Matthew decided to give chase. He grabbed his car keys and disappeared into the frosty night, clutching his lethal weapon. (Rose had given it to him for a wedding present.) He didn't manage to find the burglar at all, only the Police whom Diana had alerted.

'You're not by any chance in possession of a firearm are you, Vicar?' asked the constable, peering into the car and markedly giving Matthew the benefit of the doubt. 'Because if you were, Sir, it would be yourself I would have to arrest.'

'Are you suggesting I should return to bed?'

'Yes, Sir, I'm sure the nation will be needing you in prison one day,' said the policeman, thinking himself very amusing, 'but as a chaplain in full possession of the keys.'

When Matthew returned, frozen stiff and grumpy, Diana told him that it was just as well he didn't shoot at the bottom half of the door because the man breaking in had been bending down. He would have shot him in the head.

19th November ~ I woke up to the sound of snoring and saw that there was a man asleep in the single bed in my room. Not another tramp. I didn't know what to do.

I was busy sneaking past to find Dad to help with the situation, when I discovered the lump was James. He was sound asleep, wearing a dinner jacket and a bow tie.

I do think we should improve the security situation at home. Dad must have forgotten to lock the front door. James was driving back from a party and felt so tired when he reached Cirencester that he thought he couldn't possibly make it all the way home and tried our house instead. He just walked up to my bedroom in the middle of the night, if you please, and curled up in my spare bed. That's for my girlfriends to use. I know we're meant to welcome strangers but there is a limit. He could have been some maniac with a spade; after all Matthew seems to come across them all the time.

Rebecca declared she wasn't a bit surprised to hear about my nocturnal visitor and I'm lucky it was only James; he could have brought a horde of friends. He did. We found Alastair in Mary-Dieu's room. With nothing on. He wouldn't come out from under the bedclothes.

'What's my dinner jacket doing hanging out on the line?' Dad asked coming into the kitchen where James and Alastair were busy eating scrambled eggs and charming Mum. 'It's in a terrible state.'

'Ah well, Umm, I was going to explain about that. I got pushed into a pond,' Alastair said, rising to his feet and not knowing where to look. That's why they stopped in the middle of the night; he'd been soaking wet.

When Al eventually got out of bed Mum lent him some of Dad's clothes and had his underclothes going round in the washing machine, but what she didn't realise was that he'd been wearing Dad's dinner jacket in the first place. He'd borrowed it ages ago.

After they left I sat down to start drawing again. Rebecca says she likes the book with the vegetables. I'm sure it's the meaning that I've put into the artwork. I know exactly what being a vegetable feels like. She's given me a second one to illustrate, which is about steam and energy. I'm not sure how I can draw energy and we don't have a publisher but we might as well give it a go. 'Alastair didn't get pushed; he jumped into the swimming pool and swam about.'

'But it must've been freezing.'

'Oh, yes. He said his willy shrank to almost nothing.' So has my father's dinner jacket.

20th November ~ When he was a student, Alastair, driving back home on his moped after a party, skidded to a halt in the snow and was unable to get the machine started again. He spent the rest of the night sleeping on a traffic island wearing nothing warmer than a tweed jacket and corduroy trousers. His housemates told me that a milkman found him at 5.00am. He was fine, apart from having run out of petrol.

A year later, Diana had a birthday party in the middle of a traffic roundabout. Quite a lot of us sat there having a picnic with all the traffic whizzing round. Alastair managed to kidnap a lollipop lady, who ended up getting rather sloshed as she'd never tasted Pimms before and gulped down too much. Why she trusted him for five minutes I've no idea; Al was wearing the most regrettable pair of plus-fours. Mind you, I was wearing something that looked like an Andy Pandy suit. We were all very silly and found it amusing because a roundabout was an unusual place to be. I feel I'm sort of sitting in the middle of one now. Everyone I know is zooming about, going somewhere.

But it's no longer funny. I don't seem to be getting anywhere. I'm just drawing a boiling kettle for Rebecca.

The world beyond my window is changing. The leaves have fallen off the cherry tree and the moss and twigs are now shining in the moonlight. There is a sharp frost and a huge moon reflected in the still waters of the lake. Everything looks dead, but it isn't. It's just lying dormant. Like me.

21st November ~ Another horrid and terrifying nightmare. It was like a glimpse of hell. How easy it is to fall into hell right here and now. Heck. Why does Satan want to govern my life? I'm not important. I suppose it's in his nature to kick us when we are down.

What's confusing is that the devil does 'good' things. He does. He's a master salesman. He brings people into money and makes them feel good but it's just bait for the trap. There's no fulfilment. He can heal us of all sorts of things, but it won't last. He can bring romantic love into your life when you're committed to someone else but the consequences rip lives apart.

We don't like being caught but if we can get the better of our pride and admit we've failed we beat Satan. We regain lost ground and more. If I can overcome fear, if I can get the better of depression and rejection, ousting bitterness and resentment, if I can draw on what I know rather than what I feel without ignoring my conscience, then I'll have gained true strength. I will have shut out Satan. And I might just be of use to God.

22nd November ~ Robin came round at suppertime to find me looking a bit squiffy after another magnesium injection. Daisy was crying and Mary-Dieu was in a furious temper. We were all sitting round our dining room table, trying to eat supper. 'Don't shake that baby,' she yelled. 'She'll throw up.' I passed Daisy back.

'And what do you do?' Mum asked Robin, trying to normalise the conversation.

'Well, I'm, er, an investor. I buy and sell stocks and shares.'

'I'm getting a job,' Mary-Dieu declared.

'Oh yes, Darling?' Mum asked.

'I'm going to work for Asda.' (ASDA superstore.)

'In what department?' Robin inquired politely.

'On the till,' she said banging her fist down on the table. 'I'm going to start at the bottom and work my way to the top.'

'I'll tell the Chairman,' Robin said quickly. He later told me he'd just bought a substantial amount of their shares, and that the Chairman was a great friend of his.

Robin had come to drive me to Shropshire where he has invited me to stay for the weekend. He kindly offered to drop Mary-Dieu back in Gloucester on the way. When we stopped at a filling station, she asked him if he could get her a loaf of bread from the kiosk. He wouldn't let her pay. She suddenly went very quiet, touched by his gentleness and consideration.

Robin's family have a massive house once owned by Clive of India. I've always felt very healthy there, but it is quite chilly. I bought him a bottle of cherry brandy, for warmth, and a shepherd's crook made at Doug's walking stick factory. He has a flock of fifty sheep, only he's always losing them. He calls them 'The lost sheep of Israel'.

'You're in the room full of wheelchairs and elephants,' he told me. I was too. It's a bit complicated explaining why.

23rd November ~ Although there was a thick frost, Robin was up at 7.00am, outside rowing in the summerhouse (on his rowing machine) and making strange noises. 'I'm praying for my godchildren.' He has about fifteen and says that the only way to cram everything into his life is to do two things at once. 'Have to keep fit spiritually and physically at the same time.' I'd forgotten he used to row for Oxford.

Robin made me look at his graveyard. We trudged up through the dripping woods with his three golden retrievers bounding about and looked. There it was; a graveyard for Morris Minors. He also owns eight living ones.

I though I saw a dead body hanging in the pantry. In fact I nearly walked into it, only it turned out to be a pig's leg that had been cured for bacon. Robin was very proud of its origin. 'I was going down a lane on my motorbike and came across a piglet. It looked lost, so I put it in my pannier and got our neighbour to fatten it up on scraps.' So we ate bacon (rather fatty ~ actually almost solid fat) and some cheese ~ Stilton that Robin found in the compost bucket. He was really cross that one of his sisters had thrown it away.

Rain set in. 'Sugar.' (Robin never swears.) 'I was hoping for a frost. I want the lake to freeze over so I can see what it's like to go skating in a Morris.' (His car.) Instead he went off to an auction, his favourite thing in the world, and I went to bed with a lovely hot water bottle. They had smooth linen sheets and old horsehair mattresses, the kind you sink into. I lay looking at the elephants, which are on the wallpaper, thinking about Satan. He must want as many recruits as he can get. I don't suppose he's fussy, but I bet he's looking for people with a deep sense of commitment. 'What would I do to me if I was the devil?'

As far as I can see, there are a number of strategies he might try that don't involve sin at all. Here's one example: he'll try to distract me from reading my Bible. Of course. He doesn't want me to grow or gain direction from it – especially if the word of God is a weapon I can take up and use against him.

'What would I do to me if I was the devil?'

He'll exploit any weakness I have, won't he? Go for my Achilles' heel. But I've repented of stuff like self-pity that might have given him a crack to squeeze into. Is there something more?

I found Robin sitting at the kitchen table in a bobble hat with tears pouring down his face. He was listening to *The Archers* and roaring with laughter, dealing with an enormous mound of Brussels sprouts. He declared that he'd bought a wooden wheelbarrow, an old bike (he has about fifty already), a 'fridge-freezer and an entire 'seventies style fitted kitchen. (He managed to strap all this onto the back of a Morris pick-up but no one is sure where he's going to put it now.) He also bought an electric juice extractor for me. Kind. I asked him about my satanic theories, or rather theories about Satan's strategies.

'Well, it's clear he doesn't want anyone to go to church. Are you coming tomorrow?'

24th November ~ Robin strode off to the village church in his gumboots and a terrible temper. He'd just discovered that his mother had told an old man in the village that he, Robin, did not want to buy the Morris Traveller the old boy had treasured all his life. 'I did, it was immaculate, a beauty.' It has been sold to an outsider.

The vicar spoke about sin. He said it originally meant 'missing the target'. Ah well, in that case distraction or giving in to distraction is sin. So is giving in to anger and letting it breed condemnation, Robin. (He's still seething, especially as his mother is laughing about the whole thing.) Can anger disintegrate your health? I suppose it can give you a heart attack.

There was a great deal of shouting at lunch, not because anyone was particularly annoyed but because Robin's father has become very deaf. It was quite catching and soon everyone was shouting at everyone, and everyone got cross. The family is so big it was all rather daunting. Robin said it's always like this. They opened the house to the public once. A friend of his, who was put in charge of showing people round, said that one party peered into the dining room when they were eating and asked,

'Is it a play?'

25th November ~ I went to see my doctor again. We reckon I'm beginning to improve at last. I think it's the magnesium injections. *The Lancet* article reports favourable results, but I've not been able to find out why. Obviously Mary Loveday's treatment, my diet and the care I've been receiving must have been helping me too. I thanked my G.P. for being so supportive. It must be awful being a doctor, when you have to see ill people all day long and listen endlessly to their complaints without ever getting thanked.

Rose says vicars don't get much thanks either and they end up doing the most peculiar things. 'People never appreciate that it can be a twenty-four hour job,' she said sighing. 'Matthew was up most of last night.' They had gone to bed early but were woken at midnight by the telephone ringing determinedly.

'A man is rising from the dead.' An hysterical female was virtually screaming into the receiver.

'Rubbish,' said Matthew.

'I tell you, a naked man is emerging from a grave.'

'Calm down, you're probably just having a nightmare.'

'Look out of the window and see for yourself.' Matthew looked and, sure enough, a completely naked man was wriggling out of a squarish sort of tomb in the churchyard. The scene was illuminated clearly by the streetlights. He was holding a knife and fork.

'OK,' said Matthew, 'I'll deal with this.' It transpired that the man was retarded and had escaped from an institution. He'd decided to explore the tombs to see if he might make a little house out of one of them. Matthew found he'd brought blankets with him and all sorts of useful domestic items but then had got stuck inside. The only way the man could think of getting out was to take off all his clothes to make himself smaller.

Robin loved hearing about this and says he can't wait to get Matthias (as he calls Matthew) to give another talk at his church. Last time he gave a sermon in Shropshire Matthew spoke so *loudly* none of us could actually listen, apart from Robin's father who could hear every word and enjoyed it enormously.

I'm very embarrassed because Mum made Robin write a reference for Mary-Dieu. It's not as if he's ever employed her. He said it would be a pleasure and proceeded to dictate, 'To whom it may concern …She is an honest person and loving mother, with a very strong personality. I would consider her well able to cope with a challenging position utilising her abilities of dealing with people in a consistent and effective manner.' (ie: if they cross her she'll bob 'em one.)

26th November ~ Dad took me to Harley Street for more tests. In the waiting room was an issue of *Newsweek*, published in November 1990, which has a seven-page article on chronic fatigue syndrome. It seems to be massive in America with documented epidemics breaking out. In 1984 two hundred people went down with it in Incline Village on the north shore of Lake Tahoe in Nevada, and a year later dozens more became sick in a little town called Lyndonville on Lake Ontario. It has become 'a major public health concern', as the epidemiologists say. 'Officials at the Atlanta-based Centers for Disease Control and Prevention, the federal agency responsible for tracking infectious diseases, say they receive 1,000 to 2,000 calls about the condition every month.' (Golly, I feel as if I'm in a movie now.) While they label it 'the disease of the '90s' they say it's 'turned up spasmodically and in local clusters for more than a century,' claiming that both Florence Nightingale and Charles Darwin may have suffered.[14]

One thing's clear: I seem to be getting away with a very mild version of what can be a terrifyingly disabling condition. An enormous amount of patients seem to become unable to move for years on end or mistakenly bunged in psychiatric hospitals.

27th November ~ Bed. Daisy staying, Mary Dieu upset. More livid phone calls. It's difficult to know what to do except act as a sounding board for her. She proudly informed us that she has been to see her Psychiatrist, Dr. Knight-Webb. Mum and Dad know that he too is at a complete loss. I was wondering if she has chronic fatigue. Could it possibly be a long-term effect of polio, which she had in Vietnam when she was eighteen months old? She has ardent lassitude, sleep disorders and these irrational feelings of anger but I don't think a M.E. patient could watch so much television. But then not all the symptoms of M.E. are the same.

The good doctor had managed to persuade the Social Services to send a cleaner round to Mary-Dieu's basement, but the lady wasn't as long suffering as Mum and the arrangement sadly dissolved. The prognosis is that she'll require parental help and guidance for the next five years. If she accepts it. We are in for the long haul.

I've decided that anger, in being a natural release, is probably a very healthy way of dissipating stress, so it could be good for you but it's not much fun for those of us who have to endure the shrieking. I wish people would find non-destructive ways of channelling it. Mary-Dieu would be tremendous at fighting a cause. I'm going to mention this theory to Robin.

It's icy cold but Dad doesn't think our lake will freeze over yet. It did one year. We didn't exactly drive a Morris Minor over it but Dad was longing to try out an ice sledge he'd bought in Norway. It was like a chair on runners. He pushed Perry out over the ice and they sped up to the far end where it's quite shallow. Only then the ice cracked. Dad fell in, still holding the sledge, and ended up standing up to his chest in freezing water, sinking into the mud and unable to get out. He's still grieved that Perry didn't even get one toe wet. She'd managed to elegantly leap to the bank. Typical.

Dad caught poachers shooting out the windows of the wooden caravan in the field beyond the lake last year. When he walked over to explain that the land was designated as a nature reserve they shot at his feet with an automatic .22 rifle. He said he began to get worried, only just then Albert, who had also heard the shooting, emerged out of the mist behind Dad looking so huge, dark and ferocious, that the poachers took one look at him and retreated. Back on the road, they beat up what they thought was Dad's car. Only it wasn't, it belonged to a rambler.

28th November ~ Bed. All day. Feeling grumbly, so took Rose's advice and read Jackie Pullinger's book *Chasing the Dragon* again. She took a boat from England to Hong Kong in her early twenties and worked as a missionary in the Walled City with members of Triad gangs and others who sold themselves to opium. One of the Chinese prisoners she met defined sin as 'walking your own road.'

Mum is in a state about the neighbour's dog. Not the six sausage dogs with their slipped discs who might actually be in pain, but a big Rottweiler or something that appears to be locked inside a house where no one actually lives. The place is owned by a property developer who hasn't been around for ages. Mum has been suspicious about him ever since Albert announced that he'd been contracted to fit every bathroom with a bidet.

'I went to deliver the parish magazine three days ago,' (wanting to have a good snoop, I bet) 'and no one seemed to be around. The dog just barked and barked and barked,' Mum said getting annoyed. 'It's still barking, but I'm worried that no one has been to feed it. I can't stand it when people neglect their animals,' she went on. 'That wretched property developer, they're all the same. Just interested in money. The house must be worth a million pounds but does he care about a starving animal? Oh no.'

29th November ~ Daisy is still staying. She's quite hard work now but just adorable, blossoming every day as she discovers more about the world. I love her so much. Her greatest thing is to run and fling herself into my arms with complete abandon and absolute trust, her face shining and full of laughter. I feel that such should be our relationship with God.

Perry said she's far too busy to bring Atalanta over to play this week. 'I'm giving two dinner parties.'

'Oh, just make some salads and order takeaway pizzas.'

'It's a good thing you're not an Army wife.'

Perry even keeps a book with the menus and seating plans used at every party. A seating plan is not something I've ever devised.

Mum is still anxious about the dog next door. It's barking frantically, so it must be alive, but she says that she has nightmares worrying about it that make her toss and turn all night long. She wants to break into the house to feed it, which I don't think is advisable.

30th November ~ Bed. Daisy is with me. She's lovely. I most certainly am not; but Mum is busy. The RSPCA man, the Police and a carpenter have been summoned: Operation Dog Rescue. When they finally got inside the house there was no dog at all; just a tape recorder and two speakers. It was obviously a device triggered by anyone walking up to the front door, aimed at scaring off burglars.

Stars,
moons
planets

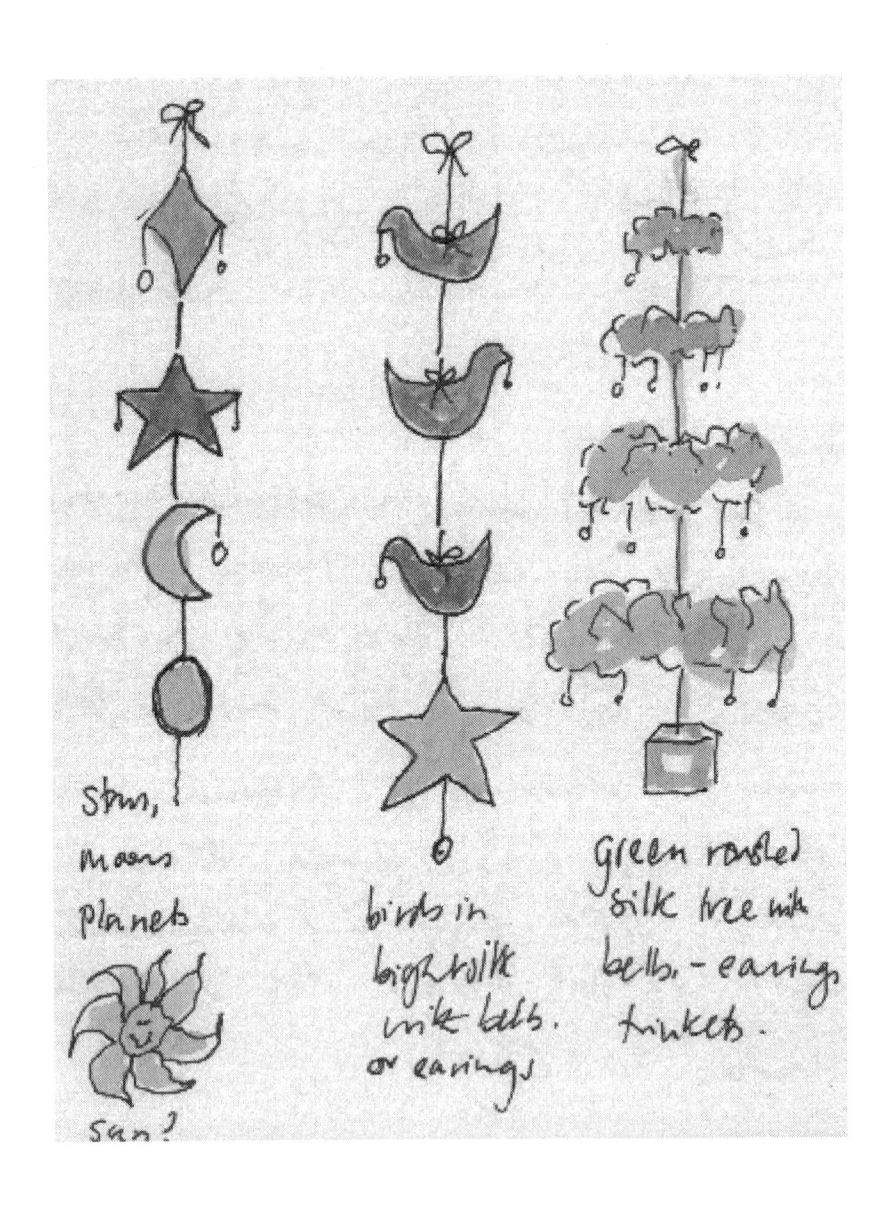

sun?

birds in
bright silk
with bells.
or earings

green rustled
silk tree with
bells, - earings
trinkets.

DECEMBER ~ He comes with healing in his wings

1st December ~

James came to lunch. We had succulent beef with crisp roast parsnips and creamy mashed potato with delicious red wine. Mum got quite tipsy. She produced crème caramel for pudding, which we ate with thin French biscuits, only Jake got mine as it fell on the floor.

James was completely perplexed by Daisy, but gallantly helped her into a boiler-suit and we took it in turns to push her down the valley, while the dogs bounded about in the field. It was rather a soggy day and dead leaves kept getting wound up in the buggy wheels. James says his contract with the *BBC* is coming to an end soon too. It's not a very good time of year to look for further employment in the film industry, but he's buying the rights to Bill Bryson's autobiography and is going to try and forge ahead as an independent producer. I know how hard that can be.

Mum went off to Evensong, going on about the new curate being 'induced' and the church being 'inoculated' by the bishop. She was thrilled to be reading the lesson to them all. 'I've got to tell them about the circumcised and the uncircumcised,' she declared with glee. I decided I would rather not go but am left alone, feeling vague and dysfunctional, like a winter turnip.

Later: Mum returned from church saying that it had all been very embarrassing.

'I'm not surprised, you were longing for a reaction.'

'No, not the reading.' It had been a special service put on for the bishop and everyone was on their best behaviour. Mum had been sitting at the side of the church near where the coffee gets set out. The urn was boiling away rather furiously during the last hymn, creating clouds of steam, so Mum decided to take things into her own hands and turn it off. Instead of turning down the knob on the side of the urn she reached down and pulled out the electric plug. There was a huge noise. A great, 'neeear-huff' and everyone stopped singing. She'd also, inadvertently, turned off the organ. Everyone thought a naughty child had done it on purpose.

2nd December ~ Bed mostly, wrote letters. Mum took Dais, Daze her father calls her now, back to a grumpy Mary-Dieu. It's still squelchy outside; mud everywhere. I made artichoke soup and dug leeks out of the vegetable garden. They're remarkably resilient, these winter vegetables. Not unlike Mum. She went on to be a clown in Gloucester for *Help the Aged* and then gave a talk at a J.P. course in Cirencester in the afternoon. 'What they all wanted to hear about was the time when those men beat up the rambler's car outside our house.' I was making her tea, which she always needs in huge quantities whenever she gets in. 'They all asked if I was worried about walking around on my own here. I explained that if anyone threatened me Bee would rip them to shreds.' She would too. Female otters can be very protective. Tamzin had a row with Mum on the lawn once and Bee bit her so hard she still has scars on her leg. 'Yes, well Tamzin shouldn't have been so beastly to me; you children attack me the whole time, I'm terrified of you.'

3rd December ~ Went over to Nicola's house and walked her Rosie-baby in an enormous old-fashioned pram through the winter parkland at Carlton where they live. I wish I had one of these contraptions for Daisy; it's much easier to push than a pushchair. It has fantastic suspension.

Fortunately we spent most of the time outside. I'd forgotten what artichoke soup can do to a body. We came across Nicola's boss, Lord Suffolk, who was putting his aeroplane away in a hanger. 'I want you back at work soon,' he shouted. 'Remember the Chinese only get three days' maternity leave.'

'Oh, no,' said Nicola calmly, 'I think they get three hours.' I was rather impressed. I would have taken great offence, but no amount of teasing seems to rile her, and she seems unfazed by the exhausting prospect of motherhood.

'Just don't let me become boring about it, Sophie. We had a woman over for dinner and all she could talk of were *her* children, *her* husband and *her* house.'

'Perhaps she has post-natal depression.'

'I don't think so.'

'It's very common you know,' said I, the girl who has now read every leaflet on depression there is.

'In that case it's a little drawn out,' Nicola responded. 'Her children are aged eleven and thirteen.'

Dick Dastardly rang this evening, sounding rather shattered. 'You cannot imagine what happened today...' Driving back from the stables Tamzin came across a lorry stuck right across the road. A huge rescue vehicle, with a crane on top, was trying to get it out of the ditch. 'The man said, "Another five minutes, Love; OK?" Well, it wasn't, and I felt like saying 'I'm not your Love', but of course I just nodded and waited.' Tamzin watched while the lorry was extracted and went on its way. The rescue vehicle started to move forward, towards her new Audi Quatro, with its crane still fully extended. 'I thought it was liable to hit the overhead cables so I pointed upwards. The driver just waved back cheerfully giving me the thumbs up sign.' To her horror the crane hit the branch of a beech tree, which fell on the electricity cables. 'There was a crack and a blue rainbow arched into the sky, sparks flying everywhere.' She thought the cable was going to hit her. 'I slammed my foot down on the accelerator, swung up on the verge, through an open gate and into a field, *Starsky and Hutch* style. I just kept driving, bouncing across the grass towards what turned out to be a school on the other side.' She skidded to a stop, got out, looked at the teacher on playground duty and burst into tears. 'They must think I'm completely neurotic; I'll never be able to send my children there.'

How odd. All these things falling on top of our cars: first the barrier coming down on the roof of my Chrysler Sunbeam, then Rose's little adventure in the supermarket car park and now this. In fact it's been a whole year of accidents: I've never known so many.

4th December ~ Ill with a bug. Drat and double drat; I must still have low resistance. My strength has evaporated. Had to cancel everything I'd planned to do, yet again.

5th December ~ Bed. My concentration has deteriorated to a span of fifteen minutes; I'm back to reading no more than one paragraph of a book at a time. I feel as if I'm wading across an estuary but survive on the knowledge that, come hell or high water, as Rose says, the Lord will always be there.

6th December ~ Bed, wondering if I shall ever get better, whether I'll be stuck with this wretched syndrome for years. Spent all my energy looking for my diary, only to find it was down my own bed. Robin thought I might enjoy reading the *Book of Job*. I managed two chapters. At least I haven't succumbed to a terrible case of boils.[xvii]

7th December ~ Bed. I can understand why people take their lives in despair, but I refuse to sink into the mud again. I'm not going to give up now or ever. I must draw on what I know rather than how I feel; problem is I feel terrible. Thoroughly uncomfortable.

8th December ~ Bed. Had to cancel lunch with Rebecca's Aunt Blottie. I'm fed up with this *unrelenting* fatigue, with lying in bed twenty-two hours a day. Will it never end?

9th December ~ Bed, but the mists are rising. Am regaining limited use of my mind. I'm trying to ignore the physical and claim a bright new future.

10th December ~ Bed, but pottering around a bit. Tamzin's doctor says it's good to potter. I'm trying to think of something amusing to do.

I've got it. Not something at all amusing but an article on dentistry. It says in yesterday's paper that the mercury in amalgam fillings can leak into your body and could be responsible for fatigue. I've got loads of fillings. I bet this is the solution. I rang my dentist straight away and asked if he could take the whole lot out.

'Are you allergic to metals?'

'Metal?'

'Do you get a reaction to wearing silver jewellery?'

'No.'

'Well, you're fine then,' my dentist said, explaining, 'the mercury in amalgam fillings is so bound up in the silver that it can't possibly get into your body. The substance has been used for a hundred years, does an excellent job and is perfectly safe.' He thought that the article in the paper was hype, based on generating business for private, cosmetic dentists who extol a full change to white fillings, which aren't so durable. He says he'll send me an article on the truth.[15]

'How's Call-me-Daphne?'

'She's fine.' Daphne is Mum. Nicola said at least she's not called 'Toni-speaking' like her mother.

11th December ~ Up and about. In fact I went to a party, held for some friends of mine who live in Papua New Guinea and are over here for Christmas. They run a scientific research station near Madang and once had me to stay. It was wonderful in Papua New Guinea. I spent my time snorkelling and helped an Oxford entomologist collect gall wasps. He promised to call one after me. A little *something nevilli*. We also went out in a banana boat to collect ant plants, a subject on which my friend Dr. Jebb has a PhD.

The Trobriand Islanders take each other canoe loads of yams when they go visiting; it's only polite. I reckoned Papua New Guinea was close enough for people to have the same customs so took along the longest yam I could find at the market. As a joke. The Jebbs just looked at me very oddly, as if I'd arrived with the groceries.

I was introduced to a chap who declared himself to be a consultant on the preservation of historic buildings. He has dogs he calls 'The Rot Hounds' ~ Spaniels and an old Labrador called Candy he has trained to sniff out dry rot. He knew all about woodworm and said that there's no point spraying it or even treating dry rot with chemicals. 'Terrible waste of money,' he said. Apparently, if you get rid of any damp source, heat and ventilate a house properly, then insects, moulds and fungi destroying buildings can't survive. And supposedly the human inhabitants will.

12th December ~ I've decided to make everyone presents this Christmas. All those with babies are getting sheep made out of black felt and sheepskin off-cuts that I bought in the Lake District. At the moment I just have naked black sheep all over my bed, but the idea is to string them up on a mobile and have them jumping fences. It's contrived as a device to help get the babies off to sleep.

13th December ~ Rebecca's Aunt Blottie has asked me to draw cartoons for a cookery book aimed at students. I have set to, drawing scenes from my own college life. Diana is the star. She always used to make amusing things like stuffed sausages. I would cheat and buy crabs stuffed by the fish shop man for

50p each. Rose, Diana and I all read Anthropology together. Once we decided to have a hunter-gatherer feast. It was a great success. Rose made everyone eat dandelion leaf salad and walnuts. Alastair wanted us to eat venison off the table. Someone bought a packet of *Fox's Glacier Mints*, which I thought was cheating until he explained that they were from the Eskimos, who are classified as hunter-gathers along with Pygmies and Bushmen. It seemed a bit complicated to draw this for the cookery book. The caption said, 'Keep it simple', so I drew Diana, with her curly hair, having seated each of her dinner guests in front of an open tin of baked beans. I hope she won't be insulted. The next illustration was of me:

14th December ~ I've just had a thought: hunter-gatherers always have a sleep in the middle of the day if they can. If man was originally designed to have two sleeps a day, why don't we now? The Spanish do. Mum always takes an afternoon rest. The dog certainly does. I used to yearn for a lie-down after lunch at work. Perhaps if I'd had the nerve to install a bed in my office and taken thirty-minute kips I might not have conked out. Alastair says I'm right (for once). He said he saw a programme about old people and all those who achieved great longevity slept at some time during the day. He doesn't. He works harder than anyone else I know. He says that I'll never guess but he's been in the Shetland Isles to recce a film about otters mating. They had very little daylight but he said it was spectacular going out with the fishing boats because so many birds flock around the catch. It must have been freezing. I felt cold just thinking about it.

15th December ~ What is happening? Why the waiting? God is probably waiting for me and I'm waiting for God. I certainly don't need any more sleep. Is God using time to reveal something obvious?

I know it's absurd, but I can't help wondering if there's anything that I've done to deserve this. Could it still be unforgiveness? Am I being silly? If you're eaten up by jealousy or resentment it's bound to exacerbate any weakness and could be the root of a stress-related condition. But can our sin cause death through ill health? I suppose gluttony could lead you to explode.

Robin says that disease is endemic in our fallen world, that it's not my fault that I have M.E. 'The world is a world with illness in it. Innocent children and animals get ill through no fault of their own.' But injury can be caused by sin. Someone else's negligence can do you in. A housewife could get frazzled if some idiot brought an overhead cable down onto her car. If we gad about like hooligans, we can hurt ourselves falling over straw bales but is there any sickness that is the direct result of someone's wrongdoing?

'Wrongdoing can't *cause* disease but it can spread it, otherwise we wouldn't be worried about biological warfare. Something like hepatitis might not be *caused* by sin, but it can be spread by irresponsible behaviour, by drug addicts sharing needles. Addictions,' he went on, 'commonly cause us to abuse our own bodies.' It's dawning on me that my addiction had been to work; and that overwork, which I'd agreed to, contributed to dragging down my health.

And I've been busy forgiving everybody I can think of, just in case. I rang Grizelda, not because I need to forgive her but to see how Paddy was, only I couldn't stop yawning. So rude. We started talking about sleep. She says that human growth hormones are released about forty minutes after you fall asleep and that it's a very good idea to take a nap at some point during the day. As long as you don't sleep for more than an hour, it shouldn't stop you getting to sleep at night.

'Gosh, how did you know?'

'A paediatric endocrinologist told me. You grow more during the summer.'

I have no idea what an endocrinologist is or does.

16th December ~ Rebecca is leaving the completed ~ and fully illustrated ~ science books with her aunt for publication and is off to the southern hemisphere. It's going to be difficult for her to work as a cook without any sense of taste or smell but she should have fun. Sarah-Jane is moving to new territory; the Waterberg mountains, about three hours north of Johannesburg. It's wild and undeveloped. I wish I could go too. I've promised to write.

Mum is in a prickly mood. She'd been asked if her otters would appear in a feature film. Thinking this would be akin to a wholesome natural history programme, she agreed. (In great excitement.) But, this was not the case. She was asked to bring Bee to meet the producer. Now Mum is very keen indeed on meeting producers, and openly admits she would rather like a part herself, but came back looking disconcerted. 'He turned out to be a sweaty, overweight Californian with revolting greasy hair scraped across his bald head and very bad breath. He's creating,' she went on, 'a sparkling *extravaganza* full of visual effects with animals dressed up as humans. I think it all sounds very dubious.' He wanted Bee to wear a tutu.

"*Ain't it cute?*" he said. "*Say! Does this little critter climb trees?*" S t u p i d man. What an ignoramus to think that an otter would think of climbing a tree.' Daphne was not pleased. 'He wanted to do all sorts of things with prosthetics. I will not have my animals exposed to such atrocities. A tutu? Can you imagine?' There's no arguing with her. 'They're wild animals and should be respected as such, even if they do happen to be very tame.'

Bee didn't get the part in the end. They cast a possum.

17th December ~ Blottie loves the cookery book cartoons and has kindly given me £100 for them. She thinks the sheep mobiles are brilliant. Perhaps I could patent them as a foil for insomnia and make a million. I've decided that forgiveness cancels sin because it begins to undo its effect.

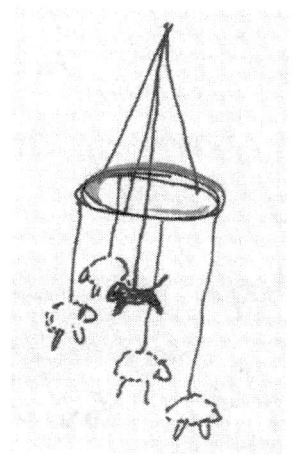

18th December ~ Why do sheep keep coming into my life? I've been reading a book about a sheep farmer in Kenya.[16] One year his animals kept getting ill and dying from a mysterious disease. His brother, who was a more experienced shepherd, advised him to move the entire flock up to the mountains. 'If they get sick and don't recover, move. You'll lose some on the way but it'll be better than having the whole herd wiped out.' Right. I'm going to radically change my environment. Off to the mountains. I have to rock myself out of this wretched condition. 'Where do I go, Lord?'

Terry, the builder is busy putting a proper roof on the parrots' cage. He suggested that I could move in there.

19th December ~ Hermione says that I must come and stay, and stay for Christmas. I don't think I'm strong enough to make it to Scotland, but Mum says it will be amusing and that I must go. Granny has very kindly offered to pay my train fare.

I've had another thought. It's about Jesus, about Christ's body broken for us. He literally offers us his body; 'This is my body ~ broken for you,' the fit, strong body of a thirty-three year old who walked all over Palestine. We accept the exchange symbolically when we take the broken communion bread. I reach out and accept his health now in exchange for mine. With enormous gratitude.

20th December ~ Train to Scotland. I have to admit I was only just well enough to climb on board and sit through the journey. Shuggie collected me from Glasgow station and bumbled me back to the house where I sat by the Aga, shaking. Granny rang to ask if I'd arrived and find out if it was cold. She sounded quite pleased when I said yes. I expect it makes her feel comforted that at least lovely warm Bedford is the right place for her to be, even if her heart is in Scotland.

21st December ~ Life is very jolly and jolly windy. My cousin Olivia, just back from Glasgow University, made us all walk up The Dumpling, an ancient volcanic plug now a small but very steep hill. When she reached the top she flung her arms in the air and started singing as she always does. Sheep sped in all directions. I was puffing and panting so much I had to sit down. Apart from anything else I'm terribly unfit.

Dad rang to report that the wild animal and Mum toddled off to Harrods yesterday as Mum had been invited to sign copies of her book there. A lady called Rita who is Head of Pets (another good title) in the Pet Department let Bee sleep overnight in the lion's cage. Not Mum, she went off to stay at the Belgian Embassy of all places.

There are no longer any lions at Harrods but there are other distractions. After a morning of signing books, Bee managed to escape and zipped off to Santa's grotto where she started bursting balloons. By the time Mum got there a portly otter, entranced by the sparkly decorations, was defying the laws of nature and making her way up the Christmas tree. None of the elves seemed to know what was happening but all the glass baubles were wobbling about on the branches and the entire queue of children were shrieking in excitement, running around uncontrollably. Santa was furious.

22nd December ~ I'm having to face the python again. I'd forgotten about him. Olivia says it's nothing but solid plaster of Paris and that since it's too heavy and too fragile to move I must just ignore it. The house is so cold that I hurry past clutching hot water bottles and sit grannifying by the fire with my tapestry. I bet woodworm thrive here.

Hermione is exporting to Germany under her own designer label and supplying terribly smart fashion houses with sweaters.

She has closed the craft shop (now a taboo concept) and the dining room is full of boxes and piles of hand-knitted garments in different colours and sizes. She sat me down to draw some designer-ish sketches to impress the Regent Street buyers.

'They say fandango is the colour for next year, so fandango it will be.'

'What are these buyers like?'

'Oh, hysterical. I love them all. They don't love me though, they love Jamie. I've *no idea* why but he certainly has much more success in securing orders than I do.' She's not that naive. No wonder he has had to flee to Madagascar. Jamie is well over six foot tall, very good looking and, although he does have a pair of pink jeans, is not particularly interested in women's clothing. All the same, the buyers adore Hermione too. They dissolve under her charm and recognise a determination to deliver come what may. She probably inherited Great-granny's tenacity.

'You have to bear in mind,' Olivia said, 'that both Daphne and Hermione were brought up by colonialists. If they want something, they just go out and lay claim. They make things happen by sheer force of character, merrily enslaving people along the way.'

I spent the afternoon sewing on labels. I see this as the dawning of a new and dazzling career in the fashion industry. Actually it's so that my aunt can get an order off before Christmas. The seamstress who usually finishes the garments failed to come in. 'I'm sorry to ask you to do this Sophie, but Cheryl says she has depression of all things.' The doctor had written her off sick. 'I can't believe it. She's been away from work for days now.' A year ago I would have found this as incomprehensible as Hermione, but I understand now.

23rd December ~ I'm feeling wonderful. Life is busy here and I keep being taken off to parties but don't feel tired at all. We're off to drinks tonight in some castle and a dinner before the carol service tomorrow. My only worry is what to wear.

Olivia is annoyed because all her underwear has gone pink in the wash. Mine went funny too but I'm rather used to it. Mum so loathes domesticity that she can never be bothered about sorting laundry which means Dad has an assortment of vests in an array of pastel shades. I'm just as bad. I put a very expensive thermal vest in the drier once. It came out miniscule and so hard you could stand it upright on the table.

I seemed to spend the day dealing with a series of fractious knitters. They rang up non-stop. 'Knitters in a twist,' Olivia called, wafting by.

'Don't let them talk for long,' hissed Hermione.

'Doo-n't let your wee are-nt leave me with noth-ing to do ooo-ver Christmas, noo.' They've no reticence, these ladies. They seem genetically pre-programmed to knit and get anxious about not having any to do. In fact they can quite persecute you for more. Shuggie explained that knitting can become an addiction. 'A lot of them are looking after infirm husbands or relatives and cope with the frustration and endless blaring television set by knitting frantically. It can become an expensive hobby unless you're commissioned.' Hermione's marketing spiel describes all this as 'sustaining a traditional craft'.

24th December ~ Olivia absolutely adores Christmas. She has found the biggest tree and is having all her friends around. Goodness they drink a lot of whisky in Scotland. I can't believe how well I feel here. The house must be full of mould but the fatigue has receded. 'Thank you Lord.'

My aunt manages to cook, stirring away at a great pan of gravy despite the fact that the Aga and the shelf above are draped with dripping laundry. Olivia says her pink underwear now smells of mince pies, and, 'Is that sexy or wot?' We heaved the boxes of sweaters into Shuggie's study and laid the table in the dining room for Christmas dinner. There's something deeply nostalgic about bringing out old decorations, even if they are falling to bits.

25th December ~ Christmas Day.

Olivia and I sat up in bed with Hermione opening our stockings like children, while my uncle made us breakfast. I've been given a lovely purple jersey. I forced Olivia to put on all her Christmas presents at once and photographed her under the tree. In dangley earrings, her new lacy vest and tartan tights she looked like a demented fairy that had fallen off the top. Shuggie was extremely pleased because Olivia's boyfriend had given him a road sign saying Shugborough. He has it pointing towards the boat.

'The hopes and fears of all the years are met in Thee tonight.' And I'd never digested the meanings of these words until now. 'He comes with healing in his wings...'

'How silently, how silently the wondrous gift is given.

So God imparts to human hearts

The blessings of His heaven.

No ear may hear His coming;

But in this world of sin,

Where meek souls will receive Him, still

The dear Christ enters in.'[17]

Something wonderful has happened: I've regained complete mental clarity. The fug has finally lifted from my brain and I can take in sights and sounds without becoming swamped. The Soviet Union has been dissolved and Perry rang to say she's expecting another baby. What a day.

26th December ~ We went out for lunch with friends of Hermione's. I sat next to a partially intoxicated man who obviously didn't want to make polite conversation. He tried to convince me that M.E. was 'all in the mind'. I don't think he was talking about cephalic symptoms either. 'I often feel as if I have M.E., especially after a night on the tiles. Ha, ha, ha.' (Ha, ha, ha.)

'It's just a matter of pulling your socks up.' Not very original or highly appreciated dialogue I can tell you. Olivia came along and saved me by doing embarrassing things with her new video camera. She says she's practising to make a film about Jamie's community projects in Madagascar. 'I need footage that captures the arrogant attitudes and debauched lifestyle of westerners to contrast with simple village life in the tropics,' she said, thrusting her lens into the face of he who taunted me.

27th December ~ Another lunch party. No one here ever rests. It's so cold your only option is to eat huge amounts and keep moving. Jamie sent a picture of himself in a dug-out canoe saying that where he is it's too hot to move in any other way.

Hermione won't stop working and is in a merry panic getting samples together for *Yves St Laurent* in Paris. It's a good thing her out-workers are manic. They're incredibly speedy and can easily complete a complicated cable pattern in a week. There are over three hundred of them now, and the thought of them all knitting into the night is terrifying. 'One of them never sleeps anyway; hasn't been upstairs for twenty years.'

'No, Hermione?'

'It's quite true. She just lies on her sofa in a pair of dreadful grey pyjamas and snoozes for a couple of hours. She has a huge Alsatian dog so everything comes back hairy, but she's a frightfully good knitter.'

Hermione seems to have all sorts of adventures with the knitters' husbands. She sat on one. He was lying in the gloom under a blanket on the sofa and she simply didn't realise he was there. She went to visit another knitter and, just like me at the Healing Centre, walked straight into the bathroom by mistake. This time there was a man in the bath. 'A big fat one. He sat up and said, "Hello".'

Another lady was a bit late with her knitting. When Olivia rang her up she said, 'Well my husband died. I haven't buried him yet, so I'll do that and then get the cardi finished. OK?'

News reached Scotland that my father has had to go into hospital. Mum got her automatic car stuck on a hill in the village. She made Dad push it but he slipped on the ice and snapped a tendon. His knee-cap shot up his leg. He rang from hospital to say that they'd yanked it back down again with a piece of wire. His leg's encased in a massive plaster cast from one end to the other, but he has a nice private room and is rather enjoying the rest. Mum said he's rather enjoying the attention of the pretty nurses who insist on giving him bed-baths the whole time. She won't go near the place. Apparently my brother-in-law Johnty had to take him to Casualty. He said he half expected to be met by Perry, looking very pregnant with a stethoscope round her neck. Her episode has just been broadcast on telly. I missed it.

The knitting orders are keeping us all frantically absorbed. I now know how to wind a ball of wool electronically. The first time I tried, the ball flew off the winder thing and hit me on the nose, but it rather fascinates me now. It's lovely working with cashmere when it's so cold.

28th December ~ I've decided Hermione is like God. He often leaves things until the last minute.

All the knitters want to talk endlessly about the weather and their health. There's a real knack to keeping phone calls short. You say: 'OK – very gud. Bye.' as fast as you can and slam the phone down. I would have never dared to be so abrupt when I worked for the *BBC*. People might have been offended and made a fuss about paying their licence fee. Hermione says the buyers can cut you short too. 'Oh, when I was in New York I spent all day plucking up the courage to ring one designer. I eventually managed to speak to her and was busy explaining how each garment is an original, carefully knitted by hand, in the traditional Scottish way, when the woman leant back in her chair and said, "I don't care if they're knitted by monkeys, I don't want 'em."'

Hermione had to grit her teeth and plough on, lugging her massive suitcase of samples through the sludge and snow of Fifth Avenue to meet another terrifying buyer. She started delivering her sparkling presentation when the man looked at her and said, "Oh, shut the bag."

Never mind, it's his loss. The people at *Hermes* like her cashmere.

29th December ~

Dear Sarah-Jane and Rebecca,

You cannot imagine the weather here – howling gales that go on and on, day after day; it gets dark at lunchtime and we can't go out. Nor do we want to as we all have sore throats. Shuggie alone, clad in his boiler-suit, is out working on the boat – under a huge transparent tarpaulin and high, high up as it sits in its cradle outside the back door. I'm wearing piles of jerseys...

(All about the weather and my afflictions; I'm no different from any of the knitters, am I?)

A woman came round to actually buy a jersey with what we assumed to be her husband. 'Lover,' she said in a husky voice, looking at Olivia with half-closed eyes. The lady had a tight perm and a glinty, inquisitive eye. I took her into the dining room where there's a sale rail, but she seemed more interested in the house and our family photographs. She was so dumpy nothing looked much good on her until I found a short knitted jacket. But it was in mustard. 'I don't take to this one.'

'Oh, but you look *very* sexy,' said the gentleman friend.

'I'll have it,' she snapped, swinging round. I wrapped it up in tissue paper (left over from Christmas) and showed them out. 'Oh, mercy,' shrilled the little lady, still spinning round. 'That was so *Serendipity*!' and they disappeared into the swirling snow.

Then, just as Olivia was choking in disbelief another minute lady came into the workroom. Defiantly no lover in tow. She was from the Dumbarton Enterprise Scheme. Hermione hadn't filled in her forms for a grant properly. 'What is *that*?' We couldn't think what she was looking at; she was just looking up.

'Oh. It's a giant chameleon.' We had all got rather used to it. It hangs in the eaves, waiting until next time Jamie has a Baobab Boogie. The Baobab Boogie is a colourful dance he puts on to raise funds for his aid work in Madagascar. The brightly painted chameleon is made of papier-mâché and is a decoration for the ball. There are also some ring-tailed lemurs.

30th December ~ Hermione is sending her output manager, Chris, off on a holiday to Mombassa as a bonus. Olivia has cheerfully lent her a snorkel, but I kept giving her too much worrying advice. 'You must swim in pyjamas.' I'm terrified she'll get badly sunburnt or eat the wrong thing, but she couldn't care; she's ecstatic. It has always been her dream to go to Africa. She has only ever been to London once and that was to help Hermione lug the sweaters about.

Poor Cheryl is still off sick with depression. I'm still winding wool. It's incredibly difficult weighing the right amount for fiddly things like gloves with seven different colours in the pattern. I explained what I was doing to Granny on the phone and found her surprisingly sympathetic. 'Oh yes, all those *wretched* little balls of wool.'

Granny wanted to speak to Hermione but she'd gone to placate an incredibly fierce knitter. 'I told *your* aunt I can't knit with black wool,' and of course every single urgent order is for cashmere *en noir*.

This company entices you to speak in italics.

31st December ~ New Year's Eve in Scotland is just the best thing. We had to dress festively so I tied a cracker to a hairband and put it on my head. I wore my genie suit, a strange, gold and sparkly creation Mum once bought in a *Caroline Charles* sale and then found she couldn't get into. A smiley man from Johannesburg, whom I was introduced to, said I must fly out to South Africa as soon as possible and invited me to stay. At this point Shuggie, in a Madagascan waistcoat, his kilt and an enormous badger sporran, whisked me off around the dance floor to jive with all the other Gay Gordons.

JANUARY 1992 ~ One step at a time

1st January ~
I waited patiently for the Lord;
And he inclined to me and heard my cry.
He brought me up out of the *horrible* pit
Out of the mire and clay: and set my feet upon a rock...
> by King David, written around 1010 BC[xviii]

I'm on the train, returning home, feeling so much better, so normal, so well, released from the hold of the fatigue.

To my surprise Dad met me at the station having driven there in Mum's automatic car. I'm sure he's not meant to drive yet. He refuses to use crutches or a stick, despite the fact it seems foolhardy not to. I reminded him that he used to hope that people would fall over on the ice so his walking-stick sales would go up.

2nd January ~ It's icy cold here. Colder than Scotland. You can't go outside at all and this house, being in a valley, gets no sun in the winter. One unemployed winder of wool and knitter-placator contemplates her future. 'What am I going to do with the rest of my life, Lord?' I ask yet again.

'It's a matter of availability.'

Dad is hobbling about telling everyone about his operation. His secondary operation. 'Another one? Dad, I would have come home earlier.'

'It was hardly life-threatening,' Mum said.

'There was a scare that I had meningitis,' he replied indignantly. It transpired that he'd had to have an operation for acne. Third degree acne. He'd developed a spotty back. And he's nearly sixty-three. 'The surgeon and hospital dermatologist decided it wasn't hormonal but couldn't think what was happening to me. Mrs. Booth, who happened to working there as a nurse, said the doctors all began to get in a terrible state about the spots and thought I might've contracted meningitis. In the end they discovered an infectious agent had been imported into the hospital. By my wife.' Instead of sending Dad in with a face flannel, as it said on the *What to bring* list, Mum had packed an old towelling beer mat so that it could just be thrown away afterwards. This is because she doesn't want any possibility of contagion entering our house. Albert had left the beer mat at home, when he came to put in a new bath after Alastair split the pink one. I think he was given it at the pub when he went to fix their toilets, and had probably been using it for unspeakable moppings.

'It was perfectly clean; I'd put it through the washing machine.'

'But washing machines don't kill beery yeast spores.'

'Well, I can't think why the nurses had to give you bed baths: quite unnecessary.' When the nurses scrubbed Dad's back with this cloth, whatever was lurking on the beer mat was worked into his skin and gave him the infection. He said that this wasn't fully explained to him, but he managed to work it out. Someone came into his room wearing a disposable white boiler-suit with a hood and a mask. They silently produced a long pair of tongs, picked up the beer mat and took it away in a kidney bowl. It was just as well. Dad had developed such painful spots that he couldn't lie on his back and they had to get a scalpel to him. My poor father, he was like Job with the boils.

3rd January ~ Olivia said that only her Aunt Daphne could try to kill someone with a beer mat. I keep thinking about availability. When I worked on dramas we'd never ask theatrical agents not whether such and such an actor was out of work, but if they were *available* for a part. 'Would Hannah Gordon be available to play the part of Mrs. Durrell? It was also a polite way of asking whether she would consider the role. It was almost an invitation.

'Yes, I'm available,' is my reply. 'What's the production called? Are there any love scenes?'

No answer.

Where does my talent lie? They keep telling us in church that we are meant to 'operate out of our giftings.' Wool winding. No, television. Television, where, now I think about it, the love scenes in the 'eighties got a bit out of hand. Tamzin said the reason why she stopped acting was that every single leading actress ended up having to take off her top – and worse. Johnty didn't want her to do that in front of anyone else. After *My Family and Other Animals* we referred to these as 'mating scenes'. Not that that was what was required of Hannah Gordon; it only involved insects in Gerald Durrell's world, specifically a praying mantis called Cecily, but some of the younger actors in that series had previously experienced what amounted to prostitution. They loathed it. Perry said that it's all out of her league now; the only vaguely sexy parts she gets to play are in gas board ads, but she still scrutinises scripts for snogging scenes.

Should I start a crusade for the media? For the consequences? Gerald Durrell said that the result of writing an innocent book on the wonders of growing up on Corfu, and telling the world how gorgeous it was, led to the island becoming a package-deal destination. A sex culture was introduced that horrified the Greeks, who previously would only allow their daughters to go swimming in knee-length dresses. It also decimated the wildlife he treasured. You hardly see a seagull there now, let alone a barn owl. He also said that he was thrilled to bits that Hannah Gordon was going to play his mother. 'She's such a beautiful woman. I invited her over to my zoo at once.' She told him that she'd just been playing the part of an otter; she'd been Bee's voice, in the film when Spike Milligan was Jake.

4th January ~ The urge to lie in bed and sleep continuously has returned. I feel drained by doing anything. I can only conclude that I must be terribly allergic to this house. But... do I have any allergic symptoms? Nope, unless fatigue is a symptom of being allergic to mould. I felt a bit wheezy in Scotland and had no fatigue at all. Doomed to wander like an albatross, I'm going to have to move on.

I think I've been looking at giftings in the wrong way. I grasped it back in June, when I was thinking of the broad-spectrum abilities God gives us to inspire or help others. What has he given me? Leadership, James tells me, a little bit of helpfulness, but most of all the gift of encouragement, only I don't know how that can do much.

Tamzin came over on a mercy mission to see Dad. He was standing by the fire, cheerfully telling her about living with a full plaster cast, when Mum let the otters into the house. Bee heard Tamzin laugh and came straight for her, snarling and baring her teeth. Tamzin, in an effort to scramble out of the otter's reach, leapt into Dad's arms. He stood there, swaying on his one good leg. Mum, of course, couldn't think what all the fuss was about.

5th January ~ Staying with Diana in London. Between taking conference calls to the States she told me she has started to go to a Roman Catholic church which surprised me. 'Sophie, it's still a secret, but I'm thinking of leaving my career in marketing and training to become a t-e-a-c-h-e-r.' I think this is great. Not surprising at all. She has always wanted to be a headmistress and most assuredly has the skills. I'm sure it would be more fulfilling than putting the polish on already glitzy City companies.

'Well, I think you would be wonderful. Don't let anyone stop you.'

'It's a lot to take on board. I'll have to spend a year at teacher training college,' she said, getting the application form out to show me. And it is. Living in London as a student with no salary must be hard.

'Yes, but if it's what you want to do, go for it whatever the odds.' Then I said, 'I'm thinking of becoming a game ranger.'

'Sophoska? You're too weedy and weak!'

'Umm.'

Diana thinks I ought to consider going into radio, but I'd be useless. The time I interviewed Gerald Durrell was a disaster, and he was one of the greatest storytellers out. When I asked him about one of his biographical books there was a terrible silence before he asked, 'How did you know about that one?' I was filled with shyness, but couldn't help telling the rather embarrassing truth.

'I rang up Broadcasting House and asked them to send me your obituary.'

'Have they written it already?' he asked, roaring with laughter. 'Can I have a copy?' When I gave it to him then and there he was even more delighted. He took out a red pen, crossed out all the bits they had got wrong, signed it and told me to send it back with his love. 'They always get me muddled with my brother Lawrence, something it seems that will follow me to the grave.' He was delighted but that sort of thing rather backfires when you're the journalist.

6th January ~ No, I lack what it takes to reconstruct my shattered career and can't just sit about praying against soft porn on *BBC 2*. They'll realise it doesn't make good television sooner or later. I need to do something completely different.

We've got to be open to change to be available. And how can we get anywhere if we aren't prepared to be flexible?

> We would rather be ruined than changed,
> We would rather die in our dread
> Than climb the cross of the moment
> And let our illusions die.
> *W.H. Auden*

The most important change people can make is not a physical thing; it's to change their way of looking at the world. We have to be overcomers. Those who survived concentration camps in the war were recognised as the ones who were determined optimists ~ those who saw beauty in every situation, who looked for humour and remained full of gratitude. It gave them strength to forbear and attracted other people to them.

How are we going to overcome the problems set before us? I'm back to where I was before: we endure, fight or seek a way through. I'm beginning to realise that the way through will probably incur change, so in my case it might as well be radical. You never know; something unexpected might happen and you have to be ready to leap into the chariot. I'm ready for something new, sure enough, ready to travel; just not well enough.

7th January ~ I arrived home to find the house on fire. Princess Michael of Kent was putting it out with salt. She was roaring with laughter and much enjoying the whole thing. 'No need to call the fire brigade,' she said. 'They make so much mess. Prince Michael will help.' And he did. He started taking burning logs from the sitting room in a metal bucket and dumping them in the river.

This sounds like another bizarre dream, but the strangest thing was that it was true. And the Belgian Ambassador was there too. Mum had invited the Kents, or the Prince Michaels, as I think I should say, to tea (they had wanted to visit the otters) only Mum, being ultra-domestic for once, had banked up the fire so enthusiastically that flames leapt up into the nether regions of the chimney. Tar in the flu caught alight. The royal party arrived back from their walk with the otters to find the house full of black smoke.

It's left a horrid smell, but there are lots of cakes to eat up. The fire inspector, who came to see the otters' enclosure, said that since Dad had put in a good quality lining to the original chimney the fire was quite safe, and would just burn itself out.

8th January ~ Another Great Excitement. Mum, never one to be outdone by Hermione, has bought a new boat too. It's not exactly new in itself but a sea-going launch from Scotland, built in 1914 from great thirty-foot long mahogany planks. For Dad. It has two cabins, a big diesel engine and is reputedly very handsome. He's thrilled. It means we'll be able to take off for weeks on the Thames, which should be fun, but he has to rebuild it first. It arrives next week: a big and inspiring new project. He's going to call it *Snapdragon*. It's to replace *Daffodil*, which he hopes to sell before the boiler explodes.

9th January ~ Granny's 75th birthday.

'*...the plans of the Lord stand firm forever, the purposes of His heart through all generations.*' *Psalm 33*

Umm. What are the purposes of God's heart? Because Granny's been ill and housebound most of her life, all she has been able to do much of the time is pray. And love us. But perhaps that was God's purpose for her. At least prayer is work never wasted. Am I inheriting this? No, we are called to do what we enjoy doing. It's not in my nature to be sedentary. I was made to move. 'What are your plans for me, Lord?' I looked back through this diary, and found:

'... I know the plans I have for you,' says the Lord. 'They are plans for good and not for disaster, to give you a future and a hope.' *Jeremiah 29 v 11*

10th January ~ Ill again. I'm finally getting used to this and I'm not going to get grumpy. Mum is grumpy though. She said she spent all morning in court arguing about what to do with some youths that were up for urinating in a public place. I didn't know this was, in fact, an offence.

'It certainly is.'

'What is the legal term for it?' I asked.

'Oh, it comes under public indecency. I do feel bad for prosecuting people who are caught short on the motorway, but they're always given fines.'

'Was the argument about that?'

'No, this was different.' Mum wasn't very forthcoming.

'How was it different?'

'Everyone said I was being too harsh on these wretched boys.'

'What were they doing?'

'They keep on doing it and it has to stop. I really think they should be locked up.'

'What do they keep on doing?'

'Peeing through the letterbox of Betty's Bun shop.'

11th January ~ Dad's Birthday. He still has one leg splinted-up and needs two walking sticks to get about. He's immensely cheerful about his injury but not very good about using the sticks. I think he's in rebellion.

It's snowing. The otters love it and have been bounding around in the woods with Jake. Luckily for me the waterwheel turbine is whirring away keeping the central heating going full pelt. It's freezing outside.

I was looking for my flute music and found what appeared to be some horrid old rags lying on some shelves in Dad's study. They were so revolting I stuffed them in the bin. 'What are you doing?' my father cried.

'Chucking this filthy stuff away.'

'Those are my trousers, the ones cut up by the rotavator.' He'd kept them and the slashed gumboots as a bizarre reminder of his escape.

'I'm keeping them to convince the insurance company.' I can't think what he can claim for.

Keep thinking about poor Betty. Betty of Betty's Bun Shop. She's about eighty. I think she ought to set a trap; spring-load the letterbox or something. At least she'd have Mum on her side. I would say the boys need a bit of a fright and think she's right to come down hard on them.

12th January ~ Oh dear, where is grace? 'Grace was a dirty girl, who didn't wash her face.' I'm still prone to vengeful thoughts. Quite childish. It's a good thing I'm not dead yet as my character still needs what amounts to piles of ironing.

The most enormous old wreck of a boat has arrived. Mum doesn't even want to look. It's filling the whole yard. My father is so pleased. He keeps stroking it.

The snow fell again last night. I'm not sure how they got the boat down into the valley but it's standing starkly against the white fields. Solomon and Leonard, the spotty donkey, are both looking on with great attention. Dad learnt an interesting thing: his vessel was originally housed in a boatshed in Scotland that once belonged to Robin's family. We'll have to get him to come aboard.

13th January ~ Went to see Dr. Prior for my last magnesium injection. I must have benefited from them. He said that women need about 350mgs of magnesium a day, men 300mgs. I should be able to absorb it naturally from green vegetables, grains, seeds and nuts ~ including chocolate. (I suppose chocolate is derived from a nut.) 'Otherwise eat ¼ teaspoon of Epsom salts a day.'

'Epsom salts?'

'Yes, or bathe in it. Fling a handful or two into your bath; you'll absorb it through the skin.'[18] I learnt that most of the body's organs need magnesium, which improves immune function, energy, sleep, blood pressure as well as cardiac function. Apparently you need vitamin D for the body to utilise magnesium. I don't see how I can sunbathe in January. 'Take cod liver oil.' All these old fashioned remedies; but they aren't a cure are they, just a treatment.

Dr. Prior said that I must still take good care of myself, as I'm likely to contract viruses very easily. He says the key to recovery is in careful pacing.

This is difficult. Daisy is ill. The snow and ice on the roads were so bad that Dad said I shouldn't drive over. But I did. She's sick with a bad tummy but we are told it's not complicated. I just sat with Mary-Dieu. She told me how desperate her depression has been, 'The darkest, greyest experience of my whole life – you're constantly wishing you weren't the way you are but can't do anything about it. At times it was torture to keep my eyes open; I felt my forehead physically bulging out, like the Elephant Man. There are emotional bits, you get in a state, worried about what people think of your parenting skills and stuff, but it's a physical thing – very real, very here.' She looked up. 'Tell people about it Sophie, so they can understand it's the most hideous, hideous thing that could happen. You couldn't be sadder if a mass murderer wiped out your entire family.'

14th January ~ My car is making a very funny noise when it moves; it's clanking. Dad says the universal joint is worn out. Perhaps I just need new universals too. I've gone down with yet another bug and can't stop coughing. It amazes me how there can be so many variants to influenza. I'm reading a book about colonial India.[19] Despite the risks of horrendous diseases like cholera and dengue fever, most British troops were healthier than they had been in England, as they rarely caught a cold. I should emigrate. At least I could live in the sunlight.

My father now tells me that he puts a cup of Epsom salts in his bathwater whenever he feels tired. He's been doing it for years.

15th January ~ It seems I've caught the bug of the week ~ everybody is down with it. My version also includes the profound exhaustion, which, frankly I'm getting used to. I'm not feeling anxious or confused any more, yet I'm not sure that I can go abroad if I'm forever breaking down like this. 'But I am trusting you, Oh Lord, saying, "You are my God!" My future is in your hands.' [xix] and little Daisy's future, and everyone's.

While it's our responsibility to do what we can, when things get beyond our control, we have to let God take over; there's often no choice anyway. Do the possible and let God do the impossible. Jesus says we must just pray that God's will be done. I suppose this means giving our free will, freely back. Relinquishment. If we 'surrender unto him' a thing, like whom we are going to marry, or whether in fact we marry at all, we jolly well surrender it. The thing's submitted. I'd be so likely to make the wrong decision myself I've got to trust God on something like that, and yet I keep thinking, 'Is it ever going to happen?'

'Nothing's impossible for the Lord.' It says that somewhere too.

16th January ~ Granny describes being ill as, 'very tiresome' or 'being under attack'. She's quite right, but I can cope with 'tiresome' now and am getting used to fighting when I feel weak.'...be strong and take courage, all you that put your hope in the Lord!' *Psalm 31*

Yes. I'm going to 'embrace suffering'; *rejoice* in the fact I'm ill. Rejoice in the blows and trials, the setbacks that are allowed to rain down on me. I'm going to thank God for his mercy. Mercy for not allowing an idiot like me to suffer one tenth of the natural consequences of my idiocy.

17th January ~ Still ill. I shall overdose on vitamin C and avoid doctors' waiting rooms. Mum is right. They're unhealthy places, full of people with viral infections.

I also need anti-freeze for my brain. Am down to my last Dick Francis book. He has a character in it called Erik. Erik's brother is a policeman called Knut and has a dog; a Great Dane called Odin.

18th January ~ Wobbly... but in a brighter frame of mind. The tide is turning. Apparently there are 57 varieties of herring in Norway and not one of them is red. I must go and see Granny, but she says she would rather not catch my cough.

19th January ~ I've learnt that the active bit about trusting God is to seek his will and pray before you start making decisions, rather than afterwards; otherwise you just end up wasting a lot of time. I need to ask that his will should supersede my own right now. And always.

20th January ~
'What if you can't come to any sort of decision?'

'When you're doubtful about your course, submit your judgement absolutely to the Spirit of God and ask him to shut against you every door but the right one.' Who said that?

21st January ~

'And if things don't work out?'

'If life is not going to plan, look to the Lord for a creative alternative, another strategy, something different. Think again ~ achieve your dream.' *Hank Overeem*

It has been snowing again, but deeply and the whole world looks different. It sounds different too. Solomon is wearing his smart green rug and, with his shaggy legs, he looks as if he's wearing flared trousers underneath. A grit lorry with five men dressed in bright orange boiler-suits came down the valley and Mum got a wolf-whistle. She's frightfully pleased.

I love walking in the snow but I think I should stay inside. Mind you, if I don't get out of the house now I never will. 'Lord, who can I go and stay with?' It's a funny time of year to go visiting.

22nd January ~

'What if I still don't have a plan?' I still don't know what God wants of me, and *where* he wants me. I could go to South Africa, the option is open, but what would I do there? I need to be certain it's the right step. I've worked out one thing. When you need direction or confirmation to prayer:

A light shines.

A way opens.

A word is given.

A picture emerges.

An assurance comes.

An inner peace settles.

Sometimes we just have to take one step at a time. It can be difficult when the mist comes down and you can only see one step ahead of you.

23rd January ~ Cock-a-doodle-doo! My muddled dreams were split in two. My parents have acquired, not one but two cockerels and they're living in the parrots' cage right below my window. (The parrots are back in the dining room.) These roosters cry ~ or whatever you call the noise ~ crow, every thirty-three seconds. Cock-a-do-dol-doo! I've timed them. It's driving me demented.

'But darling, it's a lovely country noise.'

'Why've you bought them?'

'We didn't buy them. We were given them by a sweet man called Trevor who found them wandering around in a wood. He had them at his house but the neighbours complained.' Cock-a-doodle-doo! One bird is called Albert, and the other Terry, after the local builder.

Gordon comes from South Africa. I keep thinking of the verse he gave me and looked it up:

'...how can you say the Lord does not see your troubles? How can you say God refuses to hear your case? Have you never heard or understood?' Cock-a-do-dol-doo! 'Don't you know that the Lord is the everlasting God, the Creator of all the earth? He never grows faint or weary. No one can measure the depths of his understanding. He gives power to those who are tired and worn out; he offers strength to the weak. Even youths will become exhausted, and young men will give up. But those who wait on the Lord will find new strength. They will fly high on wings like eagles. They will run and not grow weary. They will walk and not faint.' *Isaiah 40 v 27-31* Yes, please.

I decided to ring him in London. 'What do you reckon, Gordon? I'd love to go to South Africa.'

'What's that odd noise?' he asked.

'Oh, it's a rooster.'

'I'm sure,' he said, 'that God wants you to extend your experience and see the world.'

'I do have the option of staying here and illustrating books.'

'Yes, but it might be a distraction or an obstacle. If God clearly wants you to go somewhere, attractive propositions that pander to our egos tend to pop up, and later come to nothing.' Cock-a-do-dol-doo! 'Have you got a lot of hens?'

'No just two; two males.' I asked him if he ever felt unclear about the future despite asking God what to do. 'Do you ever feel you're walking in a fog?'

'All the time,' he laughed. 'Sometimes it's a matter of asking for strength as well as direction.'

'My problem is I don't know whether I'll have the energy to go in any direction at all.'

'You will. Don't do it in your own strength. When I worked in the Cape I went climbing on the coastal cliffs once by myself and fell. There was no one around. As I fell through space I resigned my life into God's hands, knowing it was up to him whether I should live or die. I woke after dark on the rocks below with a sense of peace, like after a deep and comfortable sleep. I realised that God had chosen to give me life ~ and therefore had a purpose for me. To avoid hypothermia, I dragged myself to a cave where I spent the night and then staggered slowly back the next morning and got help. My only wounds were cuts on legs and face and hip, which were stitched up. I lost a bit of blood. My teeth required root treatment but this actually straightened them out. I spent four days in the local hospital and then had a beach holiday. I certainly learnt to draw on the Lord's strength. It was quite a useful lesson.'

24th January ~ Grizelda rang inviting me up to Yorkshire where she's being lent a holiday cottage. That would be wonderful. I'll be able to get away from these birds. She told me we need to get a henhouse and put it in the field. And some hens. Her mother keeps Indian runner ducks. And llamas. One of them looks just like a Rastafarian. (I must ask Alastair if he's seen it.)

25th January ~ Rebecca has written from a game reserve in the Northern Transvaal where they've just moved with the horses. She says that I must come out as soon as I can. The area is free of malaria and I won't need any vaccinations. All of southern Africa is experiencing a bad drought this year, but she said it's still very beautiful. There was a picture of an eagle in flight on the envelope and writing paper. It's the emblem of the reserve.

Albert and Terry are fast becoming an emblem, engraved on my brain. They're impressive creatures and, I agree, look fine scratching around on the lawn but they're so noisy. Dad has been carrying them up to sleep in a partitioned-off section of the otters' enclosure where their cries are muted by the sound of the stream, but they kick and scratch when you lift them up and one nearly pecked him in the eye.

I've been put in touch with the woman who wants me to illustrate her children's books. She has written one about a carwash and is very enthusiastic, very flattering about my work. But she hasn't got a publisher. I know it would mean going back to London and endless meetings, and although it sounds like an opportunity of sorts I have my reservations.

26th January ~ Instead, I went to see Dr. Loveday and explained to her how I'd been trying to rock myself out of ill health. 'Should I go to South Africa?'

'Oh, yes,' she said, 'you'll get better in an arid climate in no time.' I asked her politely, that if this was the case, why had she not suggested it back in June.

'It's not the kind of treatment you can write out on a prescription form, but if you have friends who can look after you there, then I'd suggest this is the right time to go.' She paused. 'You'll find that people have M.E. in South Africa too. They're looking into the possibility that it's spread by parasitic ticks, but I don't know. It's probably the least understood illness the medical profession is currently facing. It desperately needs more research.'

27th January ~ I dreamt that I was on a horse looking out over rolling hills. All I had to do to start on my journey was to gently touch his sides. It wasn't a slog at all. 'But... but what about Daisy?'

'Darling, she isn't your baby,' Mum said. 'You need to get away and get well. Go, while you have the chance.'

Terry, real Terry the builder, has arrived with a chicken hutch on the back of his truck. 'Oh, you dear, kind man.' It's such a relief. It's a sort of triangular cage with a bedroom at one end. A real little henhouse. The cockerels are very happy.

28th January ~ I sat on the train staring out over the frozen fields on my way to Yorkshire, still wondering about my future. I don't want to take too big a step and end up hurtling backwards and into a wheelchair when I've come so far. I don't want to become a burden to my friends in distant lands.

Griz retrieved me from the station and took me up to the isolated holiday cottage where they're taking a break with the children. There was a roaring log fire in the grate and we ate sausages and baked potatoes with lots of butter.

29th January ~ I walked up onto the moors with my friend. She thinks I should go abroad. 'If your specialist says you should go, go. If it doesn't work out you can always come back, but I'm sure it would be wonderful.' We reached a high spot and looked out over the endless, empty country. I love wide, open spaces. It wasn't misty at all here, but clear and sunny. I felt I knew for certain what I should do.

30th January ~ I'm going for freedom: freedom and liberty. Clutching bottles of cod liver oil and Epsom salts. *The New King James Bible* footnotes define liberty as 'Freedom from slavery, independence, absence of external restraint, a negation of control or domination, freedom of access.' My secular thesaurus gives: 'Salvation, redemption, deliverance and emancipation, privilege, rescue, immunity.' How interesting.

Mum says she can't think why I don't make more use of my independence. She says she's longing to escape, but I know she'd miss her parrots. She can't exactly leave the otters either, or Dad. Being on a horse gives Sarah-Jane freedom. Freedom of a kind. I think boats represent liberty for Dad and as he's already fully absorbed doing up his new launch, he's halfway there. I rather think the root of Mary-Dieu's problem is that she wanted freedom so much but found, like happiness, it's a very elusive thing. It isn't an automatic acquisition of adult life. By the time we think we've grown up we need to be set free from ourselves. Bad attitudes set in and tangle up our lives. You're never going to be free if you harbour grudges all day long.

Liberty isn't just a physical thing; it's spiritual and born out of security that can only truly be found in Christ; by giving our lives away, whether we are healthy or not. We have to find our identity in him rather than in our work, what we do, or some image of ourselves. We need to look to God for direction and ask Him to provision our subsequent needs. He has all the resources of the world in his hands. But the choice is always ours. The handle is on our side of the door. We can only gain freedom for ourselves by relinquishing the sin and committing our lives to the Lord. Then His grace takes over, and because our sin is washed away, we can be set free. It's an eternal gift. Jesus said: 'If you abide in my word, then you are truly disciples of mine; and you shall know the truth and the truth shall set you free.' *John 8 v 31&32*

31st January ~ My last day in Yorkshire. The sun is still shining. Everything has been flung into sharp relief.

What's dawning on me is a deeper understanding of the cross, *The Great Exchange*. It's a covenant. A deal. Jesus offers to take on board our sin, effectively take responsibility for the cost and 'pay the price of sin' which is death, a horrid, painful death, so that we can walk free and be given amnesty by God. It's a legal transfer that takes place. Jesus makes it clear we have to make a decision to repent and accept the new life that follows the transaction. Our miserable old self dies on the cross with him, and we are, in spiritual terms, born all over again. The gap left by the emptied out sin needs to be filled with the Holy Spirit, God's Holy Spirit. It's a huge, overwhelming relief.

FEBRUARY ~ Out of the mire and clay

1st February ~

No. No. No! Mum is making me give a talk to the W.I. (the Brimpsford Women's Institute) with an otter. Tonight. She's double-booked and already dressed in a safari suit, hurrying off to appear as an amateur herpetologist in a film about iguanas. She knows nothing about reptiles, but when I challenged her earlier she looked at me as if I was imbecilic and said she was acting the part. Well, she's a very stressed part. 'Don't tell me I'm stressed.'

Now I'm stressed. Distressed. I've bought a ticket to Johannesburg and leave in ten days' time. 'The Lord's plans are irrevocable!'[xx] But I've decided a certain amount of stress is probably a good thing. It stops one turning into an iguana.

2nd February ~ The ladies of the Women's Institute were adorable and laughed at all the right places in my talk entitled *'Having to live with Otters'*. Luckily the Chairwoman was a *Swallows and Amazons* fan, thrilled to give me a fee of £30. I need the money.

I'm going to have to streamline my life; make it simpler. Epicurus said, 'Contentment consists not in great wealth, but in few wants.' I've decided to cut my outgoings right down to the minimum and separate myself from my possessions. This has got to be healthy. I want to do more with less. I need to fit myself into a suitcase anyway. Pippa is going to rent my flat with everything in it and look after the repairs, maintenance and insurance. A very sweet trainee production assistant called Hope is moving in to keep her company. She comes from Nigeria.

It looks as if I won't need a new car after all. Perry wants to borrow my tramp mobile, as Tamzin insists on calling it, and will keep it on the road until I come back. To Tamzin, I've bequeathed my dead sheep. This is her name for my sheepskin under-blanket, which she has been longing to try out. I'll keep clothes and things in my room at my parents' house for future use. My main expense now is decent health insurance.

3rd February ~ 'Are you the one who makes the hawk soar and spread its wings to the south?' Robin found this in the book of Job.[xxi] It's taken completely out of context.... or is it? He said that he's not at all happy that I've decided to go to South Africa but cheered up when I suggested he should come on a horse safari. He loves travelling, being detached from responsibilities.

I found a Canadian film crew in our house. Dad said he was sweating with embarrassment as they had spent the morning filming Mum in the kitchen with the otters leaping around in the sink (together with the washing up), making their own way into the 'fridge (which is always chaotic) and breaking eggs onto the floor (which is filthy). By the time I arrived they were filming Mum, bum in the air, trying to extract Jims from underneath a chest of drawers. I took a cup of tea to the continuity girl. 'Are you off to film any other interesting animals?'

'Animals? Aw no. This is a series about great British eccentrics.' I don't think my parents are aware of this.

The Producer asked me if I could possibly keep the cockerels quiet for a while. I've regressed to being a film runner. One thing I gained a great deal of experience in at the *BBC* was asking people to stop making a noise: I could stop pneumatic drills drilling, chain-saws sawing, Rastas from playing basket ball – once I even stopped the traffic going down Bayswater Road, but could I do anything about the cockerels… I found the only thing that worked was letting them out to scratch around in the field. Disaster. I went to shut them up later, when it was beginning to get dark, and found Terry running around looking flustered. There were feathers everywhere. Albert had disappeared. Mum was very upset. She was furious with me and spent hours wandering up and down to see if he was hiding anywhere, but I've got a feeling we won't find the body and am wracked with guilt.

4th February ~ Big packing-up session in London. Good-bye sofa, good-bye desk, good-bye television. Good-bye Television. I feel right about all this. Have inner peace. What really matters is what happens within us, not to us.

5th February ~ I've a funny feeling I know who ate Albert. I found an awful lot of feathers in the haystack where Jake has a hidey-hole.

Mum has handed in her resignation as a J.P. after thirteen years' service. It has been very hard for her to let go but I'm glad. She has enough to cope with in life without the addition of draining voluntary work. An invitation has arrived inviting her to attend the International Otter Convention in India, which is exciting, and she's looking forward to it already. She's passionate about conservation, and drawing on her skills as an actress, is brilliant at conveying the message to others, especially children. We feel she should concentrate on this and let others deal with delinquent youths. The delinquent pet – Jake, has been granted parole.

6th February ~ Alastair is off to the South Pole to film penguins in a thermal zoot-suit. James isn't envious at all. He gets seasick. He says he'd rather come with me, but isn't that thrilled about the idea of watching rhinoceros from horseback. I am. Alastair thinks that I would feel isolated living way out in the bush and could get very lonely, but it can't be lonelier than being ill. I can cope with that.

Tamzin said that Johnty hasn't noticed the dead sheep yet despite the fact that it makes a huge lump under the bottom sheet on her side of the bed. She gave me some riding boots, which are too small for her, in part exchange. Dad has given me a pair of binoculars and Mum has found me some old insect repellent. Granny keeps ringing to say Good-bye. I went to see Daisy. Mary-Dieu has never once thanked me for looking after her baby, but it doesn't matter. She isn't cross any more. In fact she was very funny and said she'd take the nightshift when I have kids. I hadn't thought of that. I must drive her crazy, but she loves me. Loving *despite of* is more precious than *loving because of*.

Mum and Dad went out to dinner and arrived back with the prettiest little hen you have ever seen. She is to be a girlfriend for Terry. I hope he'll be nice to her.

7th February ~ 'What has been the purpose of this time Lord? This season of sickness in my life?'

Will I only be able to see the answer clearly from a distance?

I'd been going so fast. My days had just been filled with lists of things to get done. I'd fallen into the trap of putting the merely urgent before the important. It's so easy to let our perspective become quite limited. We think our bodies so significant, and they are because we need to be healthy to operate effectively, but how much more vital is our spirit? We have eternity ahead of us. In our society we spend years educating our intellect and training our brains, and yet most parents are shy, scared of developing their children's spiritual understanding. They see it as 'Religious Education', which is either unimportant or something that must be tackled by teachers at school.

An Texan girl once told me that the word Bible stands for Basic Instructions Before Leaving Earth. B.I.B.L.E. We have the Maker's Manual, but like most instruction books few people ever read it. Until things go wrong. Then it's, 'Help, I can't understand this. Nothing's working properly. Where did you put the instruction manual?' Somehow we never find the time to read it. Well, I've had time.

I've learnt that, if Earth is our training ground, then we must expect to have to undergo trials here so that our spiritual muscle and resistance can be built up. If our body is in bad shape a virus will knock us sideways; if our spirit is in bad shape disasters will hammer us. Life is going to be full of tribulation. We're always going to need the strength and confidence, the wisdom and understanding that lie the other side of suffering.

8th February ~

'Yes, but I would really appreciate more of an explanation.'

I was given it. Jesus said, 'Simon, Simon, (Sophie, Sophie) behold, Satan demanded to have you, that he might sift you like wheat, but I have prayed for you that your faith may not fail; and when you have turned again, strengthen your brethren.'[xxii] Well that's what it's for, so we can 'strengthen and build up others.' That is my commission. 'To comfort others with the comfort I've been given.'[xxiii]

How does the Prayer of St Francis go? That we should seek not so much to be understood as to understand. Make me a channel of your peace.

9th February ~ *I've packed my bags and I'm ready to go.* I'm taking the suede chaps I had made in Farnham, a sketchbook and a hammock. Granny rang to say, 'Smell Africa for me.'

10th February ~ Fly to South Africa.

I went to see how the chickens were getting on just before I left. I opened up the bedroom side of the hutch and found two perfect white eggs. It was so exciting to find them, like a symbol of hope.

Tamzin made me a special Going Away lunch and drove me to the airport. I didn't feel at all strong; very shaky in fact, with a head full of cottonwool and rags, but I staggered onto the plane and let everything roll over me. I flew high on wings like an eagle; a steppe buzzard migrating south.

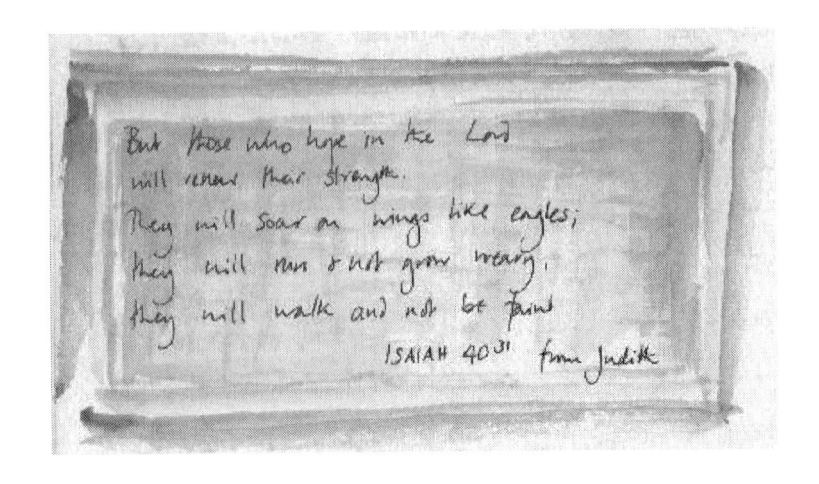

> But those who hope in the Lord
> will renew their strength.
> They will soar on wings like eagles;
> they will run & not grow weary,
> they will walk and not be faint
>   ISAIAH 40:31   from Judith

After all that

I did get well again. I arrived in Johannesburg, rang the man from the New Year's Eve party and said, 'I'm the girl with the cracker on her head.' From that moment I began to recover. It took five days. Then I climbed up to the highest point of the Drakensburg Mountains with Rebecca and knew the fatigue had gone; I felt tired rather than shattered. It was a wonderful clear day. From the top of the mountains we could see far into Natal. I felt as if I was looking out over the whole world, and it was all at my feet.

And I lived the dream. I became a safari guide for Sarah-Jane, a game ranger on horseback. It wasn't a lonely existence. People from all over the world came to ride with us; there was quite a cosmopolitan atmosphere. We sat round open fires and danced under the stars, living outside from dawn to dusk. One of my first clients was an amusing woman who claimed to have been bitten by fleas, caught off a baby heron, when she came riding the year before.

What amazed me about the bush were the butterflies. In early summer I would walk through seas of wild flowers and thousands of them would rise up around me. They migrate back and forth, making the whole landscape shimmer. I kept fatigue at bay by replenishing the magnesium that seemed to be constantly leaking from my body. The manager of the Kooperasie (the Northern Transvaal Farmers' Co-op) was most amused when I asked if I could buy Epsom salts. 'Ah yes! We call them 'Engels sout' or 'English Salts' here.' He looked at me intently. 'It's a very good cure for acne.' I didn't try this but the magnesium sulphate proved to be a good poultice for horses; excellent at drawing pus out of a gunky wound. Sarah-Jane made her pony stand in a bucket of hot water and Epsom's salts when a crocodile bit him on the leg.

The game rangers took me training and I ran with the wildebeest every night until my legs were hard. Then I raced, just ten kilometres, but along a rough road into a hot wind coming down from Botswana. I passed a few youths who conked out along the way, and these weren't wimps, they were fit Zulus. Despite this I kept contracting every virus going around. I went to see an Afrikaans doctor who declared that my immune system was overactive. He wanted to increase my serotonin levels and persuaded me to take 25mgs of *amitriptyline* at suppertime.

'It's a non-addictive drug that's been on the market for fifty years, used in much larger doses to counter depression.' Unnatural chemicals, but the adjustment worked and I started to feel normal.

The chaps Tamzin encouraged me to buy were worn until they fell apart at the seams, and even then I had new zips put in. I bought a small red horse called Sam the Great, the pony I'd always dreamt of having. We must have covered thousands of miles together. I used to play the exhilarating game of polocrosse on him wearing leather kneepads and a white helmet with a faceguard, which made me feel just like a character from a Jilly Cooper novel.

I started painting, mostly watercolours that came out of the paint box Rebecca gave me for my birthday. When I was back in England, I received a visit from the Buyer of Art for Gloucestershire Hospitals. Unbelievable. She promised me that she's doing away with the peeling posters still adorning the corridor walls and thought my landscapes would be an inspiration for sick people.

I made a nuisance of myself wandering all over Southern Africa, normally travelling alone, but friends would often join me. Robin came out to ride with the rhinos, bringing a very pretty girlfriend. James came over twice. We drove through

Swaziland and went snorkeling in the Indian Ocean, or rather I did. He lay on the beach reading the latest Jilly Cooper book. Aunt Hermione made lots of money selling sweaters and brought Shuggie and Olivia over to camp in the bush. We travelled by dugout canoe and sat watching elephant from gigantic termite mounds. Mum got to ride a stallion around the Okavango Delta. I think galloping with a herd of zebra is the only thing that's ever unnerved her, but she rose to the challenge. Dad said what thrilled him most was eating a tangerine he'd picked off a tree in my garden. Rebecca came on a trip to Mozambique when we swam from coral islands with turtles and dolphins. Diana flew out to spend Christmas with me in the Makgadikgadi Pans. I've never been so hot but it was fun. We canoed down the Zambezi past furious hippos and camped on the lip of Victoria Falls.

In all my adventures I found doing what God wanted gave me the most fulfilment. I would rush off on some mission full of trepidation and end up having much more fun than if I'd taken a holiday and tried to enjoy myself. Perhaps I was atoning for the deeds of my colonial ancestors. Perhaps they paved the way for me. In some ways I think I've regressed, held in a *Swallows and Amazons* existence like a fly caught in amber, but happily. I like riding around on African elephants and wandering along the Skeleton Coast. Snakes used to terrify me, but I'd got used to having a python in the hall. The hardest bit was coming home. Africa was where I found freedom.

Mikie did burn himself out. He developed Motor Neurone disease. I don't think anyone really knows the cause of this yet, but his father reckoned that it set in because he never gave himself enough rest.[20] He was an athlete and always pushed his body on relentlessly. He sadly died in the summer of 1999 aged forty-one.

Mary-Dieu has become a very loving mother. Once he graduated her boyfriend moved in with them permanently, and Daisy soon had a little brother – only he grew taller than any of us. We found that Mary-Dieu probably had been receiving divine protection; she'd been living across the park from a notorious mass murderer called Fred West, who preyed on young girls. We got the inside info from a *BBC* producer who stayed with us whilst making a definitive documentary on the man's life. Mind you I rather think Mary-Dieu could have given Fred West his come-uppance single-handed. She's a phenomenon all by herself.

Mum entered a competition in a newspaper and won a car. 'Oh, yes Darling; I'm frightfully good at that sort of thing. Can't you remember? I guessed how many baked beans were in a tin once and won a bicycle.' We never heard from the fur coat Alastair met in Burford, but Bee and Jims lived long and happy lives. We still have otters, there were four at one time, and Mum has been lecturing in conservation for about thirty years now, which is a feat of endurance. You have to keep at it; one woman asked if the otter was a squirrel the other day. I've just been asked if otters have legs.

As rivers become cleaner otter populations are recovering well. We found that our captive otters thrived on vegetables: they love eating peanuts and apples, carrots and oats; it helps them avoid developing kidney stones, which are a common cause of death. Mum is currently trying to put a party of people together to go down the Orinoco River in Guyana and swim with the giant Brazilian otters. They can grow up to nine feet long.

My father hasn't had any more misadventures with his machinery lately but is in the vegetable garden as I write and could be doing something frightful; it's quite a concern. We are planning to go down the Thames on his river launch this weekend. Hermione traded her yacht in for a Swan (a bigger one) and took Shuggie off round the world for six years. Her experience with the fractious knitters paid off as she had to deal with pirates and Goodness knows what else. Olivia's underwear is all purple now. I thought it was lovely and asked where she'd bought it. 'Oh no, I dyed it myself in the washing machine to elongate its life.'

Perry says her vacuum-cleaner is still going strong. Atalanta is no longer a bit interested in it, but her brother proved brilliant at clearing up his Granny's house. And has promised to come and work for his aunt. (Me) It's just as well; we are more untidy than ever. While my sisters are keen on keeping me up to date with British fashions, Atalanta says she hates shopping. Too much, too young. The Colonel (Robert) is brought them all out to ride in South Africa one New Year and they never seem to stop travelling.

Tamzin is still a slave to her own livestock. She says she has nightmares about Johnty's relatives leaving old Labradors to them in their wills. She has two energetic sons now and uses the meteorite as a door stopper in her tack shed.

Alastair's series *Life in the Freezer* proved a landmark with truly incredible, award winning footage of Antarctica. He said it's the most utterly beautiful place in the world. The book accompanying the series reached the bestseller list immediately. 'I don't think anyone's actually read it,' Alastair admitted, 'but they like giving it to each other for Christmas.' There's a picture of him in it, unrecognisable and looking like a red penguin in a thermal parka. Read all over. The great explorer in action. ('How do you do wee-wee?' Mum wanted to ask.) Alastair's since made a number of impressive wildlife films; *The Blue Planet, Planet Earth, Deep Blue, Earth* – all about oceans and extraordinary creatures. He now has his own film company called Great Ape Productions Ltd. making wildlife movies, such as *African Cats*, for Disney Nature. To our surprise Al declared that he was once a determined and expert bottom-shuffler and will delightedly discuss the behavioural genetics of the trait.

Matthew did become a prison chaplain and absolutely loved it. But after ten years he left the church to study Law and became a barrister, a profession that suits him well. Rose, who works as a psychoanalyst, still counsels prisoners and others in despair. Augustus has grown up. We last danced together at one of Diana's memorable parties. It was a James Bond party. He went as James with a scar on his face. I was Pussy Galore.

Diana became the headmistress of a leading Roman Catholic girls' school before becoming head of a London day school that always seems to be one of the highest in the league tables. I once went along and gave a talk to her sixth form and later took Mum to speak to the younger girls about otters. She says being a headmistress is an exhausting way of life, and could be stressful if she paused for a moment to let it be, but she's utterly fulfilled and very popular.

James? James married a lovely girl who likes chatting and laughs at all his jokes. Nicola, once so surprised to be pregnant, has three offspring (including a little God-daughter for me, who was born on Christmas Day). And two puppy dogs. Grizelda not only gained a degree in nutrition but runs her own company providing independent advice on nutrition for schools. It's called *Independent Nutrition*.

Rebecca writes educational children's books. Loads of them. She had just finished a series of twelve science books for the American market when I last asked. We went to see Robin; ten years to the day he still had the same leg of bacon hanging in his pantry. I took a photograph of Rebecca peering up at the monster. It was oozing. Not wanting to find another old Stilton I opened and closed the compost bucket very quickly. Robin was saying, 'Some chap wants to sell me (shares in) a machine that processes waste food. I told him we don't have waste food here; we eat it.' When I looked up, I found he was busy giving last night's vegetables to his dogs.

Pippa, my old flat-mate, married Brian. No she didn't, she married a Hollywood movie director called Jim, who comes from Dumbarton. My Granny lived there, rather grandly, in a castle (that has been made into a nursing home) until she was 95. She spent her days, as she always did, praying away for us, and is much missed. My cousin Jamie was given priceless advice when he and his wife were expecting their first baby: 'Don't let the nurses bind its arms; it'll get bronchitis.'

Henry. He was certified in the end. In his later years he got so bald we had to take him to a Psychiatric Home for Parrots. There were about thirty-six other macaws there, all shrieking away, but he was terribly happy and grew back his feathers. He needed a social life. But being with others of your species exposes you to the risks of infectious disease and his resistance just wasn't strong enough. Poor Henry.

I gather my Department at the *BBC* was severely cut back by government decree, despite the fact that a commitment to making educational programmes was in the Corporation's very constitution. Alastair said the years immediately after I left were heartbreaking for the staff and that I migrated just before the holocaust set in.

Now I stand at a distance I can see that good things did come out of my time of sickness. I was taken away from my all-engrossing career, my life in London, my flat and my possessions; the things of this world that had become so important to me. Imagey things. Materialism. Instead I was given a season to spend with my family and my friends. It was a time of enforced rest and solitude, in many ways a period of preparation for the next big step. I was given time to read, time to think, time to draw closer to the Lord, to acknowledge my dependency on him; time to bring strands of faith together and twist them into a stronger rope. A long, quiet time to contemplate things of eternal value. It was a time to pray, and as Granny always said, 'We cannot know the power of prayer.' I wouldn't have missed it for the world. You realise what it's like to be alive when you're really ill.

And afterwards I was 'taken into a wide open space.'[xxiv] I was brought to a new land and given the desires of my heart.[xxv] I flew into a season of re-growth where I was built up physically and stretched in many different directions. My life and understanding of the world were expanded in ways that I could never have imagined. Nothing can keep us from being what God wants us to be.

'When I think of the wisdom and scope of God's plan, I fall to my knees and pray to the Father, the Creator of everything in heaven and on earth. I pray that from his glorious, unlimited resources he'll give you mighty inner strength through his Holy Spirit. And I pray that Christ will be more and more at home in your hearts as you trust in him. May your roots go down deep into the soil of God's marvellous love. And may you have the power to understand, as all God's people should, how wide, how long, how high and how deep his love really is. May you experience the love of Christ, though it's so great you will never fully understand it. Then you will be filled with the power that comes from God. Now Glory be to God! By his mighty power at work within us, he's able to accomplish infinitely more than we would dare to ask or hope.'

Acknowledgements

Being ill and frail as I was, the original diary, although brightly illustrated, was only about half the length of this book and lacked pages when I gave up on it from time to time. Years years later my family persuaded me to type it up for general consumption, encouraging me to add a number of stories despite the risk of losing their dignity. I'm most grateful to all the characters I've featured who have let me publish the goings-on in their lives. If I've caused any offense, I apologise and can only hope to be forgiven.

I'm grateful to those who read through my first drafts especially Charles Foster, Zelda Perkins, Catherine Cairns, Mark Chichester-Clark, Jane Whitbread, Tiens and Hester van der Walt, Taryn Lockhart, Nina Baber, Cassian and Jane Roberts, Mark Fothergill, Leo Wynne, Willoughby Wynne, John Stitt, Hilary Reynolds, Judy Colman, Caroline Webber, Ilze Kotze, Sue Bowden, Margrit Duncan, Dave and Elizabeth Sewart, Jonathan Holmberg of CHM, Lisa McGinnis, Billy Howard, Suzanna Hamilton and Lucy Thellusson, while Lesley Wright patiently sorted out early computer problems and Lisa Scullard formatted the document. Later drafts were read by former M.E patients Julia Gard, Camilla le May, Henrietta

Mayhew and Helen Elliot while Dr. Charles Shepherd and Dr. Peter Farrant sanctioned medical aspects. I also have to thank an actor called Steve I once met at Elstree Studios and haven't seen since for his funny story about appearing in *Doctor Who*.

I want to extend grateful thanks to my doctors: Susie Weir, Mary Loveday, and John Prior. It was, however, my family and friends who cared for me when things were tough, and loved me even when I had nothing to give back, who enabled me to recover. My endless thanks goes to them.

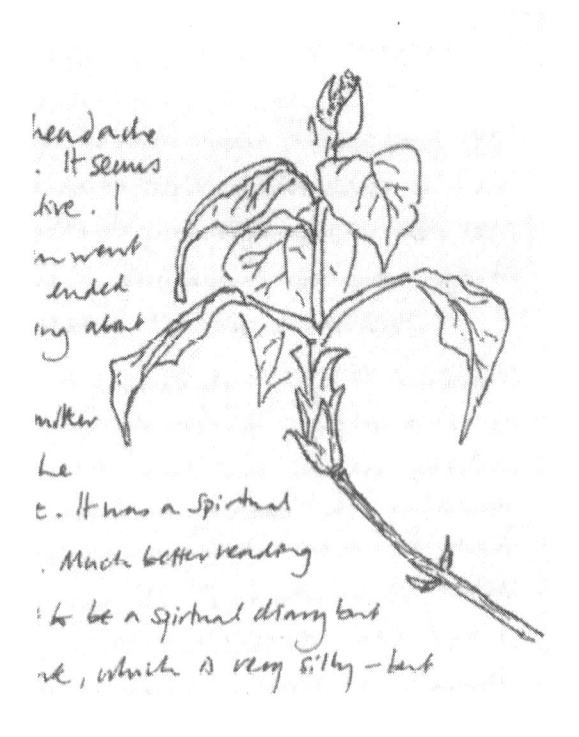

List of Characters

My Family:

- Mum and Dad.
- My sister Perry, her husband Robert, daughter Atalanta and dog Tadpole.
- My sister Tamzin, her husband Johnty, dog Maud, cat Thelma and horse Bod.
- My sister Mary-Dieu, her daughter Daisy and her boyfriend.
- Granny, Aunt Hermione, Shuggie, Olivia and Jamie.

Our animals:

- Jake, the dog. Henry, the bald macaw, Josephine the parrot, Solomon, the carthorse, and Leonard, the donkey. Bee and Jims, the otters. Snowy, the goat, and the sheep. Albert and Terry, the cockerels.

My Friends:

- James, his parents and dog Tessa.
- Rebecca, her parents, her sister, Miranda and Aunt Blottie.
- Alastair.
- Griz, Dane, Paddy and Eliza.
- Rose, Matthew and Augustus.

- Sarah-Jane, and her dog Tigger.
- Pippa.
- Nicola and Doug, baby Rosie, Polly dog, and her boss Lord Suffolk.
- Diana, her sister Amanda and future brother-in-law James Brewster.
- Robin.
- Mikie.
- Rufus Knight-Webb, his wife and his father, Dr. Knight-Webb, Psychiatrist.
- Charlie, Jane and their baby daughter.
- Raddy, her father the Field Marshall.
- Pat pat.
- Guy and Tanya.
- Our neighbours Muriel, Maggie, and another neighbour with six dachshunds.
- Albert and Terry.

Ministry:

- Gordon Crowther and John Irvine of St. Barnabas Church, Kensington.
- Barbara at the London Healing Mission.
- The Harnhill Christian Centre.

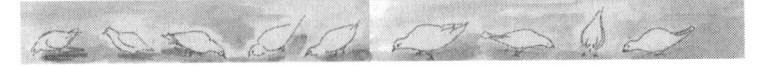

~ FUNNILY ENOUGH ~

Tapestry Map of
Life at Bakers Mill

← Mum
  Jims
  Bee
← Fisherman
← Carp
← Ducks - Coot - Grebe
← Doves
← Henry in tree
← Sophie with book
← Orvil + Josey in yard
← Jake
← Dad gardening
← Solomon
  Colts?
  Signpost.

Medical:
- My General Practitioner.
- Jeremy, Acupuncturist.
- Charlotte the aromatherapist.
- Dr. Mary Loveday, Harley Street Consultant.
- Dr. John Prior, National Health Service Specialist.
- Dr. Chris Booth, family doctor and his wife, Mrs. Booth, a nurse who had M.E.
- Hospital patients: Doris and Mrs. Doreen Hawkins

Work:
- *BBC* personnel: my Producer, P.A. and Head of Department.
- Linda my Departmental Manager.
- Paul, director of *The Velvet Claw*.

Also: Clare Francis, Virginia McKenna, Gerald Durrell, Spike Milligan, Petula Clarke, Madonna, Brian Blessed, Hannah Gordon, Rowan Atkinson, David Dimbleby, Barbara Cartland, Jilly Cooper and Claude Whatham.

~ *Some names have been changed* ~

Bibliography

Charles Allen *Plain Tales From the Raj (Futura, 1976)*
Andy Arbuthnot *Christian prayer and Healing* and *All you need is more and more of Jesus (Highland, 1993)*
Rosemary Attlee *William's Story (Highland, 1987)*
Corrie ten Boom *In my Father's House (Hodder & Stoughton, 1976)*
Michael Cassidy *Chasing the Wind (Hodder & Stoughton, 1980)*
Gary Chapman *The Five Love Languages (Moody Press, 1992)*
Joni Earekson Tada *Secret Strength* and *A Step Further (Multnomah Press, 1989)*
C.S. Lewis *The Problem of Pain (Fount, 1940)* and *Mere Christianity (Fount, 1952)*
Nanette Newman *God Bless Love (Collins, 1972)*
Adrian Plass *View from the Bouncy Castle (Font, 1991)*
Jackie Pullinger *Chasing the Dragon (Hodder & Stoughton, 1980)*
Jennifer Rees-Larcomb *Beyond Healing (Hodder & Stoughton, 1986)*
Llewelyn Powys *Black Laughter (Harcourt, Brace & Co. 1924)*

Phil Shirley *Where is the Winning Post? ~ biography of Mikie Heaton-Ellis (Harper Collins, 1998)*

Gary Smalley & John Trent *The Language of Love (Focus on the Family, circa 1988)*

D.L.Stevenson *Miss Buncle Married (Fontana, 1960)*

Colin Urquhart *Anything you Ask (Hodder & Stoughton, 1978)*

David Watson *Fear no Evil* and *Is Anyone There? (Hodder & Stoughton, 1979)*

Cox IM et al. *Red blood cell magnesium and chronic fatigue syndrome* (*The Lancet*, 30 Mar 1991, Vol. 337, pp 337, 757-60)

Samuel Pfiefer M.D. *Healing at Any Price? (Word Books 1988)*

Dr. Robina Coker *Alternative Medicine ~ Helpful or Harmful? (Monarch, 1995)*

Prayer of St. Francis *(d.1226)*

The Holy Bible (NIV) New International Version®. *(International Bible Society © 1984)*

The Holy Bible (NLT) New Living Translation

The Holy Bible (KJV) Authorised King James Version *(The National Publishing Co. © 1961)*

Other publications mentioned: *Peter Pan, M.E. and You, Paddington Bear,* Clement Freud's *Grimble* books, Burton's *Anatomy of Melancholy, A Year in Provence,* Grimm's Fairy Tales, *Polo, Day of the Triffids, Mary Poppins, The Screwtape Letters,* Arthur Ransome's books *Swallows and Amazons, Coot Club* and *The Big Six, Anne of Green Gables, Miss Buncle, Bee* *a Particular Otter*, Agatha Christie, P.G. Woodhouse and one of Bill Bryson's books. *Daylight* and *Daily Bread* books. *The Times, Autosport, Daily Mail, The Lancet, Annals of Internal Medicine, The Daily Telegraph, Sunday Times, News of the World, The Competitor's Companion, The Tatler, Radio Times, Elle, Newsweek.*

Television, radio programmes, plays and films mentioned: *Doctor Who, The Archers, Trainer, The Saint, Twin Peaks, Howard's Way, Dallas, Blackadder, The Velvet Claw, Casualty, Dead Romantic, Life in the Freezer, The Really Wild Show, The Great, Great Tit Show, The Diary of Anne Frank, Westside Story, Gigi* and *My Fair Lady, My Family and Other Animals, Bluebell, Swallows and Amazons, Cider with Rosie, Onedin Line, Ring of Bright Water, Play-Away, World Christianity, The Way Out Wacky Races, Newsnight, Magic Roundabout, Starsky and Hutch, Serendipity, Blue Peter Summer Special* and *The Blue Planet.*

Further Reading:

Dr. Anne Macintyre: *M.E. chronic fatigue syndrome: A practical guide (Thorsons Health,1998)*

Dr. Anne Macintyre: *What is M.E.?* and *M.E./Postviral Fatigue Syndrome – How to live with it*

Melvin Ramsay: *Myalgic encephalomyelitis and post-viral states – the saga of Royal Free disease (Gower Medical*

Publishing, 1988) The history of ME by the doctor who treated patients during the 1955 outbreak in London's Royal Free Hospital.

Dr. Charles Shepherd: *Living with M.E. (Vermillion, 1999)* Self-help guide by a doctor with M.E.

Useful addresses:

Action for M.E
Third Floor, Canningford House,
38 Victoria Street, Bristol, BS1 6BY
Tel: Lo-call: 0845 123 2380 or 0117 927 9551
e-mail: admin@afme.org.

The Christian Healing Mission
8 Cambridge Court, 210 Shepherd's Bush Road,
London W6 7NJ
Tel: 07570 040223
appointments@healingmission.org

Independent Nutrition
http://www.independentnutrition.co.uk

Footnotes:

[1] from Dr. Anne Macintyre's excellent book M.E. chronic fatigue syndrome: a practical guide

[2] The term myalgic encephalomyelitis was first used by The Lancet back in 1956. The journal's editorial described a group of doctors and nurses with this illness who had been looked after by Dr. Melvin Ramsay and his colleagues at London's Royal Free Hospital the previous year. The term chronic fatigue syndrome (C.F.S.) came into use in the 1980s when increasing numbers of doctorsFunnily started to recognise this illness but were reluctant to use the term M.E. The first definition of C.F.S. appeared in the Annals of Internal Medicine in 1988.

[3] By the year 2000 an estimated 422 per 100,000 people in the U.S.A. had M.E. – approx. 800,000 adults.

[4] Taken from *Action for M.E. and Chronic Fatigue fact sheet*

[5] Updated information taken from *M.E. What it is and how to get help* published in 2000 by *Action for M.E.*

[6] Subsequent medical reports show a number of Gulf War veterans developed M.E.-like symptoms. An ex-Army officer said this is probably because troops injected themselves with

too many vaccines. Ten years later I read in *The Telegraph* that 'in 1991, during preparations for Operation Desert Storm, British troops sprayed sheep dip (organo-phosphates) to control sand flies. The resulting alarming incidence of illness, including neurological damage to speech functions, cognitive powers and depression of suicidal intensity, forced the withdrawal of the preparation from military use.' (22.10.01)

[7] Leapt out of the pages of *View from the Bouncy Castle* by Adrian Plass, which I was reading.

[8] Miss Do-as-you-would-be-done-by is a character in *The Waterbabies*, which Diana reads aloud when she's allowed to.

[9] *The theory and practice of Acupuncture, a basic guide to responsible practice* from the British Medical Acupuncture Society, 2001 with notes *Acupuncture: An Overview*

[10] from *Anne of Windy Poplars* by L.M. Montgomery.

[11] Now I read in an U.S. Government publication that strong ginseng can be harmful to M.E. patients.

[12] Her instincts proved right. A horrendous bacterial infection hit Stroud Hospital a few years later. It literally ate away people's bodies. A local doctor had to have his leg

amputated. The bacteria consumed the nether regions of a political candidate for the X party and he had to have his testicles removed. My mother voted for him out of sympathy.

[13] Many doctors are sceptical about this machine.

[14] *Newsweek*: 12th November 1990

[15] Dr. John Millward claims mercury can leak from fillings. I have since had mine removed and replaced with crowns. It seems this is still under discussion.

[16] Llewelyn Powys in *Black Laughter*

[17] from the carol *Oh Little Town of Bethlehem*

[18] Dr. Sarah Myhill and Prof. John E. Davies still advocate treating a magnesium deficiency (Nov. 2000).But the U.S. Department of Health and Human Services (May, 1999) say two studies have found no difference in magnesium levels between C.F.S. patients and healthy controls.

[19] *Plain Tales From the Raj* edited by Charles Allen.

[20] see *Where is the Winning Post* a biography of Michael Heaton-Ellis by Phil Shirley.

BIBLICAL REFERENCES

[i] *The Gospel of John* chapter 3 verse 3 *NLT* also see *John 1 v 12&13* 'But to all who believed him and accepted him, he gave the right to become children of God. They are reborn! This is not a physical birth coming from human passion or plan – this rebirth comes from God.' and *1 Peter v 23* ~ 'For you have been born again. Your new life did not come from your earthly parents because the life they gave you will end in death. But this new life will last forever because it comes from the eternal, living word of God.'

[ii] *William's Story* by Rosemary Atlee

[iii] from *Paul's letter to the Romans 12 v 19*

[iv] *Paul's second letter to the Corinthians 5 v 1-5*

[v] *The book of Revelation 3 v 16*

[vi] *Paul's letter to the Ephesians 5 v 5&6 NLT*

[vii] *Gospel of Matthew 6 v 25-32*

[viii] *Gospel of Matthew 6 v 33 KJV*

[ix] Ref: *Gospel of Luke 6 v 38 KJV*

[x] *Proverbs 14 v12* and *Proverbs 16 v 25 NIV*

[xi] *The book of James 5 v 14&15NLT*

[xii] *The book of James 1 v 3&4*NLT

[xiii] *The book of Isaiah 59 v 2*

[xiv] *The Gospel of Mark 1 v 32-38*

[xv] *Paul's letter to the Romans 8 v 17* and on to *v 39 NLT*

[xvi] *Paul's first letter to the Corinthians 11 v 24 KJV*

[xvii] *The book of Job 2 v 6*

[xviii] *Psalm 40*

[xix] *Psalm 31 v 14 &15 NLT*

BIBLICAL REFERENCES

[xx] Ref: *Paul's letter to the Romans 11 v 29*
[xxi] *The book of Job 39 v 26 NLT*
[xxii] *The Gospel of Luke 22 v 31 & 32 RSV*
[xxiii] *from Paul's second letter to the Corinthians 1 v 4*
[xxiv] *from Psalm 18 v 19*
[xxv] *from Psalm 20 v 4*

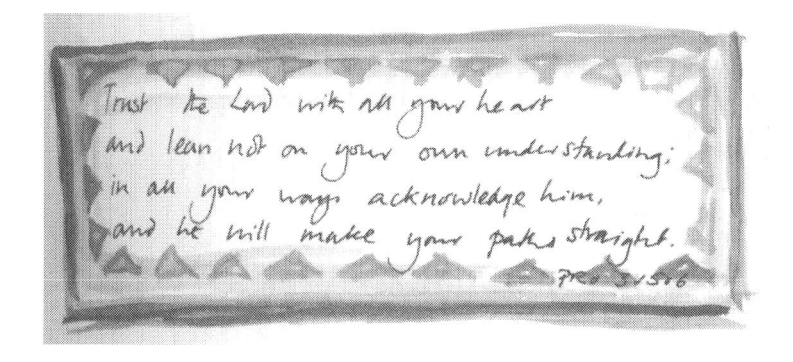

> Trust the Lord with all your heart
> and lean not on your own understanding;
> in all your ways acknowledge him,
> and he will make your paths straight.
> Pro 3 v 5+6

Printed in Great Britain
by Amazon